Yesterday's Papers
Volume Two:

Life in Edwardian England 1901-1918

From the pages of
The Isle of Wight County Press

by
Alan Stroud

THE OAKWOOD PRESS

British Library Cataloguing in Publication Data
A Record for this book is available from the British Library
ISBN 978 0 85361 684 9

Typeset by Oakwood Graphics.
Printed by Cambrian Printers, Aberystwyth, Ceredigion.

Acknowledgements

Thank you to my wife Sue and my children Tom and Kate for reading through the rough drafts. As always, their suggestions and thoughts were very important to me.

Richard Brimson also read through the rough draft, saving me from the minefield of original thought on more than one occasion.

I also need to thank the following:

Colin Fairweather for the use of the photograph on page 76
Jane and Ian Kennedy of Oakwood Press for making everything so easy.
Geoff White, my cousin, for allowing the use of three photographs taken by our grandfather, Alfred Arnold.
Zoe Stroud for arranging the use of the photographs on page 126.
Thanks are also due to Rob Martin, Geoff Allan, Robert Prys-Jones, Fred Caws and Bozi Mohacek.

I would also like to thank the *County Press* who could not have been more helpful. In particular I need to thank Robin Freeman, managing director, for generously allowing me out-of-hours access to their archive, and Ashleigh, Barbara, Gloria, Helen and David for all their kind help.

Published by The Oakwood Press (Usk), P.O. Box 13, Usk, Mon., NP15 1YS.
E-mail: sales@oakwoodpress.co.uk
Website: www.oakwoodpress.co.uk

Contents

Preface

The *County Press* archive is and always will be one of the best sources of Island history. It is only newspapers that can afford the luxury of reporting life in all its day-to-day detail and the back issues of the *County Press* are full of the facts, events and miscellany of everyday life that goes unrecorded elsewhere.

Happily, every single edition of the *County Press* still exists today in a collection of bound volumes held in the *County Press* offices. They contain over 120 years of social history recorded in minute detail and they have also been preserved forever on a more accessible microfilm archive.

Like the previous volume this book dips into that archive, this time to present a selection of cuttings from 1901 to 1918 that give a flavour of life on the Island during those eventful years.

By their very nature all the items have historical interest. Some of them are amusing while some of them are not so amusing; on occasions they have a foot in both camps at the same time.

They are first hand accounts of life in the first two decades of the 20th century, often in the smallest and most revealing detail. The articles were only ever intended to have a life of seven days but with the passing of time they have taken on a new life and become an important resource for historians. Quite simply, they are one of the best forms of local history, easily outperforming shelves of conventional history books.

The items are all introduced by some background information which will hopefully help put them in historical context but ultimately they stand or fall on their own merit.

The *County Press* reporters wrote with only one agenda and that was to provide a straightforward account of the week's news, plain and simple. They did so with surprisingly few inhibitions, and no politics or campaigning were ever allowed to intrude into the local news reports.

The columns of the *County Press* are pure and undiluted history in every sense; Island news, told every seven days, as it happened.

Some readers will have grandparents who grew up during these years. Perhaps these accounts will shed some light on their upbringing.

Introduction

On 22nd January, 1901, Queen Victoria died peacefully in her bed at Osborne House surrounded by close members of her family; the Queen was dead, long live the King. In the event, however, the King was only to live and reign for another nine years before he too died, in 1910, aged 68. Despite his short time on the throne compared with his mother's 64 years, in its way his reign was to leave almost as indelible a mark as hers, but for quite different reasons.

Both mother and son were to have the honour of having a historical period named after them, the phrases 'Victorian' and 'Edwardian' becoming part of the English language, but apart from that one common thread there was precious little else the Queen and her son had in common. His reign demonstrated only too clearly the difference between his generation's moral and social attitudes and those of the old guard, represented by his mother and father, and this attitude was to have an immediate effect on the inhabitants of the Isle of Wight. One of the first things the new King did was to dispose of Osborne House.

The King had not had a happy childhood. His mother in various letters wrote of him as 'so idle and so weak, a very dull companion; the systematic idleness, laziness and disregard of everything is enough to break one's heart'. She described the way he wore his hair as 'effeminate and girlish', and spoke of 'Bertie lounging about with a cigar stuck in his mouth'. His father, Prince Albert, was no less flattering: 'He is prone to listlessness and frivolous disputes. Bertie's propensity is indescribable laziness. I never in my life met such a cunning lazybones'.

Matters were not helped when Edward as an 18-year-old at military camp had enjoyed a young and happily promiscuous actress, Nellie Clifden, slipping first into his quarters and then into his bed as a gift from his fellow officers. Unfortunately she was as indiscreet as she was obliging and the story soon reached the ears of his father who was outraged. He wrote to the Prince telling him that he had 'sunk into vice and debauchery' and as the young King's teenage years came to end the affair set the seal on the rift between father and son. Unfortunately, within months Prince Albert died of typhoid and in the years to come the Queen made no secret of the fact that she felt the affair had somehow contributed to her husband's death.

In short then, the King had neither happy nor affectionate childhood memories and in particular his days spent at Osborne House had been far from pleasant for him. Osborne was a part of his life he was only too happy to part company with and so, despite the Queen's will stipulating that the house should pass 'to his Majesty the King for life', he declined the offer. He had already established a more than adequate royal residence at Sandringham and he had no desire for another one on the Isle of Wight. He was already in the habit of spending a great deal of time at Cowes during the summer months but never made use of Osborne House to any great degree, usually making his own sleeping arrangements in the clubhouses and residences of his wealthy friends or else on the Royal Yacht.

Osborne House had been the personal property of the Queen and accordingly she, not the state, had paid for its upkeep but the new King had no such intentions. For him, the house was an expensive irrelevance and it was very quickly shut down.

The furniture and fittings were covered with dust sheets and the staff left, for the most part to be re-employed in other parts of the royal household. Despite being asked, no other members of the royal family expressed an interest in taking over the house and so a way was devised for the King to conveniently give it to the nation. The house then began a whole new life when in 1902, two of its wings opened as a convalescent home for officers.

After 60 years, the days of the Isle of Wight as a royal residence were over.

The Island in 1901

On the Island and in the country as a whole, change and social reform were in the air. By 1901 the police on the Island had become a force to be reckoned with, comprising a Chief Constable and his deputy, two superintendents, two inspectors, seven sergeants and 42 constables (today there are over 200 police officers and 77 police staff). The postal system on the Island was in its heyday with four deliveries a day in most towns, starting at 7.00 am and finishing at 5.30 pm and consequently many letters were delivered on the day they were posted.

Life was lived at a more intimate level; people were more inclined to know their neighbours and the names of their fellow townsfolk. When the *County Press* promoted 'a relief fund for Guard Percy Peach, a much respected and very deserving servant of the I.W. Central Railway' in order to help a very ill man and his family, the implication was clear; almost certainly the townspeople knew exactly who he was.

Electricity was beginning to spread across the Island and by 1903 it had arrived in selected parts of Cowes, Newport, Ryde, Shanklin, Sandown and Ventnor. Second only to electricity in the enormous effect it was to have on peoples' lives was the internal combustion engine. By 1902 it had become obvious that like it or not, the motor vehicle was here to stay and as it became more popular so it became more tolerated, resulting in the national speed limit being raised from 14 to 20 mph. Just one year later localised number plates were introduced in Britain and the Isle of Wight was allocated the letters 'DL' which remained a part of the licence plate on Island-registered cars until 2000. In 1904 there were 46 cars and 42 motorcycles registered on the Island and driving licences had been issued to 92 Island residents.

A chain ferry, not too far removed from today's floating bridge in appearance, even then made its leisurely way back and forth from East to West Cowes and in 1904 it carried over 1½ million foot passengers and 23,000 vehicles.

Education was no longer the province of the wealthy. The benefit to Britain of a well educated population was now widely accepted and by 1907 nearly 2,000 children were being educated in Island schools. A sizeable number of the boys would end up in the shipyards of J.S. White, who by 1908 employed 1,250 workers.

Also apparent in large numbers on the Island were soldiers. They were here to man the forts and gun batteries dotted around the Island's coast. The Island has always played a major part in Britain's coastal defences and in the early 1900s there were manned forts at Totland, Yarmouth, Freshwater and Sandown, and batteries at Puckpool, the Needles, and Yaverland. In addition, there were large military barracks at Albany. Exact figures for the number of soldiers on the Island are not easy to come by, the numbers fluctuating wildly as entire regiments came and went, but it is safe to say the number must have been in the order of 2,000 to 3,000 at times. Most of the soldiers were well-behaved and disciplined but a sizeable number weren't and caused a fair amount of trouble on the Island. This troublesome minority were responsible for rapes, the victims ranging from little girls to old ladies, burglaries, housebreaking, casual theft of every description and on more than one occasion farm animals were slaughtered in the fields where they stood. The courts were filled with military offenders, week after week. They stole from shop displays, smashed shop windows to get what they wanted and on occasions gangs of drunken soldiers went on window-smashing rampages through Newport. The criminal activities of the Island's soldiers could have a whole book to themselves.

As it happened, their presence was a double-edged sword; the soldiers had money to spend and for Newport especially it meant a thriving trade for the pubs and businesses of the town. Another inevitable by-product of their presence was prostitution. Newport was able to cater for every other need of the soldiers and sex became just another commodity that the town was able to provide and South Street, then a warren of overcrowded courts and yards, became a well-used red-light district.

Local government had its beginnings in these days and by 1901 the Island had a full complement of County and Parish councillors. There was a large County Hospital at Swanmore Road, Ryde, which served the Island until the 1990s and an asylum at Whitecroft which was closed in the mid-1980s. At Ventnor, on the site now occupied by the Botanic Gardens was the Royal National Hospital for Consumption which treated tuberculosis patients. After TB was effectively eradicated by mass vaccination with BCG vaccine in the 1950s, the hospital closed in 1964.

In the weeks immediately following the Queen's death the pages of the *County Press* were filled with little else. Local news took a back seat as reports of events surrounding the Queen's death filled column after column. As a sign of respect the columns in the paper for the first few weeks after her death were bounded by thick black lines and even some of the advertisements appeared in the same mourning style. Eventually though, life began to return to normal and local events soon reclaimed their place in the paper.

The *County Press* itself went through some changes during this period. A competitor, the *Isle of Wight Express,* foundered and was taken over in 1903 and in 1904 the management invested just over £1,000 in a new printing plant in the form of a rotary press. A product of America, the rotary press had revolutionised the newspaper industry by placing the type on a rotating cylinder, instead of on a flat bed, enabling much higher printing speeds to be reached and for the *County Press* this meant that in just one hour over 8,000 complete, cut and folded newspapers could be produced.

The new press wasn't without its problems and for the first six weeks or so, to the company's embarrassment, the newspaper came off the press with smudged print, some of the pages being almost unreadable. 'We stated a fortnight ago' said the paper in a message to readers 'that the installation of the new press might involve some temporary tax. We are conscious that it has done so'. Eventually the problems were rectified, allowing the readers to see clearly for the first time the new typeface that had simultaneously been introduced. It was a change which radically altered the look of the newspaper and at the same time subtle changes began to alter the look of the front page, as logos and graphics started to creep into the advertisements which up until then had consisted solely of text.

In 1908 a new editor, W.H. Dann, was appointed following the retirement of George Lee and in 1912 came another upheaval when the newspaper moved premises. The original offices and printing works were located in corner premises in St James Square, at the junction of St James Street and Pyle Street but the newspaper had outgrown the building and so the move was made to 29 High Street, opposite the Guildhall, where it was to remain for the next 75 years.

The outbreak of war in 1914 was the start of four very difficult years for the *County Press* which saw their finances strained to the limit. Almost as soon as the war started, a shortage of paper forced the management into reducing the size of paper from eight pages to four. This carried on for several weeks but as soon as conditions allowed, a return was made to full size issues only for the situation to be reversed again shortly afterwards and for the duration of the war this became the pattern, the size of the paper fluctuating from one week to the next. As if that were not enough to contend with, the small amount of paper that was available soon trebled in price. It was a financial merry-go-round for the paper as the loss of four pages meant that nowhere near the usual number of advertisers could be accommodated and there was a dramatic loss of advertising revenue.

Eventually, unable to manage the balancing act any longer, the cover price which had stood at one penny for over 30 years was raised to 1½ pence in July 1917. Just a few months later it was found necessary to raise the price yet again and the cover price rose to twopence while at the same time the paper started printing on smaller pages. A statement in that week's issue informed readers, 'the proprietors appear to have no alternative but to increase the price to 2d. per copy and to reduce somewhat the size of the paper. They hope to retain the interest of all their old friends ...'

The outbreak of war also brought about an immediate and radical change to the contents of the paper as local news all but disappeared for four years to be replaced by news of the war.

The sheer wealth of war news in the *County Press* came as a surprise. Newspapers can allow themselves the luxury of reporting news in a breadth and depth that simply isn't possible in a history book and so it was with the *County Press* who were able to fill their pages with highly personal accounts of life at home and abroad during the war. The moving letters home from Island men at the Front are simply superb and the accounts of wartime life on the Island are fascinating. The *County Press* coverage of the war is an impressive body of work to have left behind; it is a remarkable piece of Island social history and deserves a wider audience.

To accommodate these reports, there was a price to be paid and as a direct result almost every existing feature in the paper either became a shadow of its former self, or disappeared completely in some cases, to make space for the war news. The only columns to remain largely intact were the town and village news columns and the reports of court cases. The latter part of this book reflects this turnaround in content and the last four year's cuttings consist largely of items of war news.

The World in 1901

As the new century began it was as if a tap had been turned on. Inventions and discoveries tumbled out one after another and it began to look as if technology could make just about anything possible. The century was to begin in candlelight and steam power and end with computers, satellites, and men on the moon.

History was made several times in the first three years alone. The first transatlantic radio signal was sent, the Wright brothers took to the air and the cinema industry began. Before the decade was out, Kellogg's cornflakes, the electric washing machine and plastic, in the form of bakelite, were all to make their first appearance. In 1908 Henry Ford manufactured the first of 15 million Model 'T' Fords, an impressive record that remained unequalled until the number of Volkswagens manufactured finally overtook it in the 1970s.

There were two innovations above all others that were to transform peoples' lives forever and they were the motor car and electricity. The internal combustion engine became commonplace during these years, eventually sweeping away horsepower for ever and London saw its last horse-drawn bus in 1911. Just a year later as the *Titanic* disappeared beneath the waves it was able to use the latest technology to send out a distress call call using Marconi radio-transmitters and the new 'SOS' call-sign.

By 1911 a wealthy man could travel by car, make international telephone calls from a house full of electrical appliances and if he was particularly wealthy he could fly from London to Paris. Needless to say, all this was still a world away for most people and would remain out of their reach for many years to come. The Edwardian era did see the popping of a lot of champagne corks but it was still a time of poverty for many people.

As far as wages were concerned it was as if time had stood still. The average wage for labourers and shop workers was still between 20 and 30 shillings a week, an amount that had not risen since late Victorian times. Inflation, however, had risen over those years and for many life was harder now than it had been 20 years previously. In 1901 a survey of the working population of York was published by Benjamin Rowntree. According to him, 22*s.* a week was the bare minimum needed by a family of two adults and three children, but to survive on that, he wrote,

... they must never spend a penny on a railway fare or omnibus. They must never purchase a halfpenny newspaper, or spend a penny to buy a ticket for a popular concert. They must write no letters for they cannot afford the postage. They must never contribute anything to their church or chapel, or give any help to a neighbour which costs them money ... The children must have no pocket money for dolls, marbles or sweets. The father must smoke no tobacco, and must drink no beer. The mother must never buy any pretty clothes for herself or for her children ... what is bought must be of the plainest and most economical description ... Finally the wage earner must never be absent from his work for a single day.

On the Island at that time a small cottage could be bought for £250, a housemaid could be hired to run it for £20 a year all found, and she might well have used a sewing machine in her work which would have cost her employer just over three pounds. A third class railway ticket to London was 12s. for those who didn't have a minimum of £250 to buy a car, and a good suit was to be had for 30s. A young woman teacher in a village school would expect to earn £50 a year while a more experienced teacher in a large school could earn up to £100 a year under a head teacher whose salary was £140. On the Island's councils, Newport's town clerk earned a fairly generous £250, just behind the Borough Surveyor who earned £300, and a police constable on the Island earned up to to £80 while his superintendent received an annual salary of £400. Nationally, a judge might earn over £5,000 a year and for the daughters of the gentry an allowance of £2,000 a year was not uncommon.

Perhaps not surprisingly then, between 1900 and 1918 people's expectations began to change. Britain's workforce slowly became aware of their power and began to flex their industrial muscles. In 1911 Liverpool dockworkers went on strike for more money and, in what was a first, the management eventually conceded defeat and met the workers demands. For the first time ever a workforce saw that they could use the withdrawal of their labour as a powerful bargaining tool and encouraged by the result of the strike other workers across the country followed suit and within weeks much of Britain, the Isle of Wight included, ground to a halt. Industrial action was here to stay.

In 1906 a Liberal government began to put in place what became some of the foundations of the modern welfare state. Labour exchanges were established, trades unions were given limited legal rights and for the first time modest pensions were paid to the old. Within a short time factory acts improved working conditions, housing acts slowly began clearing slums and education reforms brought free schooling to Britain's children.

In 1911, National Insurance became a reality providing a modest but welcome safety net for the sick and unemployed, and for the first time MPs were paid a salary: £400 a year.

Britain was involved in two wars during these years. Between 1899 and 1902, the Boer War cost the lives of 22,000 young men and in World War I another million were killed.

Finally, in a cruel irony for a country that had just experienced death on such a large scale, just as the war finished an outbreak of Spanish flu took hold in Britain and killed a further quarter-million.

Notes

This book covers the years 1901 to 1918, beginning where *Life in Late Victorian England* (Volume One) left off, that is to say it starts with the issue following Queen Victoria's death and ends with the issue reporting the end of World War I.

As in the previous volume the articles appear for the most part in their entirety and in exactly the same form as on the day they first appeared. Any editing has been of a minor nature and where it has occurred it is shown by the use of dotted lines.

The articles are presented in chronological order, covering a wide variety of unrelated subjects as they unfold, just as they would in a modern newspaper. The only items that do not follow this rule strictly to the letter are the items that appear in 'The Week's News' and 'Town and County Notes' where on occasion some of the lighter items have been grouped together for layout considerations rather than the order in which they originally appeared. They have been carefully chosen so their chronological place is not of great importance and are usually placed within a few weeks of their publication date.

The variety of items mirrors the contents of an average week's newspaper as far as possible and that has meant, among other things, the inclusion of some news items of a national nature. The *County Press*, like most provincial newspapers in those days, was not just a provider of local news. Reports of national events, sometimes in quite generous detail, always took up a significant portion of the *County Press* and that is reflected in these pages by the inclusion of some of the national news stories that the *County Press* judged important enough to cover. As in the previous volume, no names have been changed.

Looking at the *County Press* during these years it is clear that in the same way that Britain in 2008 is not the Britain of 1970, so there had been some distinct changes in attitudes and moral values between 1884 and 1918. In particular, stories of blood and gore seem to have lost their attraction and were quietly dropped. They had always been popular in the past; they appealed to Victorian sensibilities and were part of the staple diet of most newspapers in Britain for many years. The *County Press* had certainly printed its fair share during Victorian years but from the late 1890s onwards there is a clear break with the past and by the early 1900s morbid accounts of murder scenes or events on the gallows, and tales of 'mangled flesh' had disappeared completely.

Suicides, however, were still very much in existence. They had not diminished in number at all since the Victorian years and continued to occur on a regular basis, two or three sometimes taking place in the same week. This pattern continued unbroken until the outbreak of war when almost overnight the number of reported suicides dropped dramatically and they were to remain low for the duration of the war, a phenomenon noticed elsewhere in the world at the time and one that is still seen today.

Cruelty to animals also underwent a transformation, not in terms of the number of court cases, which remained high, but more in the nature of the cruelty itself. The whippings, beatings and starvation of Victorian times all but disappeared. There were, indeed, still the odd cases involving systematic cruelty but for the most part it is fair to say they had vanished and invariably the Island's courts now heard the same two charges over and over again. They were: 'causing a horse to work while unfit' which usually meant working a horse with open sores or cuts that had been caused by chafing reins, and the self-explanatory 'working a horse while lame'. With minor variations these two charges, unpleasant enough as they are, represent the vast bulk of the cruelty cases that now appeared in court rather than the gratuitous cruelty of Victorian days.

Finally, there are no articles or letters complaining about the state of the Island's railway companies as there were in Volume One. The reason is simple - there were none. For whatever reason, in the late 1890s the complaints which had been as vicious as they were numerous, began to tail off and eventually they disappeared altogether. Whether the railway companies improved beyond all recognition or whether the *County Press* and public simply tired of the whole thing is a matter of conjecture.

Editorially, the newspaper itself had changed since Victorian times. Over the passing years the *County Press* had become more outspoken in matters of politics and national events and were now confidently expressing their views in editorials. Their opinions, however, were strictly confined to national matters; as far as local affairs were concerned they remained scrupulously impartial, only ever passing comment on local matters that were of little or no significance.

As far as possible, subjects appear here in roughly the same proportion as they did in the original newspaper. As in the previous volume, the only subject matter not accurately represented are the Council and Local Board meetings which took up a great deal of space, covering subjects ranging from water supplies to the state of the public highways.

Just as in the previous volume, contemporary spellings and printing conventions have been maintained, i.e. the use of Newport-road instead of Newport Road and Calborn instead of Calbourne. On occasions the County Press seem unsure of the spelling of some locations; for example using 'Brook' one week and 'Brooke' the next; similarly the 'e' on the end of Merstone would sometimes come and go. These and other quirks appear here exactly as they did in the original articles; they are not misprints.

The titles used for all the articles are the original ones that accompanied them on their first appearance. None have been invented or altered in any way.

The *County Press* carried extensive advertising which ranged from large display advertisements to 'Wanted' and 'For Sale' columns. Year by year compilations of examples of all types are included and bear close inspection. They are composed of images taken from microfilm copies of the *County Press* where each page of the paper has been shrunk to the size of a 35 mm negative. For the purposes of this book they have had to be blown up again and the resulting images come complete with highly magnified scratch marks and dirt blotches. They have been restored by the author but inevitably some still show signs of their origin.

There were virtually no photographs in the *County Press* at that time, indeed illustrations of any description were a rarity. Photographs from the relevant period are dotted throughout the book to give a flavour of the Island at that time and, for the most part, are previously unpublished.

Finally, in the days before decimal currency Britain's coinage was based on pounds (£), shillings (s.) and pence (d.), and prices throughout the book have been left in this form; e.g. '£1.15s.6d.', which means one pound, fifteen shillings and sixpence. For those too young to remember, 12 pennies made a shilling, which is 5p today, and 20 of those shillings made one pound.

The County Press 1901-1918

In Ventnor a mini-crimewave was in progress. A china shop operated by Mr.Tucker had been the subject of a series of night-time break-ins, carried out by someone who found time to leave rude messages behind. P.C. Hutchins was dispatched to mount solitary guard through the night, in the darkness of the empty shop awaiting the next visit from the literary burglar ...

February 16th, 1901

A BOY BURGLAR AT VENTNOR

Ventnor has been greatly agitated this week by the arrest of an intelligent young townsman, the son of highly respectable parents, on a charge of burglary. It appears that the manager (Mr. Maurice Harold Gale) of Mr. George Tucker's china and and glass stores in High-street became convinced before Christmas that someone was obtaining entrance to the premises after he had closed for the day. One morning in January he found a corner of the pane of glass in the shop door, immediately over the keyhole, had been cut out, and the putty scraped away inside as if someone had attempted to remove the pane. On the morning of the 29th of January he found the door was wide open, the stock in considerable disorder, the till had been opened by the removal of the screws from underneath, a few shillings' worth of coppers were gone, also all the keys of the other doors on the premises which the manager had placed in the till for safety. A small bull's-eye lantern not belonging to the premises was found on the floor beneath the till. Again on the 5th inst. the manager arrived to find the door wide open, the till down again, and considerable disorder in the shop. The contents of his desk, which is over the till, had been heaped upon the floor and was saturated with wet, and inside the desk was an impudent message, badly written on a scrap of paper, and signed 'Bill Sikes'. On each occasion the manager communicated with Div. Sergt. Cass, of the local police force who now determined to station a constable every night on the premises. In the early hours of Sunday morning, between one and two o'clock, the vigil of P.C. Hutchins was rewarded. He heard the shop door being quietly unlocked, then a person entered, struck a light and lit a bull's-eye lantern, and turning on the light was proceeding stealthily down the shop towards the till in his socks when the constable grabbed him. The prisoner struggled violently to escape, but P.C. Hutchins held on and getting him outside the shop managed to get the handcuffs on, but these the prisoner slipped over his hands. The constable finally got his capture to the lock-up, when his identity was established as George Frederick Williams, 15 years of age, of Albert-Terrace, Ventnor, a clerk in the employee of Messrs. Chaplin and Co., whose offices are nearly opposite Tucker's stores. On Monday morning the prisoner was brought before Dr Robertson, JP, and remanded in custody to the Petty Sessions at Newport today (Saturday).

For Sale.

Charges for advertisements under this heading will be found at top of front page.

ARRIVALS. — Machinist's bluckbuck, emery cloth, smoke bends, Sunlight soap, turtle soap, cartridges, pincers, bits, curry combs, razors. — Upton's, Newport.

AYLESBURY Duck Eggs, prize bred, quick growing, prolific laying strain, also eggs from my splendid Buff Orpington Fowls, no better obtainable, guaranteed fertile, prices moderate. — Hucks, Dodner, Newport.

CANARIES, few good Norwich, single or pairs, pairs from 8s. 6d. — F. Bull, 37, Trafalgar-road, Newport.

CARDS, Invitation and Complimentary. — County Press, Newport.

CREAM Separators, Melotte, easiest and best Churns, Butter Workers, and Dairy Utensils of all kinds. — Linington, Market-square, Newport.

DOG-CART, nearly new, for sale. — Apply G. Goater, Bugle Hotel stables, Newport.

DONKEY, 5 years old, with Governess Cart and Harness, for sale, donkey exceptionally good. —C. Hastings, Whitecliff, Alum Bay, I.W.

EGGS. — Mrs. Fisk, Apse Manor, Shanklin, can now supply eggs for sitting from the following breeds: Buff and black s. orpington, black minorca, and boudan at 2s. 6d. per sitting. The pens contain winners, Cook and other good strains combined. Cross-bred eggs at 1s. 6d.

EGGS. — Salmon Faverolle's prize winners 5s. sitting, pure-bred buff orpingtons 4s., white leghorns from Palace cup winner 4s. 6d. — F. Dore, Newport-road, Cowes.

EGGS. — Black minorca eggs, pure, 2s. 6d. sitting; Pekin-Aylesbury duck eggs 2s. sitting, proved fertile. — Carver, Wolverton.

EGGS. — After years of careful breeding will guarantee that I have the finest winter egg-producers in the South of England; sitting 12 eggs— ancona 3s. 6d., langshan 3s., langshan-minorca cross 2s. 6d., carriage paid. — Carter, Birklands, Ryde.

EGGS, golden wyandottes, from 1st prize pen Abbot Goldsmith's strains, reduced 3s. sitting. —Chiverton, 16, Westend-terrace, Newport.

EGGS. — For sale, several sittings from Toulouse and other geese. — Apply Rowborough Farm, near Brading.

EVANS, of 44, Elm-grove, Newport, can supply large and small bundles of Firewood at 1s. 6d. to 2s. 6d. per 100. Loose wood 1s. a sack. Oak junks 6d. per bushel. Delivered free to all parts of the Island.

FIREWOOD, oak and fir, cut any length to suit customers' grates and kitcheners, by the ton or bushel, loads or half-loads, delivered any part Island; large and small size bundles for fire lights, &c. — W. Comer, wood merchant, Parkhurst Forest (entrance Bull's-farm, Yarmouth-road). Postal and Newport address, 60, Hunnyhill.

FODDER, all kinds at lowest prices. Good Hay and Straw delivered any part of the Island. — Wooldridge, corn and coal merchant, Newport.

Situations Vacant.

Charges for advertisements under this heading will be found at top of front page.

APPRENTICE to the tailoring wanted, small salary to commence. — Apply No. 80, County Press, Newport.

APPRENTICES wanted to coach and harness trade. — Apply to R. B. Cheverton, Royal Carriage-works, Newport.

BOOTS. — Wanted a strong young man as second boots. — For full particulars apply Warburton's Hotel, Newport.

BOOTS and first-class Housemaid wanted for hotel, good wages. — Mrs. Barnett, Madeira Hotel, Shanklin.

BOY wanted. — Apply J. Yelf, Hunnyhill.

BOY wanted at once, healthy and light employment. — Apply Bookstall, Railway-station, Sandown.

BRICKMAKER wanted, must be first-rate red-brick burner, to take yard per 1000, kilns and clamps. — F. Wickens, Seaview.

CANVASSER wanted, experienced, knowing the Island well, good salary and liberal commission. —Apply No. 78, County Press, Newport.

CARTER wanted, and son as Mate. — Apply Forelands.

CARTER, steady, wanted. — Apply H. Burt, carrier, 33, Orchard-street, Newport.

CARTER wanted at once for Rowborough Farm, near Brading, good cottage and garden, good wages, or single man of good character to live and sleep in house might suit. — Apply to W. H. Young, 3, Union-street, Ryde, I.W.

CARTER, steady man, wanted by 15th March, cottage and garden found. — Apply H. White, Street-place, Calbourne.

CARTER'S Mate wanted. — Apply H. Brown, Wootton Farm.

CHEMIST. — An apprentice or improver wanted. — Apply personally or by letter at Smith's Drug Stores, St. James's-square, Newport, I.W.

COOK. — A good cook wanted, two in family. — Apply Mrs. Hamilton, West Dene, Yarmouth.

COOK, thorough good, and a Housemaid wanted at once, only those thoroughly capable need apply, good wages given. — Allandale, Park-avenue, Ventnor.

COOKS, Cook-Generals, House-parlourmaids, Generals, and every other kind of servant. — Apply Miss Grainger, 82, High-street, Newport.

COOK General wanted at once, two in family, housemaid kept. — Address with full particulars to T., Culver Lodge, Sandown.

COOK-General, good, wanted end of March, small family. — Apply Mrs. Fox, 22, St. Thomas's-square, Newport.

DRAPERY. — Wanted at once young Man as junior for the Manchester department or an Improver; also well-educated youth as an Apprentice. — Hill and Company, Ryde.

The advance of the motor car had begun and it soon became clear that the unthinkable was about to happen; after thousands of years, the horse was about to be made redundant. Writing under his pen-name GHRD, Dr Dabbs, an Island GP, reflected on its imminent passing in his regular column ...

February 16th, 1901

MOTOR-CARS

I have been pretty thoroughly of late into the question of motor-car versus carriages and horses, and I seriously determined that if I could really satisfy myself that the motor was the better, I would at once do away with horses and carriages and adopt it. My conclusion is that as it took 25 years to make the bicycle perfect so we are still 15 years away from a safe enough, cheap enough motor. For a thousand pounds you may be able to get (even now) a reliable motor, but you want two, and you want an engineer who knows (and a knowing engineer means a good wage), and then you want an engine-shed. I shall be told by post that you can get motor-cars for the Isle of Wight for about one fifth of a thousand pounds. I know you can, but I am talking of a motor-car that will ascend any hill at a fair pace and not be laid up with high fever the same night or strangled with asthma the next day ... No, no; horses still hold the field, the bicycle boom is waning, and my old friend Mr. R. B. Cheverton,* of Newport, may still take heart and go on building carriages.

But - if the horse is still to be our friend, and if I am to be the friend of the RSPCA, they must show me a few more prosecutions and convictions for tourist overloading in the summer. They have no right to allow our hearts to bleed, unavenged, for the monstrous things we are allowed to see, pass unpunished.

Whatever danger might be encountered on today's streets, it probably won't take the form of a large, hungry boar pig with the strength of six men. In 1901, however, things were different and three men on their way to work one morning met with just such an animal walking contentedly along the road at Fairlee. It was vicious, it was confident and it was no respecter of umbrellas ...

March 16th, 1901

ATTACKED BY A STRAY BOAR

Harry Westmore, dealer and contractor, of Sea-street, Newport, was charged with a breach of the Highway Act by allowing a boar pig to stray on the highway at Fairlee. - William Brett, labourer, of Cross-lane, said that on the 26th ult. he was on the Ryde road in company with other men named Wickens and Grace, when he saw a boar pig on the road. It had followed a man who had his umbrella torn to pieces in trying to keep the pig off, and the man had got inside a gate out of the way of the animal, which was waiting for him at the gate. They had to throw stones at the pig, and Mr. Grace was forced to shoot at him to get the animal back into defendant's field, where the scavenge heap was. He thought defendant was the owner of the pig, but he could not swear that he was. - By defendant: The pig was upset by the man going for it with an umbrella; he went for the pig because the pig went for him. - James Wickens,

* Chevertons, forerunners of Cheverton Motors, were carriage and coach builders. Their landau carriage specially built for Queen Victoria, still exists and stands today, unseen by the public, in the Council's museum store at Cothey Bottom, Ryde.

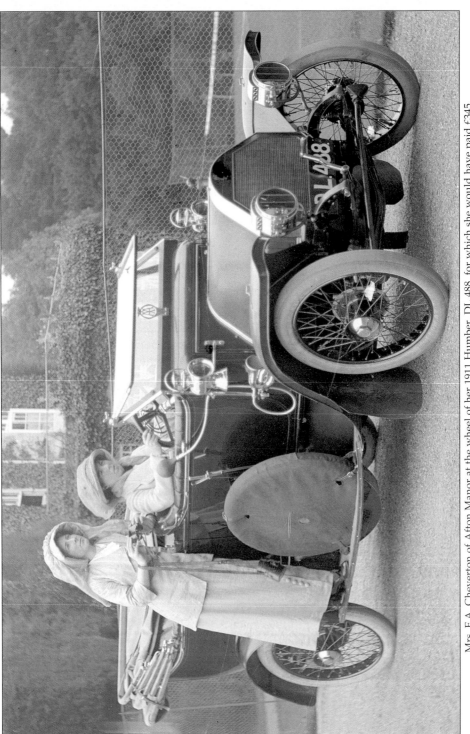

Mrs. F.A. Cheverton of Afton Manor at the wheel of her 1911 Humber, DL 488, for which she would have paid £345.

labourer, of Alvington, working at Fairlee Farm, gave similar evidence, saying the pig came from defendant's field. - P.C. Bennett said when he served the summons defendant said he had heard about the boar attacking a man and that he had sold the animal. - Defendant said he said that he had sent a boar pig away, but he did not admit that it was the same one in question. He sent them away to make sausages, which some of them might have the pleasure of eating (laughter). He said there was no evidence to show that it was his pig, which he was sure would not have left the other pigs. - Superintendent Hale said there had been complaints about that vicious animal getting out of the field. - The Bench having ascertained that the pig returned to the scavenge heap in defendant's field, fined defendant 2s. 6d. and costs. - Defendant: It is a rotten case. - The Clerk (Mr. John Fardell): You must not be rude to the Court.

———————————◆———————————

The British public's attitude to the monarchy has changed considerably since 1901 but not the interest shown in their private affairs.

The new King's first Civil List was published, detailing the sums of money to be granted to the royal family and it came under close scrutiny by both the County Press and the Times. In the same week that a maid's position was advertised at 15 shillings a week and a newly recruited constable was earning just 23 shillings a week, it was revealed that the King would receive nearly half a million pounds a year.

The gentlemen of the Press felt uncomfortable about the amount. By this time, the public were well aware of the King's lavish lifestyle and the fact that he spent vast amounts of money on gambling, fast women and expensive cigars.

The question was, would Fleet Street and the County Press be in favour of the King receiving less money or more? ...

April 6th, 1901

THE KING'S CIVIL LIST

The report of the House of Commons Committee on the King's Civil List was issued on Thursday. It proposes that the amount of the Civil List shall be £470,000 ... The committee also recommend the grant to the Duke of Cornwall of an annuity of £20,000, to the Duchess of Cornwall of an annuity of £10,000, and to the King's daughters of an annuity of £18,000; and further recommend that the contingent annuity of £30,000 for the Queen Consort, in the event of her surviving the King, be increased to £70,000, and that a contingent annuity of £30,000 be granted to the Duchess of Cornwall in the event of her surviving the Duke ... Commenting on this report, the Times of yesterday says the general feeling of the public will be one of surprise at the smallness of the proposed increase. During her long widowhood Queen Victoria lived in comparative retirement and seclusion, the reasons for which were fully understood and appreciated by her loving subjects. But from the King, in the prime of life, the public consciously or unconsciously expect a considerably greater display and a more active social leadership. Every reasonable person must be well aware that these things cost money, and a great deal of money, when done upon the only scale that is possible for Royalty.

———————————◆———————————

In the last few years there had been several escapes from Parkhurst prison and barely had the new century begun when another escape took place. Bolting from a working party, two prisoners made their way to Elmsworth, on the eastern side of the entrance to Newtown creek, where they were eventually outwitted by the simplest of plans hatched by a resourceful Coastguard who just happened to be in the right place at the right time …

June 15th, 1901

DARING ESCAPE FROM PARKHURST PRISON
TWO CONVICTS MAKE A DASH FOR LIBERTY
EXCITING CHASE AND A CLEVER RECAPTURE
BY AN ISLAND COASTGUARD

The quietude of Parkhurst was very suddenly disturbed about three o'clock on Monday afternoon by the startling alarm that two of the convicts at the Prison had made their escape. The shrill sounds of the warders' whistles rang out from within the walls of the Prison and were quickly taken up by those outside, warders were busy running about in all directions, and so quickly did the news spread that in a very few minutes convicts, prison officials, and persons living in the vicinity of the Prison were in a state of great excitement and all was bustle and activity. … It appears that a party of about 30 or 40 convicts, in charge of a warder named Keeping, were engaged in light work at the farm at the western side of the prison, which is only a short distance away from the Parkhurst Forest. The farm is fenced off by a 7ft. high wooden fence, the top of which is covered with tenter-hooks. The guards were posted at their customary positions and everything was apparently proceeding alright, when two of the convicts, who were engaged in potato hoeing, made a dash for liberty. They were William Walker, aged 24, undergoing a sentence of five years' penal servitude imposed in China for striking a senior officer, &c., and Samuel Walter Kay, a tall slim man, standing about 6ft. high, belonging to Lancaster, aged 34 years, and described as 'a clerk in holy orders', sentenced to five years' penal servitude at Lancaster for obtaining money by false pretences. The two convicts made off at top speed straight for the fence, the tenter-hooks proving no barrier to their progress. Placing their mattocks against the woodwork they clambered up the fence with wonderful agility and ease, almost before the warders and guards could realise the situation. The other convicts watched the runaways with much interest and one was heard to exclaim 'God help you!' The blowing of the warder's whistle appraised the armed guards of what had happened, and seeing the two men scaling the wall, Civil Guards Hogan and Davies each fired a couple of rounds at them. Walker got over the fence safely, but his taller comrade appeared to have been hit by one of the shots. The guns carried by the Prison guards, however, are not very dangerous weapons and failed to take much effect, and Kay, although seeming to fall from the top of the fence, got up all right on the other side, and having now obtained freedom bolted with his comrade into the thick-wooded Forest and disappeared. The news of the escape was soon made known all over the Prison and the police at Newport were quickly informed by messenger (the Prison not being connected with the telephone), and telegraphic communication was also made with the various Coastguard-stations, giving the names, numbers and description of the escape convicts. ... About nine o'clock the welcome news arrived at the Prison that the convicts had been captured, and at about 9.45, a large number of persons having assembled outside the Prison, a trap came driving up towards the Prison entrance, in which were seated the recaptured convicts, with their captors, a couple of warders and others, the party receiving ringing cheers as they passed from the avenue inside the Prison. The convicts were afterwards examined by the Prison doctor and were apparently little the worse for their experiences, though Kay was found to have been hit in the back and side by part of the contents of the guns which were fired at him on his escape. Kay had also torn his hand slightly. The story of how the convicts were recaptured is a highly interesting one and although there were several who took part in it, chief credit in the matter belongs to a coastguard named James Connell, who is stationed at Newtown Coastguard-station, and the stratagem displayed by him, resulting in the convicts' recapture is deserving of the highest praise. Connell is an old sailor and has seen a good deal of service. The Newtown Coastguard-station is not in telephonic communication with the other Island stations and consequently they had heard nothing there of the escape. Coastguard Connell was going on his usual beat from Newtown to Gurnard station to examine the 'guards'. It was about six o'clock and having crossed the river he anchored his boat on the shore at Fishhouse Point. Whether the convicts were acquainted with the custom of the coastguard to anchor his boat at this spot and had intended to obtain it to get away is not known. However, Connell proceeded some 300 yards to Polar Bank, a small copse, when his attention was drawn to two persons a few yards off, whom he took to be rabbiting. Going a little closer he discovered that the men were convicts. They were lying down flat. Connell kept a cool head and could have signalled to the station and given the alarm, but it was two against one and he adopted a very clever plan instead. Seeing that the Coastguard did not attempt to interfere with them, the tall convict (Kay) got up and went across to him and said 'Look here, coastguard, you are a friend?' Connell replied 'Yes'. Kay then said 'We are two escaped convicts and I will give you £100 if you will say nothing about this and get us some food and get us away'. 'Right you are' was Connell's answer. Kay also told Connell he wanted to get to France and there was a yacht in the river waiting for him, and the curious coincidence was that there really was a strange 'packet' in the river though whether it was for the convicts or not we cannot say. Connell told Kay that he would get them a boat and plenty to eat if they would remain in hiding till his return. The ex-stoker claimed special consideration owing to the Navy 'connection' between him and Connell, and he and his fellow fugitive, probably tempted by the promise of food after the fatiguing journey, unsuspectingly remained where they were. Coastguard Connell lost no time in devising a smartly conceived plan for the capture of the convicts and enlisted the help of another coastguard (Smith), Mr. Kemp (gamekeeper to Mr. F.T. Mew, JP), and P.C. Holbrook (Portsmouth), who is staying in the locality, the first two having loaded guns. At a given signal on Connell's return to the fugitives, Smith, Kemp, and Holbrook closed in upon them, and much to their chagrin the convicts found that it was capture instead of feeding which they were to experience. They were none too willing to 'surrender' and Kay threatened 'to do' for Connell, but acknowledged that it was a 'clever capture', then he added bitterly 'We thought we had a true friend in you, but we have found you to be a Judas'. Walker who also did not submit quietly at first was anxious to know whether the guns were as harmless as those of the Prison warders; but a warning that they would be shot if they attempted to escape again had the desired effect, and the capture was thus effected at about 6.30 p.m. The convicts, who were without jackets were supplied with coats and caps and at Porchfield they were placed in Mr. Mew's van, in which they were driven under an 'armed escort' back to prison. Their arrival was signalised by applause from the assembled company at the Prison. The reward for the capture of a convict is £5, and Connell and his assistants justly deserve such recognition of their well-planned and successful capture. Many of the search party remained out a considerable part of the night in ignorance of the fact that Walker and Kay were safely lodged within the prison walls again.

————————◆————————

A London publication, Truth magazine, seemed to have the ear of someone who moved in the King's inner circle, someone who knew his mind. When they printed a story detailing the King's apparent lack of interest in Osborne the County Press dismissed the story as nonsense but as subsequent events were to prove, Truth was indeed telling the truth …

July 6th, 1901

THE KING AND OSBORNE

Truth is responsible for the following:- 'It would not surprise me were Osborne soon to come into the market. The King greatly prefers Sandringham as a quasi-private residence, and a monarch can no more be in two places at the same time than a sparrow. The maintenance of Osborne costs about £15,000 per annum'.

What ground *Truth* may have for this statement we know not, but we take leave to question it. It is recorded of the First Edward that he came to the Isle of Wight to take possession of it. We do not think it will be recorded of the Seventh Edward that he forsook the Isle of Wight!

————————◆————————

THE WEEK'S NEWS

SANDOWN. A meteorite, weighing about 1lb. fell in the little front garden of Nevada, York-road, during the storm on Saturday night.

Lewis Wilkins, stated to be the tallest man in the world, is now at Leeds. Born at St. Paul, Minnesota in 1874, he is 8ft. 2in. in height, and measures 66in. around the waist; weighs 26 st.; in gloves takes size 14; and a penny will pass easily through any of his rings. The circumference of the interior of his hat is 27in. Mr. Wilkins is of British descent. At 10 years old he stood 6ft. high.

What has always been regarded as the largest tree in Norfolk, known as Thwaites Oak, which stood at Tivetshall, St Margaret's, has been felled and sold by auction. The trunk was over six yards long, and had the huge girth of 21ft., and when stripped it yielded no less than four tons of bark. It sold for £92. 2s.

A HUGE EEL - A huge conger eel, 6ft. 6in. in length, and weighing 61lbs., was found by the gardener to Mr. H. Adams in the sea opposite his house, Koh-i-noor, Margate. His attention was called to the spot by the quantity of seagulls hovering over the rocks.

CURIOUS NESTING PLACE – Two whip-jacks* during the winter built their nest at the bottom of an iron pipe 2ft. long and 3in. in diameter, which had been standing against a gate-post in Lower Sandown. In this pipe seven young birds have been hatched.

FRESHWATER. A FOUR-LEGGED CHICKEN – Mr. F. Crouch residing in Prince's-road, had a chicken hatched on Friday last week with four perfect legs. Two are in the usual position with the others standing out from just in front of the wings. It was hatched from a black minorca egg.

————————◆————————

The next two articles are reports of court cases where people's characters were at stake. They revolve around matters that to modern eyes might seem trivial and inconsequential but these were times when status and social standing in the community were everything, and people would go to extraordinary lengths either to defend their own reputations or to sometimes damage the reputation of others.

Perhaps a little of both is evident here.

In the first case, a Miss Thompson is being sued for slander after declaring in public that the meat she received from her butcher was rotten. Embarrassingly for her in view of her opinion, some days after she bought it the meat was taken home without her knowledge by her gardener who had it cooked for his tea and pronounced it 'very tasty' ...

July 13th, 1901

A FRESHWATER BUTCHER'S ACTION FOR SLANDER

At the Hampshire Assizes before Mr. Justice Wills and a special jury sitting in the Crown Court, the case of Hannam v. Thompson was tried.

This was an action for slander brought by Mr. Charles Hannam, butcher, of Freshwater, against Miss Linda Catherine Thompson, of independent means, residing at the same place.

Mr. Cancellor was for the plaintiff and Mr. Clavell Salter for the defendant.

The case for the plaintiff was that on January 28th one of plaintiff's men called at the house for orders and was directed to bring 2lb. of colonial neck of mutton. Being out of colonial meat - January 28th was a Monday and it was customary to clear all colonial meat on Saturday night - he sent 1lb.13oz. of scrag end of English mutton. The meat was killed on the preceding Thursday and at that time of the year would have kept a fortnight or three weeks. On the Tuesday his man told him he had been ordered to take the meat back and the same day he received a

* 'Whip-jack' is one of the old rural names for a pied wagtail.

letter from the defendant, but in consequence of the tone of the letter he tore it up. He sent in the weekly account in the usual way, and it was returned with a footnote to the effect that the mutton was bad and unfit for food, that it smelt the whole kitchen out, and that as he did not send for it, Miss Thompson had had it thrown away. About half past five in the afternoon of February 4th or 5th Miss Thompson rode up to the shop on her bicycle and, addressing plaintiff in a loud tone, said 'What do you call yourself?' He replied 'I don't know, Miss Thompson', and defendant continued 'You are more fit to be shot at by the Boers than you are to be a tradesman in the parish of Freshwater', adding that she would never leave till she had driven him out of the parish and that she would see Colonel Nixon and Mrs. Findlay and everyone she knew and get them to discontinue trading with him. There were several people passing at the time. About March 11th Mrs. Nixon withdrew her custom and on the Freshwater Bay side he now had only four customers where before he had 20; on the Totland Bay and Alum Bay side his trade had certainly decreased. In cross-examination plaintiff said he did not send for the meat to take it back and he gave his man orders not to call on the 29th. There had been a previous dispute as to 11d. He did not send his man with orders to wait at the gate till he was paid the money and to say Miss Thompson would be 'County Courted' unless she paid 1s. 10d. Other evidence on plaintiff's side went to show that defendant's gardener, named Young, when given the meat to bury decided to take it home and have it cooked, and found it very tasty, and that on March 12th defendant went to a butcher named Chapman, at Yarmouth, and told him that if he would write to Mrs. Nixon - with whom he had had a difference - and apologise he could have her custom again. He did so and had since supplied Mrs. Nixon and defendant with meat … Miss Thompson said her maidservant called her attention to the meat and she found it looked horribly black and smelt on one side … On the 29th of January she rode down to the shop where she saw the assistant and told him she must ask that the mutton should be taken back and at the same time ordered another joint. The meat was not taken away. It remained until the Thursday, when she gave it to the gardener Young to throw away and did not know that he had not done so. Q. Is it a fact that you ever went down and told Mr. Hannam that he was more fit to be shot at by the Boers than to be a butcher at Freshwater? - It is utterly false. - Q. Or that you would never leave till you had driven him out of the parish? - No such words passed me. - Q. Or that you would see Mrs. Nixon and Mrs. Findlay and get them to change their custom? - It is utterly false.

Sarah Dassonville, defendant's maid, said the piece of mutton was not nice and smelt. Mrs. Nixon, wife of Colonel Nixon, who resides next house to defendant, spoke as to overhearing plaintiff's boy say he had orders not to leave the place without the money; she considered this insolence and in consequence returned to deal with her former butcher.

The jury retired to consider their verdict and after 20 minutes' absence returned into Court and stated there was no chance of their agreeing and they wished to know if the verdict of the majority would be accepted. Mr. Cancellor said he was afraid they could not agree to this. His Lordship told the jury they must consult a little longer, and after an absence of over an hour they found a verdict for the defendant, the case having lasted from 12 noon until nearly 7 pm.

In a court case involving talk of 'blackguards' and 'good thrashings', Mr. Collinson of Shanklin was also defending his standing in the community. He was a meteorologist, although it is not made clear whether he is an amateur or professional one. Whichever it was, the fact was obviously public knowledge amongst the youth of Shanklin who had taken to taunting him as he promenaded, with 'violent and offensive epithets' such as 'Rain' or 'Showers'. He sought resort in law ...

July 27th, 1901

SHANKLIN METEOROLOGIST'S GRIEVANCE

Charles Colman, butcher's assistant, of Shanklin, defended by Mr. Calder Woods, was charged with a breach of the county by-laws by using violent language towards Mr. John Collinson of Shanklin. - Mr. J. Marsh, who prosecuted, said that complainant was a perfectly peaceable citizen who was constantly assailed in the streets by violent and offensive epithets calculated to provoke a breach of the peace, though he had done nothing to excite the hostility of the vulgar. - Complainant, who said he was a resident owner, of Shanklin, deposed that about 9 p.m. on the 10th inst. he was walking along the Esplanade and had just passed defendant and five or six others who were standing together, when he heard a shout of 'Rain' and another shout of 'Showers' (laughter). Of course he knew it was intended for his annoyance. He turned back and recognising the defendant said 'It was you who shouted'. And defendant at once said 'I was one of them'. Witness then said 'I have a very good mind to give you a good thrashing'. Cross-examined: Q. What possible violent language can you complain of in anyone shouting 'Rain' or 'Showers'? (laughter). - Will you be good enough to ask him why he did it? Q. I ask you what possible objection there can be to several lads calling out 'Rain, rain', or 'Showers, showers'. - Because it is an annoyance to me. I happen to have written a book on the question of meteorology and they do it to annoy me. Q. Have you made a special subject of rain and showers? - Yes, if you like. - Q. You think these words were meant to annoy and insult you? - Exactly. On that occasion he heard nothing besides 'Rain, rain', and 'Showers, showers' shouted at him, though when he went away he was jeered at. He had been annoyed by those lads before. He could not himself tell that it was defendant who shouted on the occasion in question, but he was certain defendant admitted shouting when in his employer's shop. Defendant was behind the counter and as witness was going out he (witness) said to defendant 'You are a dirty young blackguard'. - Q. That remark was made by you though it was quite uncalled for? - No, by no means uncalled for. I said it because of his previous offences ... Q. Aren't you a little bit sensitive with regard to this question of rain? (laughter) ... Mr. Woods submitted with a great deal of confidence that there was no case under the by-law, as though the use of the words 'Rain' and 'Showers' might be trying to Mr. Collinson, still they could not be described as 'violent language'. The Chairman said the Bench had come to the conclusion that the case must be dismissed, but at the same time they considered the practice of shouting words to the annoyance of other people should be put a stop to, and if the summons had been for using abusive instead of violent language they would probably have convicted.

Just as in Victorian times, suicides occurred in large numbers, affecting high and low-born alike. They appeared in the County Press nearly every other week and it was by no means unusual for several accounts to appear in the same edition.

It would be unwise to generalise but it is fair to say that amongst the better-off middle classes, financial ruin or loss of standing in the community was often the catalyst for suicide, while for the poor a hard life and its attendant unhappiness was more usually the cause as in the case of Mr. Jolliffe of Shanklin, who left a sad little note ...

August 10th, 1901.

SUICIDE OF A SHANKLIN MAN AT COWES
HIS LETTER TO THE CORONER

At the Grapes Inn, Cowes, the Coroner for the Isle of Wight (E.F. Blake, Esq.) held an inquest on Saturday afternoon on the body of Frederick Jolliffe, whose body was found hanging from the Esplanade at Cowes on the previous evening. Mr. Simmons was chosen as foreman of the jury.

Albert Meach, of Pelham-road, Cowes, an engineer's clerk, stated that about a quarter to 11 on the previous evening he found the deceased hanging by the neck over the wall of the Esplanade, and thought his feet were in the water ... Witness handed a letter to the Coroner, who said it was addressed to him, and he read it as follows:

This is to certify that all my belongings I leave to Mr. Fry for his extreme kindness to me, and I write to state that I don't think life is worth living as fate seems to be against me, try how I will. So I am trusting in the Lord to have mercy on me and pity for me for the rash act I am about to commit. Lord have mercy on my soul, God have mercy on me and forgive me my sins, for there are many of them. Good-bye all. F. JOLLIFFE.

PS - I wish to leave the world in peace with everyone and forgive all that have done me an injury. If everyone would do to others as they wish to be done unto them this world would be worth living in, but it's man's inhumanity to man that makes the world so wicked. Once more I say 'Good-bye' to all.

William Henry Sneath, living at 30, Chapel-street, Newport ... said he had seen the body. It was that of his wife's brother, who came from Shanklin and was a painter. Deceased had been in the Infirmary with a bad leg. After that he went back to Shanklin and was offered work, but instead of doing that he led an irregular life and had to go to the Infirmary again. He went to Cowes from there....Deceased had been lodging with the man Fry mentioned in the letter. The Coroner ... asked witness if he thought the man was sane or insane at the time he committed this act. - Witness: I should say he was insane at the time.

Deceased was a widower and about 56 years of age. The Coroner briefly addressed the jury, who at once returned a verdict to the effect that deceased committed suicide while temporarily insane.

In the same way that the shipyards of J.S White are remembered as a major employer on the Island, so it was with the Lace Factory at Broadlands in the mid-1800s. In the buildings at Staplers now occupied by the Job Centre, nearly 800 people, many of them children, were employed in manufacturing intricate and beautiful Isle of Wight lace which was sold all over the world. The factory was a major Island employer for over 40 years until Mr. Nunn, the owner, retired. He had no family to hand the business on to and the factory was closed. A former employee of the factory wrote to the County Press, some 30 years after its closure, detailing a little of its history ...

November 2nd, 1901

AN OLD AND ONCE FAMOUS ISLAND INDUSTRY
SOME INTERESTING REMINISCENCES

Many years ago one of the most important and flourishing industrial undertakings in the Island was 'Nunn's Lace Factory', at Broadlands, Newport, which was noted not only throughout England, but all over Europe, for the beauty of the lace fabrics there designed and manufactured. Mr. Henry Sheppard of Newport, who held a responsible position at the factory as machinist and designer, exhibiting in those departments the highest skill, has favoured us with the following interesting sketch of the history of this once celebrated Island industry:-

About the year 1810 a lace machine called the transverse warp machine was invented by a Mr. J. Brown and Mr. George Freeman, silk stocking weavers, of Radford, near Nottingham ... Having made a yard or two of the lace, and having no means of carrying out the invention, they took the lace to a Mr. Nunn, a banker and rich man of Nottingham, who was taking great interest in the lace trade, and asked him to assist them, which he consented to do on condition that they took his son (the late Mr. H. W. Nunn, afterwards of Broadlands, Newport) into partnership with them ... They removed the machines to Blackfriars-Road, London and in 1826 or 1827 they decided to leave London. They divided the machines, half being sent to Tewkesbury, in Gloucestershire, my father going with them. Of course I went, being only a youngster. The other half of the machines came to Broadlands, Newport ... The firm was now Freeman and Nunn. Mr. W. Freeman managed the factory only a few years and was succeeded by Mr. H.W. Nunn. The reason why they took the machines to such comparatively out-of-the-way places was that any invention they might make should be kept secret. On February 27th, 1833, the patent was taken out for the invention of French blonde lace. It was kept secret for some considerable time and was sold as French blonde, realising an enormous profit. It was said £60,000 worth was sold with a profit of £40,000 ... Mr. Nunn wrote and asked me to come to the Island, and being persuaded by Mr. George Freeman, who was still partner, I accepted his offer and arrived in the Island on January 27th, 1853. It took myself, my wife, and my son (now of Ventnor, two days to get here ... I found the machines far behind those at Tewkesbury both in construction and speed. The men had double the labour, the machines being on a very old principle, working with both hands and feet. The ones I had left were put in motion by the man simply turning a handle, like a grinding-stone, and the blonde lace made was also quite different from what I had been used to. Mr.

Nunn was very kind to me and by his instructions my first work was to alter the machines from the old principle to the rotary one, and at the same time I made myself master of the manufacture of the blonde lace. It was not all honey. I had an uphill work to do. I was by some looked upon as an interloper and an 'overner', who had no business at all in the Island; but this did not trouble me much. I knew my work and had more knowledge and experience in machinery than they had. Both Mr. Freeman and Mr. Nunn were first rate mechanics. There was at the factory one of the cleverest men I ever knew - Mr. Thomas Reason, who was self-taught in matters relating to machinery (specimens of his beautiful workmanship I still retain). In the busy time there were about 100 men, from 20 to 30 winding boys, and about 60 girls employed at the factory. The men in the factories kept themselves well acquainted with the news and topics of the day. A great many of the men coming long distances from the factory brought their dinner with them and many had theirs sent. An hour was taken for dinner, and the men at that time all met in one place, in winter round the large fire, when two of their number were told off to read the news and leading articles in the Times newspaper (each one subscribing his few pence weekly), after which there often arose some capital discussions, there being many intelligent men among them. The only holidays were two days at Whitsuntide (Newport fair), Good Friday, and at Christmas. The lace was silk blonde edging, some of it being as fine as spider web and very expensive. Mr. Nunn told me some of the silk cost a pound weight of silver for a pound of silk. The lace trade was very uncertain, going from one extreme to the other, its prosperity depending on fickle fashion. The following is an instance: there had been a very depressed trade for some time. Mr. Nunn told me he had over 20,000 cards of blonde in stock. Quite unexpectedly some very large orders arrived from America, and in about six weeks he had not 300 cards in stock. At one time I believe the men possessed sufficient votes at Newport to send what candidates they chose to Parliament. We had a strike which lasted six weeks when the men had to give in. Mr. Nunn was getting on in years, and having no son to succeed him and certain things having occurred, of which I cannot speak here, he came to the decision to relinquish the business, which he did some few years before his death (about 1870). This proved a serious loss to Newport. Mr. Nunn was buried at St Paul's (Barton) Churchyard. After his death the factory and machinery and his vast wealth came into the possession of Mrs. Capt. Harvey, of The Cliff, Shanklin, who deputed me in February, 1877 to offer as a gift the factory and machinery to a certain person, also to assist him with capital to start the factory again, and I offered to assist him in putting the machines in working order. For the benefit of Newport I was anxious that the factory should be continued, but he refused the offer. Mrs. Harvey then put it into my hands to dispose of the machinery, which I did. I have a catalogue of all the machines and description of them. The factory now is a training institution for servants and a home for ladies of limited means. I believe it is endowed by Mrs. Harvey, who died about two years ago, and who will be long remembered for her many munificent acts. Your readers may, perhaps find something to interest them in these few notes about an industry which once spread the name of Newport far and wide.

Mew Langton was the major brewer on the Island, owning many pubs and inns. They had recently enlarged their Newport brewery complex in Crocker Street by purchasing the old Bridewell, or gaol, (opposite today's Medina Railway pub) and then demolishing it to build a new brewery on the site*. The County Press described the new building and its purpose …

November 16th, 1901

THE ROYAL BREWERY

NEW MALTING PROCESS AND BUILDINGS

Inhabitants of Newport and many others, especially passengers by Railway, have marked with interest of late the demolition of an historic building near the Station at Newport, known as the old Bridewell, which having survived its period of usefulness as a place of detention for transgressors against the law, was acquired by Messrs W.B. Mew, Langton, and Co., of the Royal Brewery, whose premises adjoined, and has now been pulled down to make room for the extension of the Brewery buildings. The new building which is to be erected will be an imposing brick structure, with ornamental mouldings, 100 ft. long by 50ft. wide and some 60ft. in height, with slated lantern roof, and the interior extensively strengthened with iron. The new structure will provide convenient storage for a large supply of barley and is also designed for the accommodation of a modern plant which is to be erected for malting by the pneumatic process, and it will take the place of various old buildings. In the pneumatic system, which has been long enough in use on the Continent to demonstrate its advantages, great attention is paid to the screening and cleaning of the grain, and by the utilisation of ingenious mechanical devices in the malting process it is claimed more perfect control can be maintained throughout the various operations, a greater output can be obtained, and a product of better and more certain quality secured.

The new system will best be explained by tracing the barley through the various stages of conversion into malt. Consignments of barley on arrival are hoisted to the top floor of the building, where they are sorted and classified. Thence the grain is conveyed as required to a drying drum below, which removes the excess of moisture which exists when the corn has not been brought into condition by the natural process of 'sweating' in the barley rick. From the drying drum it is passed up through screens and separators, by which dirt, foreign matter, and broken corns are eliminated. It is then carried by a 'band conveyor' away under the roof and discharged for storage into one of eight barley bins, of from 300 to 400 quarters capacity each, situated in the central and main storage floor. This conveyor is similar in appearance to an ordinary wide leather belt, and the grain which is borne on its upper surface can be discharged at any part of its length by momentarily deflecting it from its horizontal course at the required point by means of the ingenious device consisting of movable pulleys. When required for malting the grain runs by gravitation to a band conveyor running under the bins and is deposited in

* Some weeks prior to this article appearing, a small anonymous advert had appeared, presumably from a disgruntled builder, simply reading 'Mew, Langton and Co. should compensate those who spent time and trouble in tendering to them for the demolition of the Bridewell and then doing it themselves'.

wetting cylinders on the ground floor, where it is steeped. Hence when fit, it is forced by compressed air through a tube to one of the 'germinating drums'. These drums of which there are six, are hollow cylinders of 30 quarters capacity each, through which cooled and purified air is exhausted by powerful fans, enabling the rate of germination to be controlled, the drums rotating meanwhile and keeping the grain in movement with far less damage than when moved by shovels on the old malting floors. After reaching the proper degree of germination the grain is conveyed by another band to an elevator and raised to a drying drum, the drying process being completed in a 'curing drum' on the ground floor to which the grain again navigates. This drying and curing machinery, through which it should be stated heated air is exhausted, takes the place of the kiln drying in the old system of malting. As a final step to perfection the malt, which the grain has now become, is once more conveyed and elevated to the top floor for another course of screening and polishing by which the malt dust and any unnecessary matter is removed, and thence to capacious airtight malt bins on the storage floor, there to await brewing requirements. When this demand arrives, the malt is gravitated into a machine which automatically weighs it into sacks ready for use.

The architect of the building is Mr. Ernest Flint, FRIBA., of London; the work is being carried out by Messrs. James Ball and Son, of Cowes; and … it is expected that the building and plant will be ready for work by the middle of the coming year.

The alterations now in progress on this site, we may suggest, appear to afford an excellent opportunity for effecting a much to be desired improvement in the approach to the railway-station by the removal of an awkward corner at the bottom of Holyrood-street, and it is to be hoped that the authorities concerned will not lose sight of the matter.

1902

Two single men, described in court as 'worthless characters' were found by the police, after hours, in the Five Bells public house* at Shorwell. They were actually found hiding in a cupboard in the landlady's bedroom. Mysteriously, both men had removed their boots and various items of clothing despite it being a cold February night. During the subsequent court case one of the men was silenced by the clerk of the Court as he began to tell of the arresting Sergeant committing an indecent act in front of the landlady …

February 1st, 1902
CUSTOMERS IN THE CUPBOARD

Roland Cotton, of Atherfield, and *Harry James Jacobs*, of Shorwell, two single labourers, pleaded guilty to being on licensed premises during prohibited hours at the Five Bells, Shorwell, on the previous Monday night. Mr. H.C. Damant appeared to watch the case on behalf of the owners of the licensed premises. Acting Sergeant Ryall, of the County Constabulary, said that on the 19th inst., he, with P.C. Stevens was keeping observation on the Five Bells, of which William Young was the licence-holder. In consequence of a

---

* The pub lives on today as numbers 1 and 2 Five Bells cottages, located directly opposite the Post Office.

communication from P.C. Stevens he went to the side door of the Five Bells, and on listening heard men's and women's voices inside. He knocked the door but received no answer. He went to the front door and knocked again, and continued knocking until 10.45, when he heard people inside open an inner door and go up the stairs. He continued knocking another ten minutes at the expiration of which, the manageress, Mrs. Denness (daughter of the licence-holder), opened the window and looking out asked 'Who is there?' He replied 'The police'. She asked 'What do you want?' and he replied 'I wish to come in and look over your premises'. Mrs. Denness and a servant named Laura Smith opened the door and Mrs. Denness said 'You can go wherever you like'. He examined all the rooms downstairs and the cellar. In the living-room he found bottles and glasses on the table. He then said to Mrs. Denness 'Who have you got upstairs?' and she said 'No-one; you are welcome to go up and see'. He replied 'I am about to do so', when Mrs. Denness said 'Before you go upstairs you will have to get a warrant to search my premises'. He told her that a warrant was not necessary for searching licensed premises, and added 'There are two men in this house and I am determined to find them out'. Mrs. Denness then said 'Very well, go upstairs'. He went up and searched all the bed-rooms and found no one. Mrs. Denness lifted the valances for him to look underneath the beds. On going to Mrs. Denness's bed-room she said 'Is there anyone there?' He asked 'What have you got in the cupboard?' which he had found was locked. She replied nothing but things which belonged to her. On listening at the cupboard door he could distinctly hear persons breathing inside and he asked Mrs. Denness to unlock the cupboard. She said she could not do so then as the key was at Presford, but when he told P.C. Stevens to go to Mr. Young at Presford and ask for the key she said 'I think I have a key that will fit'. She produced a key, and when the cupboard was unlocked he saw the two defendants inside (laughter). Jacobs was sitting down on the floor with his boots and jacket and vest off, and Cotton had his jacket and vest undone and his boots off. When spoken to by witness Cotton said 'Yes, you ——, we are 'all kiff' now. I have bested you before and I have bested you again. We are lodgers here, ain't we, Shinar?' (laughter). Cotton asked the question of Jacobs, to whom he referred as 'Shinar'. Witness replied that they were pretty fine lodgers, to be locked in the cupboard, and ultimately they said 'We are not lodgers; we will go'. Cotton put his boots on, and Jacobs, after hunting over Mrs. Denness's room for his boots, left bare-foot as he could not find the boots. Jacobs lived about 150 yards from the house and Cotton about two miles off. Cotton had threatened he would complain to the magistrates that he (witness) had committed an act of indecency before the manageress. On Tuesday she stopped him ——. - The Clerk (Mr. John Fardell) said they would not go into that. - Witness said he would rather for the Court to hear it. He added that there was no accommodation for lodgers at the house. - Mr. Damant said the landlord had had notice to quit. - Cotton said he went there for a night's lodging, and he had not been there long before he heard a banging at the door. Mrs. Denness thought it was her husband, from whom she had been separated, come back to the house, and they went upstairs and were put into the cupboard out of the way. Had he known it was the police at the door he should not have left the room. - The Chairman said the Bench considered it a bad case and defendants would each be fined £2. and 6s. 6d. costs; in default 21 days imprisonment. - Defendants asked for time to pay but Superintendent Ayres objected, saying they had given a lot of trouble lately at Shorwell. - The Sergeant said the men were single and had no effects. They were worthless characters. - The Bench refused the application for time and defendants stood back.

(In April the following year, Mrs. Denness appeared in court to defend a separation order brought by her husband on the grounds of her adultery. Her address was given as Melbourne Street, Newport, where she lived with her partner, 'Roland Cotton'.)

A French brig, the Russie, which initially claimed to be carrying only fishing gear and salt, became stranded on the rocks off Atherfield bay. She lingered, stuck fast for a full week until eventually being torn apart by gales, when her secret was revealed as casks of brandy, wine and spirits were washed ashore. The happy news soon spread throughout the Island and as the County Press put it, 'There were regrettable scenes ... which will not readily be forgotten' ...

April 12th, 1902

THE WRECKED RUSSIE AT NITON
REGRETTABLE SCENES ON THE SHORE. WINE AND SPIRITS
BROACHED AND CONSUMED

The mystery of the wreck of the French fishing-brig Russie deepens. That a small craft of about 250 tons should be manned by a crew of 31 hands and carry 20 whale-boats were extraordinary facts, and these in conjunction with her suspicious movements previous to being cast ashore miles out of the course to any fishing-grounds, gave her an air of mystery which many remarked upon. The statement of the crew that the only cargo aboard was salt for salting down the fish caught, contained in barrels was, however, accepted without reserve by the shoremen. Therefore, on Saturday night when a high wind and rough sea commenced to break up the wreck, comparatively only a few proceeded to the shore in search of unconsidered trifles which the tide might cast ashore. Surprise, however, gave place to suspicion, when casks of all sizes were cast up by the waves. After one of these casks had in a dark corner been 'sampled', those on the spot ignored the boxes of bloaters, polonies, pork, and other edibles which the sea continued to give up in increasing quantities, and there was a quiet stampede for bottles, buckets, tin cans, and any thing that would hold liquid. How much of this cargo of 'salt' surreptitiously disappeared in the dark hours of the night will never be known, but when morning dawned the authorities, if they did not know it before - and if they did they kept the secret well - awoke to the fact that the Russie had carried a cargo of thousands of gallons of wines and spirits. Casks of cognac brandy, white wine, red wine, claret, and cider were strewn along the shore. Some had been broached and much of the contents was missing, and those which were intact the Coastguard lost no time in rolling up the cliff to positions where they could be guarded. The casks varied in size from under nine gallons to about 100 gallons.

The scene during Sunday will not readily be forgotten. In some cases, casks had been hidden away under the shingle and their tops covered over with boulders, with which the shore is strewn, consequently P.C. Holding and the Coastguardsmen did not discover those secret hoards until later in the day. Undesirables from miles around flocked to the wreck and were soon rendered drunk by the potent spirits. Some lay about in a drunken state all day, while others fought and quarrelled disgracefully. To cope with the situation the authorities spilled the contents of all broached casks on the ground or shingle, where they stood, and kept a sharp lookout for all others that were washed ashore. Very little fishing gear was to be seen amongst the wreckage.

Saturday's blow left the Russie a complete wreck. Her masts, bulwarks, and everything above the water-line have been carried away, but it is understood that the contents of the lower hold remain to be salved.

Another correspondent writes: The wrecked Russie was the object of much interest on Saturday evening, when a large number of spectators had assembled on the beach in anticipation of the vessel breaking up as the SSW wind had increased to half a gale. The fore-part of the vessel was tightly wedged on the rocks whilst the stern twisted and swayed as each wave washed over it and the vessel soon turned on her side, releasing many barrels from the hold. These speedily came ashore and men and boys endeavoured to salve what they innocently believed to be barrels of salt. But they soon learned the real truth as to the contents of the barrels, some of which dashed against the rocks and burst and coloured the surf. Then it was realised that they contained wine and spirits, and scenes which can only be described as disgraceful ensued. Heads of barrels were knocked in, and bottles, buckets, and tins of all descriptions were utilised in carrying the wine and spirits away. Some who drank then and there became tipsy, but by this time darkness had set in. Unfortunately similar scenes were enacted on Sunday, when people from other parts came and took part in this Bachannalian orgie. Sunday afternoon saw six or seven men in different stages of drunkenness lying in the fields by the Lighthouse. The Coastguardsmen, who had been on duty since five o'clock the previous evening, were worn out by their vigilant efforts to prevent the broaching of the barrels. Timber of all descriptions, fish baskets, birch brooms, &c. washed in in large quantities. All that remained of the Russie consisted of her masts, spars, and a portion of the hull. During low tide on Monday men were busy clearing off the brass sheeting, ropes, blocks, and chains, &c., and other salvage operations have since taken place … We are informed by representatives of the owners that reports published by London and other papers as to the shore scenes and the quantity of casks of wines are much exaggerated.

THE WEEK'S NEWS

BRIGHSTONE. A white rook fell to the gun of Mr. E.H. Abraham, of Newport, who was with a rook shooting party at Brighstone last week. It is a fine specimen of a young albino and is exceedingly rare among rooks, Mr. Percy Wadham, the well known local naturalist, stating that it is the first he has known in the Island. Mr. Wadham also has four albino moles, which were recently found at Wootton.

HUNSTANTON. Friday. Mr. E. Wales, proprietor of the Railway Hotel, Hunstanton, returned home from a drive at half past 10 last night, when on entering his bar, Hubert Klee, the assistant manager, pulled out a pistol and fired at him with the remark, 'One for you, one for me'. He then shot himself dead. Mr. Wales was dangerously wounded in the head and lies in a serious condition. It is stated that quarrels had occurred recently between the two men in connection with money matters and also on account of jealousy

A lady parachutist named Miss Edith Brookes met with a terrible death at Sheffield on Tuesday night. When she left the balloon at a height of about 700 feet the parachute failed to act and she was dashed to the ground and killed.

AUCTION SALES - On Thursday of last week, April 5th, Messrs Henry J. Way and Son held a sale at the Medina-hall of interesting curios, historical relics, &c. by direction of Mr W. Ledicott, of the Old Curiosity Shop.

A RARE BIRD VISITOR TO THE ISLAND.- Mr. Percy Wadham writes, 'A white stork was seen flying over Atherfield on April 29th and seems to have dropped exhausted in a field near Shorwell amongst some cattle, where it met with a warm reception, the cattle turning on it and breaking its leg and wing. Eventually it was discovered and rescued, and after amputating the pinion joint of the wing and putting the leg in splints the stork seems to be doing well on the lawn at Northcourt, feasting on fish, frogs, snails, dead birds, and any other delicacy that comes its way'.

———————◆———————

Many readers will be aware that Brighstone's former name was Brixton and that many old maps and documents produced in the 18th and 19th century happily used either name. What may come as a surprise is that it was only in 1902 that legislation was introduced to finally drop the one and adopt the other ...

May 31st, 1902
'BRIGHSTONE' NOT BRIXTON
The General Purposes Committee recommended that the common seal of the Council be affixed to an Order naming the parish of Brighstone. This order sets forth: 'Whereas ... considerable doubt has for many years existed as to the correct name of the parish sometimes called 'Brighstone' and at other times 'Brixton'in the Isle of Wight, and after consultation with the Parish Council of the said parish we have decided that the name of the said parish shall be Brighstone. Now therefore ... we hereby order and direct that the said parish shall from and after the date of this our Order and direction be named and shall become and be known as the parish of Brighstone'.

———————◆———————

Accounts of horses bolting and disappearing over the horizon with their carts or carriages bouncing behind them were fairly commonplace and not many weeks would pass without a report of yet another runaway. Although most of them usually ended without too much harm, it was not always the case …

July 12th, 1902

ALARMING RUNAWAY ACCIDENT

On Thursday afternoon a horse and cab belonging to Mr. Smith were on the rank in the Fountain Hotel yard at Cowes when the animal slipped its bridle. It immediately bolted, and clearing the other vehicles in front of it and evading efforts to stop it, dashed out under the archway. It first collided with the shop window of Mrs. Whitman, in the High-street, smashing a large pane of glass but fortunately doing little damage to the chinaware and glass inside, and then swerving to the left, broke up a valuable bicycle belonging to Mr. Cook, of Gurnard. Tearing off along the street, the horse came to one of the narrowest parts of the narrow thoroughfare. There a trolley was standing. Unable to pass, the runaway made a wild leap onto the vehicle, and landing on it with its forelegs lost its balance and fell over into the newly constructed shop window of the Maypole Dairy Company. The framework and glass fell in with a crash. The animal, with its body in the window, lay there bleeding profusely from its wounds and evidently in great agony till Mr. H. Slade mercifully put it out of its misery with a pole-axe. A painter on a tall ladder inside the Fountain yard had a narrow escape. The cab just missed him. Another painter at work in the High-street, also using a ladder, was, fortunately, not on it when the horse dashed past and knocked it over. The affair caused considerable excitement and a large crowd gathered round the dairy premises till the horse had been dispatched and the carcass removed. Mr. Smith will be a heavy loser by the accident.*

ANOTHER RUNAWAY ACCIDENT

Yesterday (Friday) afternoon as a horse and van belonging to the Cowes Co-operative Society were in Bernard-road the horse was startled, presumably by the whistle of a train as it was coming out of the tunnel, and bolted down the road straight into the oak fence of the West-Hill Estate. Both horse and van were overturned and the groceries scattered in the road. The animal, fortunately, escaped unhurt.

———————◆———————

Truth magazine didn't always get it right …

August 2nd, 1902

TOWN AND COUNTRY

The *World* announced last week that Osborne house 'may become a convalescent home or a sanatorium', and *Truth* this week characterises this statement as an invention of the most extravagant character. 'We shall hear next', says *Truth*, 'that Buckingham Palace is to become a barracks and Windsor

---

* The Maypole Dairy Company eventually sued Mr. Smith for £ 8. 6s. 11d. damages and the case came to court in April the following year. Since they were unable to prove negligence on Mr. Smith's part, the court found in his favour and Maypole Dairy not only lost their claim but were ordered to pay Mr. Smith's costs.

Castle and is to become a model prison. Last year the *World* stated that Osborne would shortly be sold. The fact is that Queen Victoria left Osborne to the Crown, intending the domain to become one of the permanent residences of the sovereign. The estate could not be alienated, and it would be as well if the publication of absurd fictions on the subject of Osborne were discontinued, as the circulation of such tales causes much annoyance to the King and the Royal Family. The Princess of Wales and her children will go shortly to Osborne for a stay of several weeks, and it is very probable that the King and Queen will reside there for some time next winter'.

———————————◆———————————

Public displays of affection or physical contact of any kind were rarely if ever seen 100 years ago, especially ones involving the royal family. Then as now, they were not known for indulging in physical contact, either in public or with the public, and to this day physical contact with a member of the royal family is strictly taboo but as this obituary of an 82 year-old Osborne estate worker reveals, not everyone followed the rules …

November 22nd, 1902
DEATH AND FUNERAL OF OLD OSBORNE SERVANT
SOME INTERESTING REMINISCENCES

As briefly announced in our last issue, Mr. William Jackman, who for many years was employed on the Royal Estate at Osborne, died at the Royal almshouses at Whippingham on Thursday, the 13th. He was 82 years of age. He commenced work at Osborne in the year 1842 as the servant of Lady Blachford, and on the property being purchased by the late Queen Victoria, Jackman remained and continued his work there till he became unsuited for further service. He then retired to the almshouses and there became the recipient of the benefits graciously provided by the Queen for old servants of the estate. Jackman was the oldest employee at Osborne. He occupied the position of head carter and ploughman for many years, carrying out his duties with faithfulness, which won the respect and regard of those with whom he was daily brought into contact. He, moreover, was endowed with a spirit of good humour which broke through any troubles of his life to the last. Members of the family of the late Queen Victoria were fond of him, and the Princes when boys would sometimes go into the fields where he was ploughing and ride occasionally upon the horses which were in his charge. He was frequently visited by the late Queen when he lived at Barton since his retirement, and he has not been forgotten in these later days. The King in the early summer this year paid a visit to Whippingham in his motor-car and saw the residents of the almshouses. His Majesty had a short and lively conversation with Jackman, who could not refrain, remembering past years, from putting his hand on the King's shoulder and saying 'I be glad to see ye'. This touch of cordiality from an old and familiar servant evidently pleased His Majesty.

———————————◆———————————

Cycles and Motors.

CYCLIST! Now is the time to select your new m/c. Ah! what is your mount to be for 1903? Remember, it all depends with whom you entrust your order whether you cycle with pleasure or disappointment throughout the coming season. We have not a single m/c left of 1902 pattern, and therefore customers can rely on getting right up-to-date goods, a point which intending purchasers should be very particular about. We have again selected the very cream of the cycle production for our coming year's trade, and have every confidence in recommending the following renowned makes : Triumph, Centaur, Osmond, Hobart, Calcott, Hazelwood, Raleigh, and Sunbeam, all of which turn out a good mount, with free wheel, 2 brakes, and plated rims, from £10 10s. To those who *will* have a cheaper machine we are offering a mount with all on at £8 8s.; but our advice is—purchase the best m/c you can find and you will soon save the extra cost in repairs. Any m/c can be had on easy terms; old m/c's taken in exchange at Cheverton's, the home of the cycle, close to Town-hall, Newport. Travellers will wait on intending purchasers in any part of the Island on receipt of post-card. The noted house for repairs.

For Sale.

GREYHOUND for sale, cheap.—Apply Merston Manor.

GUN, bargain, double-barrelled, 12-bore, central fire, breechloader, top lever, extension rib, rebounding locks, left choke, pistol grip walnut stock, splendid killer, beautifully finished, new, £1 18s. 6d., approval.—F. Coote Reynalds, 48, Devonshire-street, London, W.C.

HAMS! hams! hams.—The right size, the right quality, and the right cure at the right price if purchased from the right firm—A. W. Abraham and Co., bacon factors, Upper St. James's-street, Newport, I.W.

IRONMONGERY, Oils, and Colours at clearance prices, prior to removal into the wholesale department as previously announced.—Upton's stores, Newport.

LANDAUS, two, for sale, in good working order, painted chocolate, picked out red, lined blue cloth and morocco leather, with poles, bars, lamps complete, one with luggage cradle.—Apply R. Bartlett, New-road mews, Shanklin, I.W.

LAWN-MOWERS at store prices for cash; machines ground and repaired; garden rollers, Tamlin's Nonpareil incubators.—Linington, Market, Newport.

LIME.—Grey lime daily for building purposes at Standen pit, near Newport; also good lime and fine chalk at Castle pit, near Cemetery; white and grey lime sold at yard, Chapel-street, Newport, or delivered by rail or road to any part of the Island; also lime sold for land purposes.—Proprietor, E. Rogers, Chapel-street, Newport.

PARLOUR Billiard Table, small size, cheap, cash or terms.—Cheverton's furniture stores, Newport.

TO LET.

ALVINGTON.—To let, large 6-roomed Villa and 300ft. garden, gas cooker, rent 6s. 6d.—Roberts, Eastern Villa, Carisbrooke.

NEWPORT.—6-roomed Cottage at Merton-terrace, Worsley-road, Hunnyhill, to let, rent 4s. 6d.—Witham, Pyle House, 137, Pyle-street.

SANDOWN.—Very pleasant furnished Cottage, close to sands, newly decorated, perfect sanitation 6 rooms, 15s. weekly.—"Ivanhoe," Martin's library, Sandown.

TWO COTTAGES FOR SALE, by MESSRS. WALLIS, RIDDETT,—AND Co., in an excellent situation in Ryde; main-road; midway between railway-station and town. Both let to good tenants, who have been in occupation several years. Long leasehold; ground-rent £3. Price £220. (S.R. 737.)

Apply at TOWN-HALL CHAMBERS, RYDE.

£420 will purchase a small but very conveniently placed Residence in the flourishing town of Shanklin; near church, railway-station, sea, and shops. Arranged on two floors; in good repair. Long lease; low ground-rent. Fixtures at valuation. Or would be let unfurnished on lease. Immediate sale desired. (S.R. 675.)

Apply to Messrs. Wallis, Riddett, and Co., Ryde.

NEWPORT.—To be let, a small Cottage known as Round House, with a large garden thereto, situate on the Fairlee-road, Newport.—For particulars apply to J. Beverton, Stuart House, Holyrood-street, Newport,

Messrs. Marvins.

Re Caroline Wall, deceased.
PORCHFIELD,
in the Parish of Calbourne, about three miles from Newport.

Sale of Household Furniture, Linen, China, Pictures, Jewellery, Gold, Silver, and Plated Goods, and other Effects.

STANLEY WADHAM has received instructions from the executors under the will of the late Caroline Wall to Sell by Auction on WEDNESDAY, FEBRUARY 11, 1903, at 12 o'clock (on account of the number of lots), the whole of the HOUSEHOLD FURNITURE and effects contained in the residence, comprising bedsteads and bedding, 4 prime goose-feather beds, bolsters, and pillows, a large number of blankets, counterpanes, and bed linen, mahogany and japanned chests of drawers, an antique mahogany cabinet commode, a ditto pierced brass fender, antique barometer, gilt chimney glasses, a fine old engraving of George III., dated 1771, easy and other chairs, dining and other tables, valuable grandfather's clock, a ditto, capital grey talking parrot, a ditto paroquet, mahogany glazed chiffonnier bookcase, six single and one arm antique Chippendale chairs, lady's valuable gold watch and long chain, 3 silver watches, 8 ditto earrings, 13 ditto brooches, rings and studs, large patent wringing and mangling machine, pots and plants, china and glass, kitchen and scullery utensils, and numerous effects.

On view the morning of sale, and catalogues may be obtained at the place of sale, at the offices of the Auctioneer, St. James's-hall, Newport, and at 60, High-street, Cowes.

The valuable LIVE and DEAD STOCK of the DAIRY FARM will be Sold by Auction at 11 o'clock precisely on the same date.

Separate catalogues issued.

1903

Bloaters sailed through the air in Ryde one evening as Mr. Wolfe, a local fishmonger, let his hair down as Christmas 1902 approached. Refreshed and invigorated by repeated visits to a nearby public house, he provided an entertaining sideshow for late night shoppers as he sold his fish from the pavement in Ryde High Street. At the same time he managed to add a new word to the English language. ...

January 3rd, 1903

THE MOST 'SENSIBLEST' MAN IN THE WORLD

Henry George Wolfe, dealer, of High-street, was summoned for loitering on the footway without reasonable excuse. P.C. Denness deposed that on the 20th of December he was on duty in the upper part of High-street, and at about 6 o'clock he saw defendant out in the street with a crowd, many of whom were boys and girls, around him. He was the worse for drink, and he was singing and calling attention to his show in language which was not very choice. He asked some of the people 'What do you think of my — show?' Witness called defendant's attention to the fact that he was blocking the street but he only replied that he was the boss and should do what he liked. Several bicycles and carriages came along and it took witness all his time to get them through the crowd without an accident. Defendant paid a visit to the neighbouring public house, and when he came out he still continued his objectionable conduct. He held up a herring and shouted 'Who will give me a penny for this?' He then got a box of bloaters and threw them about for the people to scramble for, and he was not particular whose face he threw them into. Defendant kept this sort of thing up till 9.30. He cautioned defendant more than once. There was a crowd there practically all the evening. - P.S. Watson corroborated. There was such a crowd that the street was quite blocked. When Wolfe was behaving in the manner described witness said to him, 'You are acting very foolishly Wolfe, and will get yourself into trouble'. Defendant replied 'When you are talking to me you are talking to the most sensiblest man in the world' (laughter). - Defendant said he was working very hard all the evening, in picking and trussing birds and in serving people. No doubt he might have had a glass, but he was too busy to be out in the road; in fact he was not in the road more than 25 minutes all the evening ... There were five previous convictions against the defendant. The mayor said the Bench considered defendant was guilty of behaving in such a manner as to interrupt traffic in the street. They would deal with the matter as leniently as possible, but he would have to pay a fine of 10s. and the costs 12s.6d. He advised defendant not to offend in this way again.

The annual licensing sessions for the Island presented some interesting statistics ...

February 14th, 1903
ANNUAL LICENSING MEETING AT RYDE

Supt. Hinks reported that there are 65 fully-licensed houses, nine beer on and off, three beer off, three refreshment houses, three chemist's, and 13 grocers' licences; total 96, which gave one licence to every 115 persons according to the census of 1901. Forty-eight persons were apprehended or summoned for having been drunk or drunk and disorderly and all were fined. The licence of the St Johns-road railway station had been granted by the magistrates but the excise licence had not been taken out for several years. The Lamb Inn, Brunswick-street, at present requires some internal alterations for the accommodation of the public. The brewer had promised that the requirements should be carried out immediately.

February 14th, 1903
NEWPORT BOROUGH LICENSING SESSIONS

The Clerk (Mr. W. H. Wooldridge) read the annual report of Supt. Ayres to the justices as follows:- I beg to lay before you the following report, showing the number of licensed houses, &c., within the Borough, namely: Fully licensed houses, 56; beer and spirit, 4; ditto six day off, 2; beer and wine, 1; beer, 11; beer six day, 2; beer, six day off, 1; grocers' licences, 5; chemists' wine licence, 1; billiard licence, 1; total 84. Two houses have been closed during the following periods: The Old Inn, Hunnyhill, from about 31st of January to the 24th of March, 1902, the Dolphin, Quay-street, from about 27th September to the 20th October, 1902. The Anchor Brewery, Mill-street, is apparently not used at all for business and one chemists' wine licence has not been used since March 1902. 44 persons have been proceeded against for drunkenness and other offences in connection therewith since the annual licensing meeting 1901, 42 of whom were convicted and fined, and three dismissed, one male with a caution, being of weak intellect. Four licence holders have been proceeded against, namely: William Hills, Shoulder of Mutton, for serving a drunken person, and dismissed with caution; John A. Creal, the Eagle, unstamped measures, fined 1s.; Alfred Beck, the Britannia, adulteration, dismissed on payment of costs 18s.; James Bridge, the Sun, unstamped measures, fined 1s. The population of the Borough is 10,911 according to the census of 1901, and there being 83 licences to sell on and off the premises, this gives one licence to about 132 inhabitants of all ages, the number of licences in my opinion being excessive to the requirements. The licensed houses have been well conducted generally since the annual licensing meeting of 1901.

———————◆———————

Electricity had arrived in Cowes, Newport, Ryde, Shanklin and Ventnor although it was still beyond the means of most people and for the moment remained the reserve of the wealthy. It had recently reached Sandown and for the residents able to afford it, it had quickly become a part of everyday life, so much so that when the town experienced its first power cut life almost ground to a halt ...

February 21st, 1903
LIGHTS OUT!

SANDOWN. The town was in a state of almost total darkness on Thursday night owing to the failure of the electric current, the fuses attached to the main cables failing. All the lamps, arc, incandescent, and private, went out at 7 o'clock, and the necessary repairs could not be effected at the works at Lake in time to switch the current on again the same night. In fact, the workmen could not discover where the fault lay until yesterday (Friday). The tradesmen who depend on the electric current for lighting purposes suffered some inconvenience, though in the majority of cases the failure did not occur till near closing time. A number of tradespeople had to resort to other means of shop illumination - oil lamps, lanterns, and candles. An old public servant jocularly inquired of our representative the way to the Post-office. Yesterday the defect was remedied, and last night the lighting was fairly good. The Electric-light Company have sent a letter of apology to all their customers for the fault which suddenly developed in one of the Sandown mains.

———————◆———————

To this day there are front doors in Carisbrooke High Street that open directly onto the road, with no pavement at all to separate them from the traffic. So it was one Saturday afternoon in 1903 when the well-known landlord of the Eight Bells stepped into the road from his pub door just as an 11-year-old boy came down the hill on his bicycle ...

February 28th, 1903
FATAL CYCLING ACCIDENT AT CARISBROOKE
WELL-KNOWN ISLAND COACH DRIVER KILLED

We record with much regret the death which occurred on Sunday evening, of Mr. Alfred William Burt, the genial and esteemed host of the Eight Bells, Carisbrooke, who was the victim of a bicycle accident which occurred outside his home in Carisbrooke High-street on the previous (Saturday) afternoon. It appears that deceased had just left his front door to go to the yard above when he was knocked down by a bicycle ridden by an 11 year-old boy, Reginald Cantelo, of Carisbrooke-road, who was riding down through the village. He sustained severe injuries including the fracture of two ribs and collar-bone and injury of the shoulder and face, and he was picked up bleeding and suffering from great shock. He was removed indoors and attended by Dr. Castle, who, owing to the fact that deceased had been in ill health for some time, regarded his patient's condition as very grave from the onset. Deceased lingered on through the night and next day, but towards evening gradually sank and died as already stated. A familiar island personality has thus been removed, for Mr. Burt was known far and wide, not only as the landlord of the Eight Bells, but as a veteran coach-driver, in both of which connections he was constantly in contact with visitors from all parts. Just over a year ago we published in our columns an interesting note from the *Road*, recording the noteworthy fact that Mr. Burt had just completed his 'golden' as an Island coachman. The writer of this note stated: 'this season recently finished was his fiftieth. He has driven over half one million miles. ... He is a master of his art and possessed of a good fund of reminiscences in coaching'. As supplemental to the note quoted above we stated then, what will bear repeating now, in regard to so notable a personality, 'that in a chat we once had with Mr. Alfred Burt he told us that during his half-century of coaching he has had six runaways, the most alarming of which was when his team bolted down Union-street, Ryde, many years ago. The corner into Pier-street was safely turned, and then Mr. Burt found immediately before him three carriages, two on one side and the third on the other side of that somewhat narrow street. With consummate coolness and skill the coachman steered his team through and the runaways were shortly afterwards pulled up, no casualty of any kind having resulted. This has been Mr. Burt's record throughout - a complete absence of any serious accident'. Mr. Burt commenced driving on leaving school, going first to Freshwater, from which place he drove an omnibus to Newport for some years. Then he went to Ryde and was for some time coaching between Ryde and Newport. His principal route, however, was between Ventnor, Newport and Freshwater, and it was between the Ventnor and Freshwater, we believe, that he drove his last team. He was landlord of the Eight Bells for the long period of 38 years, and it is stated that, with the exception of Mr. Frank Creeth, of the Griffin, Godshill, he was the oldest licence holder on the Island.

THE WEEK'S NEWS

SOMETHING LIKE A CRAB -- On Wednesday Messrs. G. Spencer and Sons landed a crab which turned the scales at 8lb. and measured 20 in. from tip to tip of the claws.

PARKHURST CONVICTS' DASH FOR LIBERTY - At about 5 o'clock on Monday afternoon, as the working parties were being marched back to the prison for the night, four prisoners suddenly bolted away ... but all in vain for quickly the clang of the Prison bell, the shrill chorus of warders' whistles and finally the crack of rifle shots proclaimed their attempted escape was discovered ... Rifle shots were fired by the warders and the prisoners were exposed to a nerve-shaking peppering. However, as the object of those holding the rifles was to merely frighten the runaways into submission, only two were struck by a stray shot and were slightly injured ...

THE MASSACRE OF THE TREES - *To the Editor of the Isle Of Wight County Press.* Sir, - The trees forming that magnificent avenue just before you get to Brading are all to be cut down by order of the 'powers that be'; also every tree on the high-road through Whitefield-wood; indeed, the latter are mostly down already and lying about like fallen giants on a battlefield. The elm avenue is to follow shortly, so that there will not be the slightest shade on that hot road between Ryde and Brading. The idea is that the road will cost less to keep in good order when unshaded, but what a pity it seems - It is quite a wicked massacre to cut down such splendid timber and make the country look so bare and ugly. - Yours faithfully, J.M.F. Ryde.

LOST AND FOUND - *Jacob Reason*, of Freshwater was summoned for allowing six cows and two heifers to stray on the Yarmouth and Freshwater road, near Westhill, on the 25th ult. – P.C. Bain proved the case. – Defendant said 'They were lost and I did not know which way to go for them. I was lost once but the Lord found me and I knew where I was at once; but I did not know where the cows were'. – Defendant was fined 6d. for each animal, namely 4s., and 4s. Costs. – Defendant: One more little word I would like to say, and that is —— . Police officer: 'Stand down'.

Until the late 19th century Ventnor had its own mill, sited just above today's Winter Gardens. The water course which drove the mill wheel eventually cascaded down the cliff face where it then ran to the sea below. Following the closure of the mill, the outfall was allowed to form a waterfall, which tumbled down under one of the brick arches supporting the road to the Esplanade. On reaching the bottom the stream formed a water feature in a pretty ornamental garden. Today the garden and the stream are long gone, both buried under municipal concrete, but in 1903 different sensibilities prevailed and the amenity was more highly thought of, and so concerns were raised when the flow of water noticeably decreased. Steps were taken to restore it to its former glory ...

May 2nd, 1903
VENTNOR'S NIAGARA
The waterfall at the eastern approach to the Esplanade having seriously decreased in volume of late, Mr. Gibbs, the energetic chairman of the District Council, induced the town's surveyor to make a careful investigation this week, and his efforts were on Wednesday rewarded by the discovery that the great body of water which once formed the old mill stream was passing into the sewer from the catch-pit opposite the Alexandra-gardens, where there was formerly a connection. This water has now been turned into its proper channel, and the result is a splendid waterfall, such as has never been seen there before.

Newport was no stranger to prostitution. The Island was home to army forts and barracks and enjoyed a military population of several thousand men in its midst and inevitably sex became just another of the many services on offer to the soldiers. A discreet blind eye must have been turned by the authorities on many occasions as prosecutions were few and far between ...

May 23rd, 1903
GRAVE OFFENCE AND HEAVY PENALTY
Katherine Bartlett, an elderly woman, was charged on an adjourned summons with keeping a disorderly house at 67, South-street. – P.S. Adams gave evidence to the effect that during the last week in March and also in April he saw soldiers - as many as 11 on one night - enter the defendant's house with women of loose character. Some of the soldiers left at very late hours and others sometimes remained all night. On the 30th of April he visited the defendant's house with the provost-sergeant from Parkhurst and found four soldiers downstairs and one

'Ventnor's Niagara.' The waterfall to the Esplanade. 1907. (*See page 45.*)

upstairs in the bed-room, underneath the bed. On the other summons being served defendant said 'I have done this to keep me out of the Union. These girls come here and take part of the proceeds'. There had been many disorderly scenes at the place and it was a perfect nuisance. - P.C. Stone gave corroborative evidence, as did Sergt. Harry Foulds, of the 2nd Sherwood Foresters, who said the soldier found upstairs under the bed was drunk. - Defendant, who pleaded 'Not guilty', said she had been ill, but could get no relief from the parish. She was obliged to do something for a living. She did not have the soldiers in. There were plenty of houses besides hers in South-street where such a thing was done. – Supt. Ayres said that defendant promised to give up the house and go to the Union on April 9th, but she did not go till after the summons was served. - The Mayor said the Bench was satisfied that the charge was proved, and it was a very grave case. Defendant's statement that there were plenty more of such houses was no defence to the case. The Bench had decided to impose the full penalty of £20 and costs; in default, three months imprisonment with such hard labour as defendant was capable of performing.

The Workhouse at Parkhurst had come a long way over the last 20 years. During Victorian times it had been regularly and roundly criticised in the pages of the County Press but by 1903 its reputation had changed and there was now barely a hint of criticism of its affairs. Just eight years before, evidence from the head nurse Miss Biles, had led to the dismissal of the Master of the Workhouse. In the intervening years she had gone on to become the Superintendent of the Workhouse and cake was now on the menu …

May 30th, 1903

EXTRA CAKE ALLOWED

The Classification Committee recommended that 2oz. extra of cake be allowed the women working at the laundry, &c., on Tuesdays and Thursdays, Mr. Minter stating that the women were now getting 4oz. but as they worked hard it was thought desirable to allow 6oz. - In reply to Mr. Manning, Mr. Minter pointed out that formerly the women had lunch, but at their own request a quantity of tea and sugar was served out and substituted for the lunch, and they could brew the tea when they wished to. - Mr. Manning thought that women brought to the wash tub at 7 o'clock in the morning and kept hard at work all day should be allowed something extra. He had frequently visited the laundry and had never seen a woman idle, and that was more than he could say of a great many other people in the House. He suggested that they should be allowed a reasonable amount of cake and a cup of cocoa. He asked whether 4 oz of cake and a cup of cocoa would be sufficient for these women, who were the persons above all others, who deserved to be looked after. - Mr. Ball said the suggestion of the Classification Committee showed that they were looking into the matter, and the Board might leave it to them. - Mr. Morris said he should think this cake was very rich (laughter). For his part, he should feel very much better off with half a pound of beef steak (laughter). It might be a question of whether they should not give them a little solid beef. - The Chairman said if they took a walk round the House they would find that the inmates were living pretty well. If they went there any day they would see a dinner served up which they could not see equalled, at any rate not surpassed, in nine tenths of the mechanics' houses in the Isle of Wight (hear, hear). They had a good joint of meat and invariably two vegetables. The dietary scale that was formed made provision for those people to have a lunch in the morning, but at their request the lunch was taken out of the scale because they said they could generally save something from their breakfast to do for their lunch, and they did not want additional food served out each lunch time; but they asked to have something to drink. The Board therefore supplied them with dry tea and sugar so that they might have something to drink with their lunch. He (the Chairman) had been told by a Carisbrooke person the 'cake question' was becoming intolerable. The children who attended the Carisbrooke Board-school insisted on having cake given them by their parents, because they said the children from the Union were sent to school with a piece of cake (laughter). He hoped every poor soul outside the House would do as well as those did that were in. - The proposition was carried.

--------------------◆--------------------

Doctor Dabbs was well known on the Island. Besides being a local GP, through his poetry and other writings he also enjoyed a reputation as a literary man. His column in the County Press showed him to be a man of some wisdom and refinement, in short, a pillar of the community, so it is hard to imagine the shock that must have been felt when the good doctor confessed to being a reformed drug addict ...

June 20th, 1903
NARCOTICS: A WARNING AND A CONFESSION BY DR DABBS
Dr Dabbs, who is contributing a weekly article on 'Health and Hygiene' to the London Argus, devoted his page last week to the subject of narcotics, against the use of which he uttered a very strong warning. In the course of his article he says: 'If I have had my dark hour with narcotics, and have emancipated myself from their foul tyranny, I become a guide as well as a critic. So let me make a full confession - I have. It was in the year 1868, and I was working for honours for my degree. I was working like a machine, not being one. I thought (as many think) that a high degree was everything; it is a good thing, but very far from being everything - very far indeed. And I began to take a little laudanum to get sleep, and I at last reached a personal dosage of I am afraid to say how many grains of opium a day. I had fully grasped the fire I was playing with, and had determined to stand it out on the night-journey home from Aberdeen to London. I reached Perth half-demented, and missed a train to get opium; ditto at Edinburgh, ditto at Peterborough, and at London I went in for a prolonged debauch of it ... One night I set to work to cure myself. I left all my money at home, my watch - everything that I could sell or part with for opium. I took a meal of raw cakes and milk; I took my bulldog with me, and I set out to walk through the early summer night. I started at 7 p.m.; my next opium hour would be 8 p.m. I remember very little of the night. I know that my dog got home alone at 2 a.m. and seemed too tired to even crawl into his kennel, and I know that at 7 a.m. I was standing haggard, wild, and exhausted, with torn clothes, battered hat, and briars all over me, leaning on a gate looking over Carisbrooke village, and I know also that my head dropped on my hands and I slept - slept for about 20 minutes, and woke up well. Since that day I have never touched (in health) a narcotic.

July 4th, 1903
THE WEEK'S NEWS

THE MACKEREL HARVEST - Mackerel has been most plentiful in the Island this week, consequent on the large shoals which have been caught at Chale Bay, and the price has varied from threepence to less than a penny each. The disturbance of the quiet of Sunday by the shouts of mackerel men hawking their fish might have been a little startling to those who remembered the Sunday-trading prosecutions which took place last year in the Island, unless they were aware that the obsolete Act of Charles II., under which those proceedings were taken, specially exempts the vendors of Sunday mackerel, provided that the hawking does not take place during the hours appointed for Divine service.

POLICE SERGT. AS NURSE - Some curiosity was excited on Sunday afternoon by the sight of a police officer wheeling a little two-year-old boy up Hunnyhill in a perambulator. The explanation was that the child, whose mother had been arrested and has since been sentenced to imprisonment, was being taken to the Workhouse to await its mother's release from custody. Unfortunately, this hapless little one, who seemed quite happy in charge of the police-sergt., has been compelled to spend a considerable part of its short career within the Workhouse walls.

A NARROW ESCAPE -- On Saturday afternoon, as a pair horse-brake was turning from Lower St James's-street into High-street, a little child, straying away from its mother, ran into the middle of the road in front of the horses. Fortunately the driver saw the little one's peril and pulled his horses up with almost incredible promptitude, the animals being on their haunches in an instant, and the fact that their fore-legs came down on either side of the child sufficiently indicates the hair-breadth escape from a serious if not a fatal accident. The little one was picked up none the worse for its alarming experience.

The presence of several thousand soldiers on the Island, a community within a community, could hardly fail to have an effect on Island life. Unfortunately, it was often the wrong effect. A hardcore minority of the soldiers were responsible for a relentless catalogue of crime, some of it violent. In December 1903, Newport town itself became the victim late one Saturday night when over 200 menacing soldiers went on the rampage ...

December 12th, 1903
RIOTOUS SOLDIERS AT NEWPORT
MAYOR'S THANKS TO THE POLICE

Before the commencement of the business at the Newport Borough Police-court on Monday, the Mayor said he wished on behalf of the Bench to thank Supt. Ayres and the police of the town for the excellent services they rendered on Saturday night when there was quite a riot in the town, caused by a large number of soldiers from Parkhurst, there being, with civilians, more than 200 in the street at the time. It was only becoming that he should thus acknowledge those services of the police, services which were a very great strain upon the small staff of police which they had there (applause).

The central figures of the riotous scenes referred to by the Mayor were some 50 men of the 2nd Sherwood Foresters from Parkhurst, who evidently visited the town on Saturday night with some comrades with the intention of making merry on the eve of their departure with a strong draft of the battalion for Hong Kong on the following Monday. Dressed in khaki, with slouch hats, they attracted a great deal of attention as they went about in parties of about a dozen, each singing and shouting. As the evening wore on merriment gave place to rowdyism, culminating in extensive window-smashing and ugly horse-play, during which police and civilians, who were called upon to assist in restoring order, were assaulted by blows from military sticks, kicks, and stones thrown by the soldiers. It being Saturday night there were more of the civilian population in the street than is usually the case between 11 and 12, when the more disorderly scenes were witnessed. The presence of so many crowding round the military and following them about was additional incitement, if such were needed, to the soldiers to commit the excesses of which they were afterwards guilty. One party of the soldiers were said to have invaded a fried-fish shop in the High-street and to have been allowed to clear off a large quantity of fried fish without compensating the owner, who preferred that loss to horse-play in his shop. Window smashing was freely indulged in by another party, who were said to have eluded the picket and to have returned by way of the Grove into Sea-street, panes of glass in dwelling houses and public-house windows being broken, in addition to a plate-glass shop window in Mr. Cooke's premises at the bottom of Holyrood-street. The disorder was at its worst in Lower St James's-street, where the offenders 'concentrated' on their way to Barracks and offered a stubborn resistance. The police, who had been doing their best with the separate parties to get them away to Barracks as quickly as possible, were now powerless to quell the disturbances of the 'combined forces', and the intervention of the military police and picket was not as effective as might have been reasonably expected, though arrests were made. The civilians were called upon to assist the police and they responded by forming a line across the road near the Star and forcing the soldiers back towards Barracks. Supt. Ayres, Sergt. Sharp, and P.C'.s Edwards and Bungey were in the thick of it hereabouts. At Town-gate matters got so serious that truncheons were drawn by the police, whilst the rowdy soldiers made a fierce attack with their canes. Several of their numbers were 'laid out' and the turbulent Tommies were forced to continue their retreat followed by the police and civilian reinforcements. The military offered further resistance on the top of Hunnyhill and resorted to stone-throwing, but they were eventually got into Barracks. Fortunately no one was seriously injured, though many were struck. Compensation for damage to property, which includes over 30 broken window panes and a plate glass shop window, has, we understand, been guaranteed by the regiment.

There was quite a crowd in the street on Sunday night in anticipation of further disturbance, but the soldiers were less boisterous upon this occasion and the efforts of the police, assisted by a specially selected picket, prevented further riotous scenes.

1904

Today there are no Isle of Wight Harriers and no railway line at Godshill, but once there were, and one day they came together on a January afternoon in 1904 ...

January 23rd, 1904
HARRIERS' ALARMING EXPERIENCE
Mr. Frank Mew's pack of Isle of Wight Harriers had an alarming experience on Monday afternoon, when pursuing a hare near Kennerley Farm, Godshill. The hare bolted up the railway line, and in the cutting the train made a sudden appearance, dashing into the pack. The brake was promptly applied to the train, but it was found that two of the harrier bitches had been cut to pieces, whilst another was so badly injured that it had to be destroyed. The animals lost were three of the most valuable in the pack.

———————◆———————

There was a time when the pages and letter columns of the County Press were regularly filled with criticism of the railway companies. Curiously, the persistent complaints noticeably and abruptly stopped in the mid-1890s. The reason is unclear after this passage of time, but it remains a fact that something happened, and from that point on only the occasional withering protest appeared, such as this one ...

February 27th, 1904
I.W. RAILWAY FARES
To the Editor of the Isle Of Wight County Press.
Sir, - I hear everywhere that the expense of travelling in the Island is said to be excessive. How can people bear out this statement when my experience of today is cited? I had occasion to take a Monday special cheap-ticket return from Brading to St Helens. The distance is quite over a mile, and I imagine under a mile and a half, and I actually had only ninepence to pay.
Yours obediently, J.F.C. HAMILTON. Spencer Lodge, Ryde, February 22nd, 1904.

———————◆———————

On occasion young offenders were birched by order of the courts. It comes as no surprise to learn that the age of the child had a direct bearing on whether they could receive the birch or not. What is surprising is that the birch was reserved for the younger children, not the older ones ...

February 27th, 1904
COWES BOYS IN DISGRACE - THE AGE LIMIT FOR BIRCHING
Frederick Poland, Frank Flaxmer, and *Harry Tribbick,* Cowes boys, were charged with stealing a bag of swede greens, valued at 2s. 6d., the property of John Henry Butchers, farmer, of Broadfields Farm, Northwood. Prosecutor said about midday on the 12th. inst. he picked a bag of swede greens, put them in the sack produced and left them by the hedge under some hurdles. About 3 p.m. he returned for the bag and both bag and greens were missing ... Prisoners

pleaded guilty and in reply to questions they each said they were over 14 years of age - the age limit for birching. The Chairman, however said in the opinion of the Court, Flaxmer and Tribbick, the two smaller boys were not 14, and they would each receive six strokes with the birch*. With regard to Poland, the Chairman said that unfortunately he appeared to be past the age at which he could be ordered to receive the whipping which he richly deserved, and he would be fined 5s.; in default five days.

—————————◆—————————

In some parts of the country during these years, publicans as a matter of course supplied free ale to policemen on the beat as a 'perk'. Certainly a Cowes policeman, while on duty, was given free beer one night by a pub landlord, apparently in front of other customers. He then returned to the pub after hours and entered by the back door to stay for nearly another hour. The landlord was prosecuted for his part in the events - but not the constable, it seems ...

April 9th, 1904

PUBLICAN AND POLICEMAN
'HARBOURING' AND SUPPLYING A CONSTABLE ON DUTY

William S. Spranklin, landlord of the Horse and Groom Inn, Union-road, at Cowes, was charged with a breach of the Licensing Act by knowingly harbouring on his premises a police constable when on duty.... Defendant pleaded not guilty. On the the application of Supt. Ayres all witnesses were ordered to leave the Court.

Inspector Matthews stated that on Wednesday, the 23rd, inst. from instructions he received from Supt. Ayres, he watched defendant's house. At 11:23 p.m. he saw P.C. Prout enter the back door - the yard door of the Horse and Groom. Shortly afterwards witness heard the side door open and shut. Witness watched until 18 minutes after midnight, when the police constable came out and went on his beat. The following day witness went with Supt Ayres and saw defendant at his house. Supt Ayres asked defendant if he could give any explanation as to why the police constable was in his house the previous night after 11 o'clock. Defendant hesitated for some time and then said 'Well, he came into the house early in the evening'. The superintendent asked him at what time, and defendant said 'Shortly after 8. He came in and had a pint of beer, and I spoke to him with regard to a matter the Inspector had spoken to me previously about, and as he could not stop I arranged with him to come back after 11 o'clock'. The Superintendent had previously told defendant that in giving his answer he wished him to be careful, as what he said might be repeated hereafter. Defendant said 'That is quite right'. Supt Ayres then asked defendant how long the constable was there and defendant said about 10 minutes. Witness added that he was watching defendant's house from 8.15 p.m. till 10 minutes to 9. The constable passed where witness was watching at 8.15, and he lost sight of him opposite the house and did not see him come out during the time that he was there ... Supt Ayres stated that on the 24th ult., about 6

* How the Island birchings were carried out is never referred to but certainly in the rest of the country they were carried out by the police immediately following the court hearing, sometimes in the court building itself or at the nearest police station. Boys under 14 years of age could receive a maximum of 12 strokes.

p.m., he visited defendant's house in company with Inspector Matthews. He saw defendant and told him he had come to see if he could give any explanation as to a constable being on his premises between 11 and 12 o'clock the previous night. Defendant said the constable was in earlier in the evening and had a pint of beer. Witness asked him who it was, and he said P.C. Prout. Witness said 'What about his coming in here after 11 o'clock?' Defendant said 'Well, I wanted to see him to try and find out who had made a complaint against my house'. Witness said 'Well, don't you know it was very wrong of you to encourage that constable here? If you wanted to know anything why did you not go to the Inspector?' Defendant said 'Yes; I see I have made a mistake'. When witness was leaving the house defendant said 'Will this go any further?' Witness said he was sure he could not say. The matter must be reported, and he could not say what the consequence would be. Defendant again said he was very sorry it occurred ... Defendant gave evidence saying the constable came in and asked for a pint of beer, with which he was supplied. The constable tendered the money for the drink but witness gave it to him back. He did not know the constable was on duty ... This concluded the case for the prosecution ...

P.C. Prout, who attended on subpoena, said that on Wednesday, the 23rd, he had occasion to go to defendant's house in the evening about 20 past 8 ... By Supt Ayres: There was no other reason for going there except an ordinary Licensing Act visit. Had a pint of beer there. That was not a usual thing when on duty, but it was done. When he visited the house again after 11 o'clock he found the yard door open ... Q. Did you give any reason for going there on Thursday night after 11 o'clock? – No. - Q. Did you make any entry in your diary? - No, sir; I did not. - Q. Did you make any entry as to Wednesday night? – 8.20; that is all sir. - Q. After you visited the house after 11 o'clock did you make any entry in your diary? - No, sir. - Q. Did you make any report to your Inspector? - No, sir. Q. And yet you say you were there in the ordinary course of duty? - At 8.20, sir. - Q. After hours were you there in the ordinary course of duty? - No; at his request. - Q. Do you know that is strictly against the regulations? - I do, sir. - Q. Do you remember what you said in answer to the charge of being on licensed premises? - I said it was quite right. I was sorry and I knew it was wrong. I think I brought him to this. I am sorry. - Q. You knew you were doing wrong when you went on these licensed premises? - I did, sir. This concluded the case for the defence ... Mr. Hiscock, for the defence again submitted there was no case against defendant of having knowingly served the constable on duty. The Chairman: The Bench consider there is very much of a case ... Defendant would be fined £2 in each case and the costs, making £5. 8s. in all; in default of distress one month.

Mr. Hiscock did not know whether the Bench would give an expression of opinion as to the desirability of removing the man. The owners were anxious to secure the best of tenants. The Chairman: I hardly think it comes within our province to make any suggestions as to that. The law no longer allows us to endorse his certificate, which we otherwise should have done. Mr. Hiscock: After that, I do not ask for it.

THE WEEK'S NEWS

PIGGY'S DIVERSION AND ITS ALARMING SEQUEL. A pig which escaped from the Newport Railway-station yard on Wednesday afternoon caused considerable diversion by plunging into the deep stream at the foot of the station hill and careering about in the water in the vicinity of the Royal Brewery premises until captured by Mr. Cooper, of St. Cross, who by means of a boat and rope got piggy safely out of the water. A number of spectators, who crowded onto the footbridge leading to the Grove, had a narrow escape from serious accident, as one end of the bridge suddenly began to collapse. Fortunately the occupants of the bridge were able to get off in time. The bridge has since been closed by order of the acting county surveyor. It is desirable that the bridge should be speedily repaired, as the foot-way now obstructed is much frequented by the public.

HORSE OVERBOARD. On Saturday afternoon a horse attached to one of Messrs Shepards' trolleys was startled by a train passing over the Railway-bridge and backed over the Quay into the river. Fortunately, it was low water and the animal was rescued after considerable difficulty, little the worse for its mud bath.

LATE ITEMS. Miss Charmley, of Accrington, was found gagged and bound in a coal cellar, with a note 'Revenge is sweet' pinned on her dress.

BLACKWATER. ROOK SHOOTING. At the invitation of Mr. J. R. Scott Blake a rook-shooting party enjoyed some excellent sport at Stone Farm last week, when nearly 400 birds fell to the sportsmen's guns.

A COMMON CHARGE - *Frank Scovell,* a cripple, of Newport, was summoned for having used obscene language at High-street, Niton, on the 18th May. – P.C. Bennett said defendant used most filthy language to a respectable tradesman because he was carrying a light. Defendant said the constable let fly at him and knocked him down spinning. If that was not true, he hoped the Lord Almighty would never let him leave that box. - Fined 1s. and 9s. costs.

———————◆———————

For some parts of the Island, electricity didn't arrive until the late 1950s, but as long ago as 1904, the wealthier residents of Shanklin and Sandown were already hardened veterans, having had the benefit of electricity for over two years. Electricity, like the motor car, was clearly here to stay, as the Isle of Wight Electric Light Company were keen to show ...

July 23rd, 1904

SHANKLIN AND SANDOWN ELECTRIC LIGHT WORKS

By invitation of the Isle of Wight Electric Light Company, the members and officials of the Sandown and Shanklin District Councils, together with their friends, made a special visit of inspection of the works at Skew-bridge on Tuesday afternoon. The visit proved both interesting and instructive, special

attention being given to the new boilers and 350 h.p. Generating engine which have recently been installed by Messrs. Davey-Paxman and Company......
Trains from Sandown and Shanklin stopped at the County-ground to set down passengers. A cursory inspection was first made of the works, after which an adjournment was made to a large marquee, erected by Mr. R.C. Gray (Sandown), and prettily furnished and decorated, the decorations comprising bunting and greenery, with variously coloured electric jets intermixed with the greenery. Col. Hamilton said how pleased the Electric-light Company were to see so large a gathering on the present occasion. When the electric light was first mooted in the Island it was very encouraging to know that the people were so interested in it and had supported the Company splendidly. These particular works were started in 1901, and at the end of that year they had 4,380 lamp connections in the district. Now the number had increased to upwards of 11,000 connections. That showed that the necessity existed for this magnificent light. The latest contracts the Company had received were at Sandown - lighting the Ocean Hotel and St. John's Church. The Company were confident that the more people saw of the electric light and the more they saw of its advantages, the more would the light be used in the district. Col. Hamilton then asked Mr. Rayner, on behalf of the Shanklin Council and Mr. Board on behalf of the Sandown Council, to switch on the light to the tent. These gentlemen each used a small silver switch, and in an instant the spacious marquee was a blaze of light, the bulbs of red, white, and blue glass having a charming effect among the greenery. At the same time several electric fans were also set in motion. The silver switches are to be suitably inscribed and presented to Messrs. Rayner and Board as a memento of the occasion ... After tea the guests were photographed by Mr. Ancell.

------◆------

Opinions differ as to whether fortune telling is a harmless diversion, an exact science or the work of charlatans. For the Chairman of the Bench, it was the latter so when Madame Lemain, palmist extraordinaire, came up before him he was able to tell her her fortune ...

July 30th, 1904

PALMISTRY IN THE ISLAND

Madame Lemain, Shanklin, whose name was stated to be Florence Mansfield was charged with pretending to one Alfred Hutchin to tell fortunes by palmistry, on the 10th inst. - Mr. John Marsh defended. - Acting Sergt. Hutchin deposed that on Wednesday last, in consequence of instructions, he went to Shanklin in plain clothes. At about 3 p.m. he was on the beach, accompanied by his wife. He saw the defendant at a small tent on the beach near the Chine. Outside of it were advertisements of palmistry. His wife and he were looking at the advertisements when defendant came to them and asked would they have theirs told. Witness advised his wife to go in and she refused. Defendant said 'I will give you full particulars. I don't tell you anything dreadful'. He said 'Do I understand you will tell my fortune?' She said 'Yes'. She said her fee was 2s. 6d., but for full details she charged 5s. Witness said 'Then, for the larger fee, you will tell me more?' She said 'Certainly'. After examining his hands, principally the right, she went on to tell him what would happen in the future, notes of which he made shortly afterwards

… He paid her and left. Witness read from his notes of what defendant had said. She told him he had a splendid business hand; he would make a first-rate colonist [*sic*]. She asked if he had been abroad and he said he had. She told him he had three children and one of them would become very clever and would make a good architect; she should like to see his hand. He was happily married. His occupation was something to do with the soil. He did little of the manual work himself but would superintend and arrange things splendidly. She asked if he speculated and said that in about two years time he would make a lot of money as the result of his speculation. He was kind hearted and would rather do good to others than himself. She asked if both his parents were alive and said it looked as though he would have some trouble but she never said much about deaths. He would live till 75 or 80. He had had an accident and injured his head. Witness added that he saw defendant's advertisements about Shanklin.

Mr. Marsh: Have you, as a matter of fact, any children? – No … Q. Do you believe in palmistry? - Well, I don't know: I believe some of it. - Q. Do you pretend that you were deceived by what she told you? - There is no doubt I was deceived. It was true that he did not do much manual labour. He certainly did not say he was a landscape gardener. He signed the book produced … Had no idea what was in the book. Mr. Marsh said witness had signed the following: 'Having consulted you, I hereby again declare my belief that in all you have said or written you have had no intention to deceive or impose on me or to take my money under any false pretences and I pay you my fee accordingly'. Witness said defendant held her hand over this statement when she gave him the book … Mr. Marsh called the defendant, who said she was a scientific palmist, a pupil of a well-known man, and that she had studied palmistry from a child. - Q. Do you believe in palmistry? - Most certainly I do. - Q. In any of your operations do you intend or desire to impose upon or deceive anyone? – Not at all. I many times give a free reading … The Clerk: You only tell character from the lines of the hand? - Character and capabilities. - Q. Supposing they have a good life-line, you judge the distance and tell them? - Yes; I judge if they will live a long life. - Q. Didn't you tell the sergeant he had three children? - Yes, three children. I always say 'Three children are marked'. I don't say you have them. On a gentleman's hand it is very difficult to tell children. I said 'Three are marked'. He said 'I have four'. She did not say that in two years time he would make a lot of money, the result of speculation. She did not think he did much at it. She knew he was not independent. She remarked that he had a soft hand, which denoted that he did not do much manual labour. She said 'You are not fond of work'. He laughed and said 'No, I am not'. Mr. Marsh: That was a very safe observation … She had done very badly since she had been in Shanklin. This week she had taken 15s. Of that, 12s. were paid to a man, and 2s. to a girl to take the baby out, leaving her 1s. It was not a very lucrative position at present. Defendant was fined 5s. and 5s. costs.

The Chairman said the Bench had dealt very leniently with her because they simply wished to put a stop to that sort of thing going on here and to His Majesty's subjects being imposed upon by a pretence of telling fortunes through the aid of this palmistry (applause).

Louise Barnet, known as *Madame Louise*, was charged with a like offence at Sandown on the same day … Defendant was fined 5s. and 5s. costs.

Madame Lemain, outraged and humiliated by her conviction, put pen to paper ...

August 13th, 1904

A LADY PALMIST ON HER CONVICTION

To the Editor of the Isle of Wight County Press.

Sir, - My recent experiences in the Town-Hall, Ryde, make it difficult for me to believe that I am living in the 20th century in dear old England - a land which I have been taught from my cradle was synonymous with the land of justice. Justice has been denied to me today. On the uncorroborated evidence of a police officer, which I on oath denied, I am convicted and fined. I have always admired and respected the police force, though I have never been before inside a police court ... I protest against fraud and charlatanism, and the fullest assistance and co-operation of the League is offered to Scotland Yard and the police throughout the country to stamp out humbug and expose sham. I am a scientific palmist and no fortune teller, and my clients come to me of their own free will, with no coercion on my part. I have studied palmistry from a child and perfected myself under one of the most famous authorities on the subject, who has been consulted by many of the most learned of the day. Phrenology has had its persecutions, but is now recognised as an exact science, and until something definite is done to protect us, and Parliament undertakes the matter, we shall always be in danger of misrepresentation. I flatter myself I was very accurate in my estimate of this man's character. I told him he had great powers of imagination. He certainly showed them in the witness box. I wonder a hysterical halfpenny daily paper hasn't unearthed this treasure; he would make a valuable addition to the staff ... Nothing will ever shake my belief in scientific palmistry. It is said in Holy writ, 'and God made markings in the hands of men, that the sons of men might know them'; so why people should be punished for studying those markings is an enigma to me ... Apologising for taking up so much of your valuable space, believe me, yours faithfully, F.R. LEMAIN.

THE WEEK'S NEWS

BRIDEGROOM'S STRANGE CONDUCT. A Cowes wedding which had been fixed to take place at the Congregational Church on Monday did not take place consequent on the strange act of the bridegroom. A short time before the hour fixed for the ceremony the bridegroom was nowhere to be found, and everyone was very much astonished when he was conveyed home in a cab from Gurnard, where he had been discovered in the water. He was insensible, but was soon brought round by medical attendance. The cause of his strange act appears to be a mystery.

ADGESTONE. At White House Farm is a hen which has taken very kindly to a litter of pigs. The hen laid her eggs in the piggery but they were taken from her. When the pigs were born the hen remained and ever since has manifested much affection for the little piggies, and she shelters several of them at a time under her wings.

The British public were aware by now of the King's wayward lifestyle and his involvement with scandal as Prince. He had narrowly missed being named as co-respondent in a notorious divorce case, eventually suffering the indignity of having to appear as a witness, and several years later he had been forced to appear in court again, this time to admit being involved in a famous gambling scandal.

However, he was the only King Britain had. Whatever his shortcomings he was universally acknowledged to have an affable and kind manner and the newspapers, County Press included, generally stood by him although in this report he is damned with faint praise, being described as only 'essentially popular' ...

August 20th, 1904

'It is an open secret', says to-day's *Lady's Pictorial*, 'that the King is getting tired of being mobbed and stared at wherever he goes, and an incident at Cowes annoyed him thoroughly. His Majesty is very good-natured and the soul of courtesy, but for some time past he has felt that a little more consideration might be shown to him in return'. King Edward is an essentially popular monarch, and it is natural that he should attract all eyes whenever and wherever he appears in public, but, so far as our information goes, there was no such breach of courtesy* at Cowes as that to which our excellent contemporary has referred, no doubt misled by a report published by a London halfpenny Journal, which occasionally exhibits a weakness for relying upon its imagination for its facts!

There is no way of knowing the nature or true circumstances of any of the individuals featured in these court cases of 100 years ago. In this case, an 11-year-old boy is said to be a thief and 'out of control' and at one point is found on the streets of Cowes late at night looking for lodgings. How a child ever came to be in such a situation in the first place will never be known now but there was obviously more to the story than met the eye ...

September 17, 1904

AN INCORRIGIBLE BOY

Douglas Arthur White, a 11 year-old lad, of No 2, Pyle-street, Newport, was charged with stealing a purse containing 6s. 7d., the property of Mrs. Elizabeth Lockyer, a widow, lodging at the house of prisoner's father. – Prosecutrix said on the previous afternoon, about 2.30, she left her lodgings to go for a walk. She left a purse containing 6s. 7d., and a key in the pocket of her skirt, which was hung up behind the door of her room. When witness returned about half-past 4 she saw the prisoner on the stairs. He asked her if she had seen his 'dad' and she said 'Yes', and he replied 'I am just going out', and he went out directly. Witness went into her room on the ground floor and noticed the flower stand had been taken away from the window, the curtains disarranged and the skirt shifted. She examined the skirt pocket and found the purse was gone. Witness went into the next room and told the father what had happened. Information was given to the police. Witness locked her door before going out. She always left the window open a little way at the bottom. – P.C. Lavery, stationed at Cowes, said that at 6.30 p.m. on the previous night, from information received by telephone that prisoner had

* The details of the 'breach of courtesy' were not revealed.

stolen some money at Newport, he made inquiries, and that at 10 p.m. he saw prisoner in Medina-road, Cowes, standing outside the Alexandra Bar public-house inquiring for lodgings. He told witness his name was Douglas White, of Newport. Witness told him he believed he was wanted at Newport for stealing money, and he replied 'Yes, I know; I stole it yesterday afternoon'. Witness took him to the Police-station, searched him, and found he had 3s. 3d. Witness charged him with the theft and locked him up. That morning he told witness he threw the purse and key away. Witness went to the spot, but was unable to find the purse. - Prisoner pleaded guilty, and his father said he had a great trouble with the boy, who had got quite beyond his control. He had tried all he knew to make the boy behave properly. It would be utterly useless to give him the birch. He thought the only thing to do with the boy would be to send him to an industrial school. He was continually playing truant and sleeping out. He could do nothing with him. A fortnight ago a friend brought him back from Eastleigh. He was willing to contribute towards his support in an industrial school. - The Mayor said the Bench had decided that prisoner should receive six strokes with the birch, and he would be remanded to the Workhouse for a week while arrangements were being made to send him to an industrial school until he was 16 years of age. The Bench made an order accordingly, the father to pay 2s. per week towards the support of his son. The costs were remitted.

Just as the coming of the railway had altered peoples' lives forever, so did the arrival of buses. Suddenly the Island shrank even more and the little towns and villages across the Island became only minutes from each other instead of hours, and life no longer had to be taken at the walking pace of an animal.

The Isle of Wight Express Motor Syndicate announced the imminent arrival of their new bus service. 'The scheme is likely to prove a distinct commercial success' wrote the County Press* ...

November 12, 1904
MOTOR OMNIBUSES FOR THE ISLAND

We are informed that a Company, named the Isle of Wight Express Motor Syndicate, has been incorporated for the purpose of providing an express motor omnibus and parcel service in the Island. Particulars placed in our hands for publication show that nearly half the required capital has been subscribed by the directorate, which includes some well-known Island names and their friends, and the balance will be publicly issued in the Island on Saturday next. It is the intention of the promoters to run five services of cars through or near the following towns and villages: Ryde, Cowes, Newport, Ventnor, Shanklin, Sandown, Yarmouth, Freshwater, Bembridge, Seaview, St Helens, Brading, Wootton, Whippingham, Osborne, Carisbrooke, St Lawrence, Whitwell, Godshill, Sandford, Spring Vale, Calbourne, and Newbridge. Double decked Milnes-Daimler cars, of the type used by the Great Western and other Railway Companies, as well as by the Brighton, Eastbourne, Hastings, and various Corporations throughout the country, with seating accommodation for 36 passengers, will be employed for the traffic and the makers will guarantee them to run at an average minimum rate of 11 miles an hour.

---

* Not quite. The company went into receivership after just three years.

It is stated that the fares will compare very favourably with those ordinarily charged by Railway Companies. Such a system, running daily, at intervals of an hour or an hour and a half, with the facilities it affords for putting people down at convenient centres, should prove of great public convenience. Books of tickets will be issued at reduced rates to those desirous of frequently travel by the cars, which will be luxuriously fitted up and lighted. Many of the routes taken will open up fresh natural beauties for the delight of the hosts of visitors to the Island, and this, it is thought, cannot fail to promote the prosperity of the service. Apart from the great advantage which will accrue to residents by a cheap and convenient method of locomotion to points not now readily reached, anything which improves and lessens the cost of communication in the Island is worthy of public support, and in this case there is not lacking evidence to show that the scheme is likely to prove a distinct commercial success.

1905

When an Island priest died leaving £10,000 to each of his two servants the story attracted the attention of the national press. Fleet Street reporters descended on the house and surrounding area at Bonchurch and in scenes that bear an uncanny resemblance to today, the photographers hunted as a pack, even taking to the trees with their cameras to get the pictures their editors demanded ...

February 11th, 1905

FORTUNES FOR TWO BONCHURCH SERVANTS

The Rev. Father William Edmund Roope, of Underrock, Bonchurch, a retired Roman Catholic priest, who died on November 23, left estate of the total value of £48,725. The testator gave to his servant Cecily Guy £10,000, his household effects, and the use of Underrock, and directed that, on her death, Underrock is to go to William Gerard Roope. Subject to £10,000 to his servant, Ruth Blaza, the testator leaves his residual estate to the children of the late Gerard Roope and children of Charles Henry Roope. These handsome legacies to the deceased's servants have attracted wide notice, and the recipients have, since the news was first published last Saturday, been subjected to much annoyance. London daily papers sent their representatives to obtain interviews and write it up sensationally, the *Daily Mirror* on Monday produced the portraits of Miss Guy and Miss Blaza (from a photograph taken by a Ventnor photographer a year or two ago) on the lawn in front of Underrock; begging letters have reached them wholesale, also about a dozen offers of marriage, the writers in some instances mentioning that they were not particular which of the ladies they married, and persistent photographers, amateur and otherwise have hung around with their kodaks taking snapshots at every favourable opportunity. It is even said that some of the most persistent have perched themselves in trees in the lovely grounds attached to the house in their efforts to achieve their ends. Altogether the ladies have not spent a very happy week since their acquisition of wealth became known, but for their sakes it is to be hoped that after the usual nine days' wonder they will be allowed to live in peace and enjoy the reward of their long and faithful service.

RYDE LECTURE SOCIETY.

OPEN LECTURE.

TOWN HALL, RYDE.

DR DALLINGER ON "ANTS,"

WITH LANTERN ILLUSTRATIONS.

On Wednesday Afternoon, Nov. 29,

At 3 o'clock.

Reserved seats 3s.; Second seats 2s.; Back seats 1s.

Members of the I.W. Lecture Society half-price
to 3s. and 2s. seats only.

SPECIAL ARRANGEMENTS FOR SCHOOLS.

Plan and Tickets at W. Watts', 29, Union-street.

For Sale.

149, HIGH STREET, AND THE SWAN HOTEL
YARD, NEWPORT, I.W.
Two useful hack mares, 5 spring carts, 4 vans,
4-wheel phaeton, 4-wheel dickey trap, grass-cutter
in good order, portable forge, pair of double blast
bellows, horse clipping-machine, tyring platform,
1½-h.p. gas-engine in good working order, 40
gallons of axle oil, 3 iron vice, 300 spokes, quantity
of drums, cans, &c., pair of rubber-tyred wheels
and axle complete, quantity of wheels, axles,
shafts, poles and bars, 5 sets of double and single
harness, wagonette head, glass frames and firewood, and miscellaneous items.
HENRY J. WAY AND SON are instructed by
Mr. R. Bull, who is reducing his stock previous to alterations of premises, to Sell by Auction,
on MONDAY, SEPTEMBER 18, 1905, a large
portion of the STOCK-IN-TRADE.
On view the morning of sale and catalogues
obtained of the Auctioneers, Newport and Freshwater, I.W.

STONE STEPS
FLOWER AND TEA GARDENS,
CALBOURNE.

Now Open Daily for the Season (Sundays excepted).
ADMISSION 3D.   TEAS FROM 6D.
Swings, &c. Stabling on premises. Three minutes'
walk from Railway-station.
A Delightful Country Holiday Resort.
Grounds 12 acres in extent.
G. WHITTINGTON, Proprietor.

MARVELLOUS OFFER.

THE MIDGET PHONO
(a genuine Phono, NOT A TOY)
and
12 RECORDS
in
RECORD BOX,
Complete 17s. 6d. only.

COME AND HEAR THEM
AT
MURDOCH, MURDOCH, & Co.'s,
NEWPORT AND COWES.

Official and other Notices.

I FLORENCE FURNEY, of 14, High-street,
Newport, tender my public APOLOGY to my
husband and also to Mrs. Wilson for the false
accusations made against them by me.
(Signed) FLORENCE FURNEY.
February 17th, 1905.

NOTICE TO BUILDERS AND OTHERS.
MEDINA DOCK.

DRY RUBBISH may be shot in the above Dock;
cart entrance, Bridge-road.
J. S. WHITE AND COMPANY, LTD.

WILLIAM FLOYD DECEASED.

ALL Persons having any Claims against or
Owing Amounts to the Estate of the above
named deceased late of "Milton" Villa Newport-
road Cowes butcher are required to forward particulars of their Claims or to Pay their Accounts to us
the undersigned within seven days from the date
hereof.
DAMANT AND SONS,
Solicitors to the Executors.
Cowes, I.W., 15th July, 1905.

ISLE OF WIGHT RURAL DISTRICT COUNCIL.
HIGHWAYS.

THE Council Hereby Give Notice that COM-
PLAINT has been made of obstruction being
caused to Highways in their district by stones,
placed by carters under the wheels of their carts
when resting on hills, being left on the surface of the
road.
Notice is also given that damage is caused to the
surface of the roadway on hills by the careless and
improper use of drag shoes.
The Penalty incurred in both of the above cases is
the sum of Forty Shillings.
By order,
H. ELDRIDGE STRATTON,
Clerk to the Council.
12th July, 1905, Newport, I.W.

The new bus service took to the road; or rather, in a hint of what was to come, it didn't ...

April 22nd, 1905

INAUGURATION OF THE ISLAND MOTOR CAR SERVICE

On Thursday, the I.W. Express Motor Syndicate inaugurated part of their service of cars under most promising auspices, four being started from Ryde on journeys to various Island centres. Today's proceedings began with a luncheon followed by speeches ... The Lady Adela Cochrane started the service of cars in the afternoon from the Esplanade. Here a very large crowd had assembled, and the four cars were manoeuvred with the greatest ease ... Lady Adela took up her position in the front of the leading car and then started the car amid great cheering, and the others followed around the Canoe-lake and back. The cars subsequently started running to Newport, Cowes, Shanklin and Bembridge.

The motor-buses started running on their prescribed routes yesterday (Friday) morning, but owing to only four of the seven cars having been delivered the times could not be kept. In consequence, the directors have decided to suspend running until the whole of the seven buses have reached the Island. The very wet weather was unpropitious, and early one of the cars sank in the newly-made road near the head-quarters at Ryde and a tyre came off. A second car, when near Carpenters, was taken down the wrong road and stuck in the mud. With the assistance of horses and people it was extricated.

The following week the new bus service merited a mention in the news pages ...

April 29th, 1905

ISLAND MOTOR BUS SERVICE

The available motor buses of the I.W. Express Motor Syndicate have been running since the end of last week and have apparently secured a very good share of the Easter holiday traffic, principally between Ryde and Carisbrooke Castle. Much interest is being manifested in the introduction of this new means of travelling and a definite announcement as to a regular service on the different routes will be welcomed by the public. This will be forthcoming when the Company have their full complement of cars available, and we are informed that it is hoped shortly to arrange for full running over the regular routes and the particulars will be advertised in the County Press, thus putting an end to the feeling of uncertainty which exists as to the intended service.

They were also the subject of a letter ...

SPEED OF MOTOR-OMNIBUSES

To the Editor of the Isle of Wight County Press.

Sir, - I have received two complaints in regard to the speed of the motor-omnibuses - one from Wootton and the other from an inhabitant of Ryde. I should be glad if you would allow me to publicly state that very stringent orders have been given to our drivers that the speed in passing through towns and through villages is not to exceed, under any circumstances, eight miles per hour. By inserting this letter you will oblige, - Yours faithfully, for the Isle of Wight Express Motor Syndicate, Ltd, CLEMENT RUTTER, Secretary.

THE WEEK'S NEWS

SANDOWN. - BIRDS' NESTS IN SEWER VENTILATORS. - It was thought that birds' nests rendered practically inoperative the ventilators in the roofs of the Baptist Church and Schoolroom, and on Saturday a man was engaged to proceed on a voyage of discovery. In one ventilator five sparrows' nests were found, with young ones fledged; and in the other there were three nests with 11 eggs. The nests were destroyed, and the place of entry to the ventilators wired. In the ventilator in the schoolroom-roof, a nest of jackdaws was found, and evidently they had built almost for eternity. From top to bottom the nest measured 4ft. 6in., and the material of which it was constructed was sufficient to fill a lady's large travelling trunk. There were five eggs in the nest. Throughout the day the homeless birds were perched on the chapel roof chirping plaintively, and Jack and his mate looked disconsolate.

NEWPORT - AN EXCELLENT COW – A cow belonging to Messrs. Tutton and King, of Broadfields Farm, during the week ending May 27th gave no less than 5 gallons 3½ pints of milk per day, whilst 16lb. 7oz. of butter was made from the week's milk. The feed was grass only. This cow, which calved on March 2nd last, is now for sale for 21 guineas.

A WIFE TALKS TO HER HUSBAND.* *Jane Goodcliffe*, Shanklin, was charged with having used profane language in Orchardleigh-road, Shanklin, on the 4th inst. – Div. Sergt. King proved the case and said defendant had been previously convicted for a like offence. P.C. Sibbick said defendant used the language to her husband while standing on her doorstep. She continued the language inside for two hours and could be heard out of doors. - Fined 5s. and 5s. costs, or seven days.

THREE GLASSES OF BEER LESS - Morris and Cowdery, bootmakers, Newport, v. Charles Ash, Scarrots-lane, Newport. - This was a judgment summons for a debt of 9s.6d. - Debtor complained that the summons was not in the right name. He was summoned as Martin, but his name was Charles. – His Honour: You are the man, aren't you? - A. I might be. - His Honour: You have very little doubt that you owe the money? - A. I might owe it. - Debtor further complained that the debt had grown to 10s.3d., which was a bit hard, and said he objected to pay because plaintiffs sent the bill openly and the postboy showed it to everyone all over Newport. - His Honour: You don't find that people have avoided you through your owing the money, do you? They will come and have a glass of beer, if you will pay for it? - Debtor said he did not offer to pay for it. He offered 1s. a month. He was a drover and had a mother and family to help keep. Last week he earned 7s.6d. – His Honour: You must pay 2s. a month, 6d. a week, that is three glasses of beer less (laughter).

---

* Whoever wrote this and other captions for court cases over the years obviously had a dry sense of humour. A report of a drunk fighting in the street was captioned 'A Pugilistic Inebriate', while an account of two Cowes women smashing each other's windows in an argument which got out of hand was captioned 'Neighbourly Amenities'.

In a very odd coincidence, two Cowes men decided to commit suicide not just on the same day but also at the same place. If this report is correct, the two men were complete strangers and neither could have known the intentions of the other but despite that they somehow decided to drown themselves in the Broadfields, Love Lane, reservoir at Cowes within hours of each other. The first suicide took place on Sunday morning and the second followed a few hours later in the evening ...

April 1st, 1905

SHOCKING DISCOVERIES AT COWES
BODIES OF TWO MEN FOUND IN A RESERVOIR

The people of Cowes have seldom been more shocked and horrified than they were on Monday morning when they became aware of the fact that the body of one man had been recovered from the water of one of the reservoirs of the town and that dragging operations were going on for the purpose of finding another. The reservoir in question is known as No. 2. and gives the principal water-supply to the town. It adjoins the well and pumping machinery and is of considerable capacity, holding something like five million gallons of water or more. The reservoir is of large area and occupies the greater portion of the fenced space in which it has been constructed. The fence is a wooden one about 5 ft. high. A wide gateway at one corner is the only means of gaining entrance and this gate is generally kept locked. It is supposed that the two men climbed the fence and that one entered the water on Sunday morning and the other the same night. It is very remarkable that two cases of the kind should have happened within 24 hours of each other and in the same body of water. Dragging operations were quickly proceeded with, a floating bowler hat having given the first tragic sign, and the body of Alfred Chambers, 27, was recovered but it was not till Wednesday morning that the corpse of Charles Jacobs, 31, was brought to the surface, a floating cap being the evidence on which it was correctly suspected that another besides Chambers had been drowned. Both men are well known, and public sympathy for the families has been general, but that feeling is, perhaps, more deeply recognised with regard to Jacobs who is a member of a widely-known and esteemed family in the town. The Deputy Coroner for the Island opened the inquiry into the deaths of the men on Wednesday afternoon at the Kingston Arms, Cowes .... Verdicts were returned in both instances that the deceased committed suicide while temporarily insane.

THE WEEK'S NEWS

'Brusher' Mills, the famous New Forest snake catcher, has been found dead at Brockenhurst. Mills was familiar to visitors to the Forest where he practically lived the life of a hermit. He caught thousands of snakes during his career and during that spell that he earned his livelihood by disposing of them in various ways. He was quite an original character, and until recently lived in a small hut in the heart of the Forest.

A few days ago a dog visited the London Hospital with an injured leg, and had the limb bandaged. He has since called every day to have the injury examined.

A tramway engineer at Hastings was pointing out the dangers of live wires to an assistant on Monday when he touched one and was instantly killed.

AN OMISSION EXPLAINED. A few of the streets of Cowes only being lit with gas on Wednesday night is explained by the fact that the men of the town's Gasworks were having their well-deserved annual outing, a pleasurable event which they happily contrived to make coincide with the full moon. This gave ample light for the streets of a peaceful town. The Gasworks employees drove via Shanklin to Ventnor, where they had an excellent dinner, and afterwards returned through Godshill to Cowes. The weather was fine and the excursionists spent a most enjoyable day.

--------◆--------

Everyone should have a hobby …

September 9th, 1905
A BEETLE'S RESURRECTION
To the Editor of the Isle of Wight County Press.
Sir, - Your entomological readers will be amused at an experience I have just had of the resurrection of the male of the stag-beetle, which I could have sworn had departed this life, as all captured beetles do, some three months ago. It had then been mounted on its proper card, its feet fastened with seccotine and the card hung on a nail in the wall of my bed-room. Yesterday, however, my attention was called to a stag-beetle on the front doorstep. I concluded it was a fresh specimen, looking wonderfully like my old one. As it was alive however, I dismissed the suspicion, took it in my fingers against its will, and carried it up to my room to the poison bottle. When I looked on the card on the wall it was empty! After three months! It would be amusing to have the experience of other entomologists. - Yours obediently, E. Dugdale, Freshwater. Sept 6, 1905.

--------◆--------

A casual observer might be forgiven for not noticing that Newport town centre has a river running through it. Various public works over the years have ensured that for the most part the Medina and its concrete river banks have been successfully hidden from view. It wasn't always so.
At the bottom of Hunny Hill was the picturesque Town-gate Mill pond,* the subject of many a picture postcard. It proved attractive to humans and animals alike …

September 9th, 1905
PERFORMING SEAL IN A MILL-POND
Considerable interest was aroused in the vicinity of Town-gate and St. Cross yesterday (Friday) afternoon and last evening by the antics of a performing seal, which had been rather unwisely allowed by its owner to take a swim in the mill-ponds there. The inevitable result was that the seal so enjoyed its 'dip' that it was loath to leave the water, disregarding all appeals of its owner to become captive again. For something like five hours the seal darted and dived about in

---

*   Thanks to some imaginative restoration the mill-pond area has recently been transformed, showing the river off to its best advantage.

the stream, to the intense interest of a considerable crowd of onlookers, who were highly amused by the unsuccessful efforts of the man, who waded into the stream to capture it. As a last resort the hatches were raised, but it was not until 8 o'clock when nearly all the water had been run out of the stream, that the seal was eventually caught.

Mr. Scovell of Cowes passed by Hillier's the butchers, one day. As he did so a lump of meat sailed through the air and landed on his panama hat. Was Mr. Scovell simply a victim of innocent circumstance or was Mr. Hillier a deliberate and reckless flicker of meat? …

September 30th, 1905

A STAINED PANAMA

William Parsons Scovell v H.J. Hillier, Cowes. - Mr. A.T. Ivens was for plaintiff, a retired superintendent of H.M. Customs, of Cowes, who sued defendant, a local butcher, for £1 damage under somewhat amusing circumstances. - Plaintiff excitedly explained that as he was passing defendant's shop in St Mary's-road, Cowes, in July last, he was struck on the top of his new 30s. panama hat by something which came out of defendant's window, and his hat was stained with blood, necessitating special cleaning, which cost 1s. He looked inside and saw defendant in a crouching position with the thing he flicked flies off the meat with, in his hand and when he told defendant to keep his hands to himself, defendant laughed in his face. - Defendant said he did not know that he hit plaintiff, but if he did it was accidentally done, as he was flicking the flies off the meat, and if plaintiff had come to him and told him about it, instead of sending him a lawyer's letter, he would have apologised and paid for the cleaning of the hat. - The hat was produced, and His Honour, having inspected it, asked what was the matter with it. – Plaintiff: There is nothing the matter with it now. - His Honour said it was perfect rubbish, when what was apparently an accident happened, for an irate old gentleman to think he had been terribly injured and to incur legal costs. If he wanted to indulge in the law in such a matter he must pay for it. Judgment for the defendant, with costs.

(Mr. Scovell seems to have been a driven man with time and money to spare. He wouldn't let matters rest and some weeks later went back to Court to seek leave to appeal against the verdict. The Chairman refused, describing him as 'silly'.)

At Cowes, one September night, a dinghy, with four sailors aboard cast off from Watch-house slipway to return them to their yacht anchored nearby. As it did so, one of the men in the boat, John Kitchen, was violently attacked by another in full view of several witnesses on land. When the dinghy reached the yacht Kitchen was no longer in it; he had disappeared. Subsequently William Hockings, also on board and the man seen to attack Kitchen, was accused of killing him. Within two days one of the other men on board committed suicide, leaving Hockings and a man named Barton as the only witnesses to what had taken place in the dinghy that night.

At the inquests and subsequent trial it was obvious that not everyone wanted to tell the truth about what they had said or done that night ...

(The case attracted great attention and became the talk of the town and was reported at great length on many occasions over the subsequent weeks. Those reports have been condensed into this one account).

September 30th, 1905

YACHTSMAN CHARGED WITH MANSLAUGHTER AT COWES
SAILOR DROWNED UNDER REMARKABLE CIRCUMSTANCES

A sensational case at Cowes has largely occupied the public mind there during the past week. In view of the fact that the whole of the details are to be laid before the proper tribunal, it is unnecessary at this moment to go into all the details of the case. The substance of the matter, however, appears to be that on Monday night last, three sailors belonging to the steam-yacht Iolanthe were in a rowing-boat and put off from the Watch-house slipway to go on board their yacht. It was past 10 o'clock and very dark, with a choppy sea, and altogether a nasty night. The boat had got but a few strokes away when one of the men, named Kitchen, it is stated, jumped overboard. From that time, he was missed till his body was found on Thursday afternoon in shallow water near the slipway from which the boat put off on Monday night. As to why Kitchen left the boat as he did, it is stated that there was some fighting in her before she put off and the one of the men was seen to knock Kitchen about. Whether this treatment caused Kitchen to jump out is not at present known. Another singular feature of the case is that one of the men left in the boat declared that he had seen Kitchen land on the slipway and go ashore ... Yesterday (Friday) morning William Hockings, seaman, of the yacht Iolanthe, was charged at the Cowes Police-station 'on suspicion of feloniously killing and slaying John Wesley Kitchen, at Cowes, on the 25th inst, by striking him on the head'.

A few days later, one of the men in the boat committed suicide ...

October 7th, 1905

COWES TRAGEDIES
MYSTERIOUS DEATH OF A YACHTSMAN
SUICIDE OF A PRINCIPAL WITNESS
INQUESTS AND VERDICTS

There has been a sensational development this week in connection with the mysterious death at Cowes of a yacht's seaman named Kitchen, excitement having been intensified when it became known on Wednesday morning that Albert Dallimore, who was in the boat with the deceased and the man accused of killing Kitchen, had committed suicide by hanging himself on the steam-yacht Iolanthe ... Before his death, Dallimore had told a witness that he had seen Kitchen swimming ashore after he jumped from the boat ... Alfred Luter, Trinity pilot, living at the Union Inn, Cowes, of which his father holds the licence stated that he was on the Watch-house causeway and remained there till about midnight ... Iolanthe's boat was there. Kitchen was in the stern of the boat. No one else was there with Kitchen. He was holding the boat onto the causeway, and apparently waiting for someone else to come. Hockings (the accused) and Mr Barton, the steward, were on the causeway. Hockings was having an angry argument with a man named Cotton from the Hermione but witness did not hear what they were saying. Saw the Iolanthe's people get into their boat - Hockings, Barton, and another man, whose name he had since ascertained to be Dallimore. The last named was sitting on the fore part, Barton and Kitchen were in the stern and the accused took up the oars to row. They all appeared to be sober. When the boat put off Hockings said to Kitchen 'That was your -- chum, and I will serve you the same if you say two words'. Witness heard Kitchen say 'I've done nothing'. Then Hockings threw the oars in and went for Kitchen, and knocked him about a great deal, striking him very heavily. Kitchen was rather a small man, and he appeared to be in the bottom of the boat. The boat drifted off while this was going on. Did not see deceased try to hit him back. Did not see that Barton and Dallimore interfered to stop it. Accused was standing up when striking Kitchen, who was either lying or sitting down … Witness heard Barton call out 'Take me ashore'. Webb came out in his boat and fetched him and said he was a length away when he saw the blows struck … Mr Barton was sitting facing the men and could see better than witness. The prisoner was continually punching the other man, and therefore witness could not say how many blows were struck. Henry Caws, Trinity pilot, living at Sun-Hill, Cowes deposed that he had just arrived on shore when he saw the four men in the boat. The first thing he saw was one man punching another unmercifully. He had never heard a sound before that. The other man could not defend himself because he was sitting down in the stern, the other man standing up. Witness told him it was a cowardly bit of work, and he should come on shore and do it. He saw deceased take out his handkerchief and wipe blood from his face just as the boat put off.

… The Foreman of the jury: The verdict is 'that the deceased received his injuries in consequence of fighting with William Hockings, and that he met his death by drowning, but that there is no evidence to show how he came into the water'. The Coroner said there was only one question that he felt disposed to ask. The jury did not wish the charge of manslaughter to be preferred? The Foreman said they did not. The Coroner: Then I receive your verdict accordingly (applause, which was immediately suppressed).

After the closing of the case several of the accused's friends went up and shook hands with him. But he was not discharged from police custody. He has been charged with 'killing and slaying' Kitchen. A large crowd assembled outside the Town-hall, notwithstanding the late hour, and the accused was cheered as he emerged into the street and went away.

SUICIDE OF AN IMPORTANT WITNESS.

The Coroner on Wednesday afternoon held an inquest at the Royal Oak Inn, Cowes concerning the death of Albert Dallimore, a yachtsman, of Seaview, who was found hanged on board the steam-yacht Iolanthe, at Cowes on the previous evening. Unusual interest attached to the case, as Dallimore, who was in the boat when the fatality occurred to Kitchen, was to have been called as a witness of what took place in the boat that night … Captain E. F. Love, of the steam-yacht Iolanthe, identified the body. Deceased was about 29 years old.

The Coroner: Have you had conversation with him as to what took place in the boat on the night of Monday, the 25th September? – Witness: Yes, a good many conversations. Did the deceased make any explanation of what took place the evening? - He continued to make the same remark all along as to what transpired in the boat. Will you repeat what that was? - I questioned both Hockings and Dallimore on their arrival in the boat on Tuesday afternoon as to what they had done with Kitchen, and they stated that he had jumped over the stern of the boat. And disappeared? - Well, they tell me he got on the causeway. You saw Dallimore several times after that. Did he seem low and depressed? - He seemed low and depressed on Monday morning when I talked to him ...

The Coroner asked Acting-Sergeant William Simmons, who had known Dallimore for nine years: Did you have any conversation with Dallimore? What did he say? Witness replied that he would rather not state what deceased said. It was hardly necessary. After a pause, witness went on to say that deceased asked him how he thought he would get on. 'I said', continued the witness, 'tell the truth whatever you do, and that will carry you through. Don't keep anything back to try and save other people'. He replied 'No, Simmons, I shall see you again before Thursday'.

Answering the Coroner, the witness said he was not exactly surprised to hear the deceased had committed suicide. Deceased was a man who would take anything much to heart ... The jury returned an open verdict that deceased died by hanging ...

At the next hearing Barton took the stand. He had been present in the boat alongside Kitchen and so had witnessed all that took place at close quarters. It immediately became clear that he was determined to give nothing away ...

October 21st 1905

THE COWES TRAGEDY
MAGISTERIAL HEARING COMPLETED
ACCUSED COMMITTED FOR TRIAL
CHAIRMAN CAUTIONS A WITNESS

At the County Petty Sessions at the Guildhall, Newport, on Saturday, the magistrates were occupied for some 5½ hours in hearing the adjourned charge of manslaughter arising out of the recent tragedy in a yacht's dinghy at Cowes ...

William Barton, steward of the yacht Iolanthe, of Briston, said he heard Hockings say to Cotton as they were going to the boat 'I don't want anything to say to you. If you touch me I shall blind you in five minutes'. He heard Cotton say 'I am a good man'. They all got into the boat, witness being in the stern. He could not say in which part of the boat Kitchen was.

The Chairman: Do you understand the oath you have taken? - Yes, sir.

The Chairman: To speak the truth, the whole truth, and nothing but the truth? - Yes, sir.

The Chairman: Then take care you do it. It seems to me you need a caution very badly.

By Mr Damant: You say you do not know the position Kitchen took up? - No, I don't. I merely stepped into the boat and tried to find a chamois to wipe the seat. – Q. Did you hear any fighting or quarrelling going on? - I never heard anyone speak at all. - Q. Did you see any blow struck? - No. I did not. My back was towards them when the boat had a list. - Q. Then am I to understand that you kept your back towards them? - No, I turned round when the boat had a list, and then I saw the two men closed with each other, fighting. - Q. Just now you said you never saw a blow struck? - They were closed with each other. I never saw a blow struck. They were in a bended attitude. - Q. Which one was on top? - I could not say. I saw the other boat on the starboard side and I was trying to keep my eye on the boat I had hailed. - Q. You could see another boat, but you could not see what was going on in your own boat? Is that all you saw or heard? - Yes. Mr Damant: That is all the account you can give of what took place that evening? - Yes ... Q. Is that all the information you are going to give the Court? - I cannot give you any more. Q. And we have it in evidence that you were there all the time the blows were being struck and that you were nearest to these two men and could see what was going on. ... Q. I must caution you that you are liable to be tried for perjury if you don't tell the truth. - That is the truth. - Q. You want the Bench to believe that you were close to those two men and yet did not know what passed? - I don't know what happened. I was looking at the man in the other boat and was trying to get away from them ... Hockings was formerly committed for trial at the Hampshire Assizes.

Finally, in December, the trial took place ...

December 2nd, 1905

THE ALLEGED MANSLAUGHTER AT COWES

At the Assizes at Winchester, on Monday last, before Mr. Justice Lawrance, *William Hockings*, on bail, a yachtsman, of Exmouth, Devonshire, was charged with the manslaughter of John Kitchen, of Newlyn, Cornwall. Prisoner pleaded not guilty ... As soon as he got into the boat, having taken the oars to row off, he said to Kitchen (alluding to Cotton), 'That fellow is a ---- chum of yours. If you say anything I will serve you the same', or words to that effect. To that, Kitchen, it seemed, made no reply. Then it seemed from the evidence that would be given that Hockings pulled in his oars and made a violent attack on Kitchen. Dallimore was sitting in the bow, and Barton and Kitchen were sitting on the seat in the stern. Witnesses would say that Hockings struck Kitchen violent blows about the head to such an extent that a man on the quay shouted 'You coward. If you want to fight him come on shore'. After the assault the prisoner put out his oars again and rowed away. The last that was seen of Kitchen from the shore was when he was wiping the blood off his face with his handkerchief, and then the boat disappeared into darkness. Before the boat left, however, Barton came ashore. When the boat arrived at the yacht the officer on board asked where Kitchen was, and Hockings replied that he had had a 'scramble' with him in the boat and that Kitchen had jumped overboard. Hockings also said that Dallimore had seen Kitchen go up the causeway, and Dallimore supported the statement ... After the body was found a police officer saw Hockings, who said he thought they (the police) would be after him as soon as the body of poor Jack (meaning deceased) was found. Dallimore was not called at the inquest, for he had committed suicide by hanging himself on board his yacht, the Iolanthe, and the only man who knew how Kitchen met his death was Hockings ... Hockings then went to the witness box ... He was sent that night to fetch Kitchen, Barton and Dallimore. After making the boat fast at the causeway he got out and went to the public-house and had a pint of beer. That was all he had that day. They were not supposed to have anything on board the yacht. He came back from the public-house and was perfectly sober. He looked for his boat and found it was far away from where he had made it fast. It was three or four lengths from the slipway. Kitchen was in it. He said 'Jack, bring the boat in so as me and the steward can get in'. Kitchen got one paddle out and was not bringing the boat in as he (witness) thought, and so he said 'Why don't you put the other paddle out and bring the boat alongside?' Then the other man (Cotton) came down to him and said 'What are you talking about?' Hockings replied 'I was not talking to you but to Jack in the boat'. Cotton said 'To little Johnny?' and Hockings said 'Yes'. Cotton said 'Well, talk to me. I'm a good man'. He (Hockings) replied 'I don't want anything to say to you, but if you strike me I'll blind you in five minutes'. Cotton was coming towards him as if he would strike him. The steward then came up and stopped the conversation. By that time Kitchen had just got alongside. He (Hockings) and Barton and Dallimore then got into the boat. He told Kitchen that he had no business to cast the boat off the land, and Kitchen replied 'You've got a lot to say in this boat'. He (Hockings) replied that he ought to have, as he was in charge …

Mr Giles then addressed the jury, pointing out that the men who witnessed the assault substantially agreed, and the only evidence that at all disagreed with them was that of the prisoner. The witnesses had no interest in saying anything more than what they clearly saw. He contended that the evidence showed that there was a premeditated and brutal assault on Kitchen by the prisoner … The Judge, in summing up, told the jury that if they believed the Hockings did not strike deceased before he went into the water the whole matter was at an end so far as that inquiry was concerned. The questions for the jury were two: Was the deceased man struck before he entered the water, and if so was the person who dealt him the blow the prisoner? If what the deceased man did was to voluntarily jump into the water for the purpose of not going back that night, and if his death resulted from a blow from some obstruction in the water, a post or something of that kind, their verdict would be one of not guilty. The jury retired for 20 minutes and on returning announced that they had found the prisoner not guilty, and he was discharged. There was some attempt at applause in Court, which was immediately suppressed.

———————◆———————

A honey-buzzard was an unusual sight on the Island and there was great excitement when one took up residence in Seaview. It was sighted, it was studied, it was shot …

December 16th, 1905
SEAVIEW
A honey-buzzard was recently captured by Mr. Walter Nash, of Salterns. It is said to be a very rare visitor to the Island. How it came to get out of its course in the migration is a matter of some speculation. It is a fine specimen and the owner has had it preserved and mounted. Can any reader inform us if there has been any previous capture of this particular class of buzzard in the Island? If so, when and where?

The answer came the following week …

December 23rd, 1905
TOWN AND COUNTY NOTES
In reference to the paragraph under our 'Seaview' heading last week, relating to the capture of a honey-buzzard, we have received a note from Mr. Henry Johnson, of Winchester, who takes great interest in local ornithology, stating 'Dr Cowper, in the 'Hants Court Guide', records one shot near Sandown by Mr. H. Jacobs while it was in the act of plundering a wasp's nest. The date was October 7th, 1878'. A correspondent writing from Haylands, Ryde, says a honey-buzzard was captured in Whitefield Woods on or about the 14th June, 1898, and he believes it is still in the possession of the owner of the Woods. Mr. H. Grimes of the Vineries, Upton-road, Ryde, writes that he will be pleased to show anyone interested in the matter a beautiful specimen of the honey-buzzard, which was driven through the window, he thinks, of Wellington-Lodge, Spencer-road, Ryde, in the snowstorm of January 11th, 1881.

1906

A patient at the Ventnor Consumption Hospital attacked another patient with a knife one morning. The police were called and he was arrested and the follwing morning he was put on a train to Newport in the custody of a police sergeant. The train set off from Ventnor West station and shortly after leaving St Lawrence, it entered the tunnel that ran under the downs to Whitwell. In the carriage, the two men sat opposite each other in pitch-black darkness. When the train emerged into the daylight, one of them had gone …

February 10th, 1906
ALLEGED MALICIOUS WOUNDING AT VENTNOR HOSPITAL
PRISONER'S SENSATIONAL ESCAPADE
JUMP FROM A TRAIN
Herbert Beard, a patient at the Royal National Hospital for Consumption at St. Lawrence, was brought up in custody charged with maliciously wounding another patient named Herbert Bull. It appeared from the evidence that on that morning, at about 8.45, as the patients were mustering for breakfast in the dining-hall, the prisoner and Bull were engaged in cutting up bread. Without any warning the prisoner slashed out with the knife he was using. This blow falling short and only cutting Bull's collar, the prisoner slashed out again, and before Bull could get out of the way, the knife reached his neck, inflicting a wound on the left side about three inches long and skin deep. Bull and another patient grappled with the prisoner, and took the knife away from him. The Police were communicated with, and Beard was arrested. He gave as his reason for the act that Bull had annoyed him and he had had his revenge and was satisfied. On the other hand, Bull said they were on the best of terms, and only the night before they had been smoking their pipes together. The magistrates remanded the prisoner to the Ryde Court on Tuesday next.

Chapter 2

Things that make life easier

It used to be thought impossible to speak to people hundreds of miles away or to wash clothes without boiling them.

That was before the telephone and Fels-Naptha.

Now you can do both.

But you can't do the talking by shouting or the washing with ordinary soaps. You must use the telephone in the one case and Fels-Naptha soap in the other.

Modern science is making life easier for both men and women.

Official and other Notices.

I, EMMA JONES, of 33, Fitzroy-street, Sandown, hereby give notice that I have NOT contracted any DEBTS in the name of my husband, Arthur Jones, now living with his father, at 3, The Lindens, Brading, and that his advertisement in reference thereto has no justification whatever.

A startling sequel to the occurrence detailed above occurred while the prisoner was being taken to Newport on the following morning. He was in charge of Div. Sergt. W. Cass, who took him to the Ventnor town station at Steephill, where the Sergeant entered the last carriage; there were, however, several goods trucks behind this compartment. The prisoner took a seat in the far corner facing the engine, the Sergeant occupying the corner seat opposite. There was one other passenger in the carriage, namely, Mr. W.A. Hart. The prisoner was very quiet and there was nothing whatever in his demeanour to arouse suspicion of any intention on his part to attempt to escape from custody. Nothing occurred till after the train entered the tunnel and the carriage was in darkness. Then the prisoner must have noiselessly opened the window, reached through, seized the handle, which was on his side of the door, and turned it, and rising from his seat silently sidled out through the partly opened door without touching the Sergeant's knees, which must have been within an inch or two of him. The first intimation the Sergeant had as to what was happening was hearing the click of the door as it came to. Thinking the prisoner was then opening the window, the Sergeant leapt forward to prevent him doing so, but all he 'felt' was empty space, for the bird had flown. The Sergeant put his head out of the window, but could see nothing in the darkness. However, as soon as the train was through the tunnel, the Sergeant took measures to stop it, and it was brought to a standstill at the level crossing at Dean. Accompanied by one or two others, the Sergeant made his way back to the tunnel as quickly as possible. It was a bright day, and the light penetrated the tunnel for some distance. As soon as the searchers entered, the Sergeant discerned the prisoner sitting up on one side of the tunnel. When the party reached him, however, he was lying down, apparently dead. They turned him over to ascertain what injuries he had sustained, and all they could discover was a slight scalp wound, from which the blood was flowing. A hurdle was procured and the apparently dead man was placed upon it, and carried to the Whitwell station. Before reaching the station, however, the bearers had suspicions that the prisoner was shamming, and depositing him, still on the hurdle, in one of the waiting-rooms, the party pretended to move away. The Sergeant, entering the room quietly immediately after, discovered the prisoner sitting up, and realising that he was not much the worse for his adventure, gave him to understand that he would not have an opportunity to escape again. When the next train came up, the prisoner walked to a carriage, the doors of which the Sergeant had locked. The police authorities at Newport had been apprised of the occurrence by telephone, and at Shide an ambulance was in waiting, together with members of the local corps. In this the prisoner was conveyed to the lock-up at the Police-station, where he was medically examined, and found to be uninjured except for the scalp wound. The prisoner's coat tail was torn, showing that he had a narrow escape from being run over by the trucks in his leap from the train.

(Mr. Beard appeared at the Hampshire Assizes in April and was found 'totally unfit to undergo prison discipline due to his state of health'. He was bound over and for reasons not made clear he was sent to a workhouse infirmary in Lichfield.)

St Lawrence and the railway line to Whitwell with the tunnel just off picture on the right. (*See page 73.*)

With figures that would bring a tear to the eye of a modern-day policeman, the Chief Constable for the Island presented his annual account of the crime statistics for Ryde ...

February 3rd, 1906

POLICE WORK IN THE BOROUGH OF RYDE

In his annual report the Chief Constable (Mr. C. Greenstreet) states that the number of crimes reported to the police last year was 19, the same number as in the preceding year. For these offences 14 persons were proceeded against, 13 males and one female. All were convicted. The crimes were: Burglary 1, larceny by a servant 4, simple larceny 8, receiving 1, embezzlement 3, and false pretences 2. In the burglary reported only a few farthings were stolen. The only undetected crimes were three cases of simple larceny. The total number of persons proceeded against and dealt with summarily for non-indictable offences was 110. The following is a list of the offences: Adulteration of food and drugs 1, assault on constable 3, common assault 7, Betting and Gaming Act 3, cruelty to animals 6, obstruction of highway 6, Heavy Locomotives Act 1, Motor Car Act and bicycles 2, drunkenness 36, other offences against the intoxicating liquor laws 5, Shop Powers Act 1, damage to trees, shrubs, &c., 1, Army Act deserters 3, Commons and open spaces 2, Towns Police Clauses Act 25, hackney carriage regulations 4, Vagrancy Acts 3, Sale of Pistols Act 1, Petroleum Act 1 ... There are 95 premises licensed for the sale of intoxicating liquor. Six clubs were registered. Nine premises are licensed for the storage of petroleum, 4 for carbide of calcium,* and 4 for the sale of game. The following licences were issued by the police: 29 cabs, 15 omnibuses, 6 wagonettes, 56 cab drivers, 45 bus drivers, 66 boats for the Canoe-lake, 10 boatmen, and 7 luggage porters ... Eight inquests were held, three lost children were restored to their parents, 263 premises were found insecure at night, 204 street lamps were reported defective, and 25 stray dogs were seized. The authorised strength of the force was 15, but there was one vacancy which it might not be necessary to fill, in consequence of the increased efficiency of the force due to the replacing of old and worn-out constables by younger and energetic men. 69 days had been lost by sickness from natural causes.

THE WEEK'S NEWS

HOSTILE DEMONSTRATIONS BY LONDON UNEMPLOYED. The unemployed made hostile demonstrations at the Guildhall, London, yesterday. Hundreds of policemen guided the approaches. Several men were arrested.

THE QUEEN'S UNEMPLOYED FUND. This fund now amounts to over £100,000, at which Her Majesty has expressed her delight.

A fishing boat belonging to Mr. Frank Mursell, of Bembridge, has had an extraordinary adventure. During a heavy gale on the night of the 6th of January it was blown out to sea, and Mr. Mursell heard no more of it until an announcement in the Shipping Gazette informed him that on the 5th of February it was found washed ashore on the coast of Norway.

---

* Used in early car headlights. Water was drip-fed onto the powder to produce acetylene gas which was then ignited to provide a bright light.

A sailor dressed as a fashionable lady badly beat 3 constables who tried to arrest him at Croydon on Tuesday.

———————◆———————

The provision of public services took a huge leap forward in these years as government and councils across Britain continued the work of the Victorians by investing large amounts of money in the water and sewage systems of Britain. The sinking of a well was a demanding civil engineering project and on completion of a well for the people of East Cowes, the County Press complemented the Council on a good job, apparently well done …

February 24th, 1906
THE WATER SUPPLY OF EAST COWES

The East Cowes District Council, on Thursday afternoon last, started their new system of water supply for the district. They have for years been handicapped by an indifferent supply, although they have spared no pains in obtaining professional assistance and spending large sums of money in well-sinking and providing machinery. With the population of the district growing rapidly, and the need of additional water becoming an absolute necessity, the District Council consulted the well-known engineer, Mr. W. Brown, C.E., of Tottenham, and the result has been the finding of abundant and excellent water and the completion of a splendid system of supply which promises to meet the requirements of the town for many years to come. The work is practically finished throughout, and the Council and the ratepayers generally have reason to be highly satisfied with what has been done for them by the engineering and mechanical experts who have been engaged. By the side of the old well from which so much was at one time hoped, but which has proved so disappointing, a new well has been sunk to a depth of 107 ft. It had been intended to go much deeper than this, but a sudden inrush of water which no amount of pumping could exhaust, brought about the decision that the sinking of the well should go no further. The well is 8ft. in diameter, lined at the top with cast-iron cylinders to a depth of 25ft., and at the bottom there are more cylinders to a depth of 40ft. Brickwork lines the space between these two sets of cylinders. A set of pumps has been fixed at the top of the well by Messrs Duke and Ockendon, of Littlehampton. Covering the pumps and well is a newly erected building which has been added to the old engine-house, and a roomy and well-lit and suitable place is thus provided for the new gear…. From the well a new water-main has been laid. This main is some 600 ft. long, and rises to a height of 150ft. to the tank of the new water-tower which has been erected at the top of Victoria-grove, better known as Tower-road…. The whole scheme has cost about £6,000…. The water-tower tank could be filled in 2½ hours, and it holds 29,700 gallons or a three days' supply for the houses for which it was intended.

(Unfortunately, just two years later the new well was said to be 'unable to keep up a satisfactory supply of water' and the Council, in what was described as 'an animated discussion' heard embarrassing accusations that the new well had simply tapped into the old one located nearby. The cost of the work was described by Councillor Floyd as 'money flung away; it might just as well have been thrown out into the English Channel'.)

———————◆———————

The first commercially available banana didn't arrive in England until 1880. Before that their import had not been practical because they ripened and spoilt during the long voyage to England. The problem was solved by the arrival of refrigerated holds on ships and almost overnight bananas became part of the British way of life. Fyffes, the banana importers, opened a cold store in Pyle Street Newport, which some readers will remember still being in existence well into the 1970s …

March 3rd, 1906
BANANAS FOR THE ISLAND
Due to the increased demand for Jamaica bananas in the Isle of Wight, Messrs. Elders and Fyffes, Ltd, of London and Bristol, have opened a store at Newport fitted with two special banana ripening rooms. They have this week commenced forwarding consignments of the fruit by specially built cars, which, under the arrangements made by the firm, will be enabled to reach Newport 13 hours after the arrival of their ships at Avonmouth Dock. Some particulars concerning this growing trade may be given next week.

———————◆———————

Just as in Victorian times, the pages of the County Press were still full of court cases involving cruelty to children. This one is selected at random and is no worse or better than any other. The cases were all depressingly similar but it is fair to say that only very rarely was there physical harm done to children, the prosecutions being almost entirely due to neglect or hunger rather than any act of deliberate violence towards the children …

June 16th, 1906
MOTHER'S HEARTLESS CONDUCT
Mary Ellen Queenan, a married woman, described as a hawker, formerly of Newport and latterly of Portsmouth, was brought up on a warrant charged with deserting her three children aged 13, 7, and 5. P.S. Hy. Hawkins said that at 3 a.m. on the 23rd of April last, from what he was told, he went to Sea-street, where he looked through the window of the tenement formerly occupied by defendant and saw the three children in question huddled together on some dirty rags and clothing. They were crying, and they told him they were frightened and very hungry. They said they had not seen their mother for two days, and they had no food or firing. Later he took the children some food and gave them something to get some milk. The matter was reported to the relieving officer and the children were removed to the Workhouse during the day. On Saturday, the 9th, he received prisoner into custody at the Portsmouth Police-station. In reply to the warrant, she said she did not intentionally desert the children. The children were in a very bad state of neglect. Inspector John Marshall, NSPCC, said on the 23rd of April he visited defendant's little cottage or shed place in Sea-street, Newport, and saw the children there in the room where there was an old bed, broken chairs, and a table. They said their mother left them on the previous Friday morning and they had not seen her since. Finding the children had no food or firing, and no means of getting any, he communicated with the relieving officer, with the result that they were removed to the Workhouse. About a fortnight before, he called on defendant

and the man named Durrant, with whom she had been living, and warned them to look after the children, as he had had some complaints. They both promised to look after the children. After the children had gone to the Workhouse he saw defendant with a baby and her husband at Ryde, and told her what happened and again warned her to go and look after the children … Defendant said she hoped the Bench would deal with her leniently as she had had a hard cruel life. She was married in that town at the age of 14 to an Army pensioner, and they parted 15 years ago. She was the mother of 15 children, and she had not had a husband to support her and her children all through, so she had to work hard and tramp miles and miles to maintain her family. She had two sons doing well in Australia and a daughter married very comfortably at Southsea. She would have taken the children out of the House if she had been able. She had to get out of her house in Newport and she was looking for a house in Portsmouth when the children were taken to the Workhouse. She had no intention of deserting her children; she loved them too much for that. She loved her children as she loved her life. She again appealed for leniency owing to the hard life she had experienced in bringing up her children, and said her husband was now willing to take her back. If they sent her away it would break her little baby's heart. - The Bench sentenced defendant to one month's imprisonment, with hard labour.

As Mrs. Queenan left the dock to begin her sentence, her place was taken by Mrs. Langman who was accused of using her house for prostitution. The two ladies were to share another experience; they received the same sentence. Mrs. Langman, however, wasn't prepared to accept her punishment before she had given a spirited account of herself …

June 16th, 1906

ANOTHER WOMAN IMPRISONED

Jane Langman, a married woman living apart from her husband at Orchard-street, was summoned for permitting her premises to be used for habitual prostitution. – P.C'.s W. Collins and A. Clark, who, in consequence of complaints, concealed themselves near the defendant's house in Orchard-street in the evenings between the 17th and 23rd ult. and kept watch on the defendant's premises, gave evidence as to the visits of soldiers and others there, and also of an unknown woman. Defendant said she was being run down as by a lot of bloodhounds. She challenged a statement of P.C. Clark that she did not know she was being watched by the police and said, 'I don't like to call you a liar, but you have got a false pair of jaws'. - Inspector Cass proved the arrest of defendant, who said 'Can't I have a friend or two if I like, to come and see me?' - Defendant, who protested that she should have been warned before such proceedings were taken, was sentenced to one month's imprisonment with hard labour. – Defendant: Thank you; I am very pleased'.

———————◆———————

Ventnor residents had a surprise one sleepy afternoon in June, when their peace and quiet was shattered by a loud explosion. The Fire Brigade were trying out their new device for calling out the fire crew; a bomb …

June 30th, 1906

FIRE AND BOMB

Much interest was created at Ventnor on Thursday, just before five o'clock, when a loud explosion brought residents to their doors and windows in more or less alarm. It appears that the Fire Brigade, not being satisfied with the fire Bell, which cannot be heard in all parts of the town, had decided to experiment with an aerial maroon or bomb; and it was entrusted to the keeping of Mr. H. Humphries, West-street, Longdown, with instructions to explode it on Friday evening. On Thursday afternoon however, Miss Jolliffe who resides in a cottage near the Rifle Volunteer Drill-hall in South-street, was burning some old letters and papers when during her temporary absence downstairs, some of the burning paper fell out of the grate and set fire to the mantelpiece and hearth. On the fire-bell being rung, Mr. Humphries exploded the bomb, which was heard in all parts of the town and brought the Brigade together in double quick time. The fire however, had been promptly extinguished by the application of a few buckets of water before much damage had been done, and when the facts became known there was general laughter. The bomb has evidently come to stay as a fire call.

———————◆———————

THE WEEK'S NEWS

A GOOD CATCH - With a hook and line, a lobster weighing 7½lb was caught from Yarmouth Pier-head on Saturday last by Mr. T. H. Doe.

The Emperor of China has issued an edict ordering the abolition of the use of opium within ten years. The revenue from opium represents 7% of the revenue of the Indian Empire.

OPERATION ON A DOG - Mr. F. Halsted, of Union-street, Ryde, had a dog run over by a coach last week. As he did not wish to lose the animal, he took it to the County Hospital, where one leg was amputated and another put into splints. The dog is doing well.

CAPITAL PUNISHMENT - Capital punishment for burglary recalls the old-time severity of the law, as illustrated by the following paragraph from the Hampshire Telegraph of August 18, 1821: 'John Brookes, 22, a native of the Isle of Wight, was hanged at Winchester this day for having committed a burglary at the residence of Capt. J. K. White, in Jubilee-terrace, Southsea, and stolen property to the value of £300. He was the first man to be hanged on the new drop which had been erected on the tops of the walls of the prison, so that a distinct view of the awful ceremony might be obtained. While in the condemned cell he most ingeniously constructed a ladder of faggot sticks long enough to reach the top of the wall and strong enough to bear his weight, and he would certainly have effected his escape but for a timely discovery by the turnkey'.

VENTNOR - THE WATERFALL. Ventnor's lovely waterfall at the approach to the Esplanade is to be again illuminated with coloured electric lamps, and the current was turned on for the first time this season on Tuesday evening. There is a larger volume of water than ever, and the effects under the coloured lamps are pretty in the extreme.

———————◆———————

The Workhouse continued to improve ...

August 4th, 1906

THE CARE OF IMBECILES

The Local Government Board forwarded the report of Dr. Needham, visiting Commissioner in Lunacy, on his recent visit to the Workhouse, stating that he found 14 men and 17 women of unsound mind in the wards, and all were dressed neatly and bore every evidence of being well cared for. None complained of their treatment. The day-rooms were light and very clean, but more bare than was customary, and he should have liked to see in each ward a small open book-case with a few simple bound books and a musical-box, and perhaps a few plants ... Mr. Hayden, speaking with his recollection of 12 years as a Guardian, said that when they remembered that what was once described as 'the black hole of Calcutta' - verminous and unfit for human habitation, as their imbecile wards were in the old days - had been transformed into what, by comparison, was a palace, it seemed really almost unbearable red-tapeism to have an inspector recommending the small things suggested in his report. He thought the time had come to stop, after the enormous improvement brought about by the huge expenditure incurred in their new wards (hear, hear) ... The Chairman said there was a beautiful library in connection with the House, but what was wanted was a supply of picture books and illustrated papers ... One's mind went back to what the place was in the old days. It should be a palace for those poor people (hear, hear). - Mr. E. Morris: You will be getting another letter in the *County Press* (laughter). The Chairman: Oh, I can put up with the *County Press* letters. They won't hurt me (laughter). - The proposition was carried.

———————◆———————

Back in September the previous year, a performing seal had caused problems with its antics in Towngate mill-pond (see page 66). Perhaps it was the same seal which brought Cowes High Street to a halt one summer's day afternoon a few months later ...

August 11th, 1906

PERFORMING SEAL OWNER'S OBSTRUCTION

Charles Winter, Great Yarmouth, did not attend to answer a charge of obstructing the highway at Cowes. – P.C. Sheates said on the previous Tuesday, about 4 p.m., he was in the High-street, Cowes, where he saw the defendant with a truck, on which was a tank containing a performing seal. - The Chairman: What, a seal? - The Magistrates' Clerk explained that it was a tame seal, about 4 ft. 6 in. long. - Continuing, witness said the truck was standing at the entrance to the Town Quay. He asked defendant to move it, as it was causing an obstruction, but he refused to do so and remained there for 20 minutes. During that time a performance was given by the seal in the presence of about 100 people, who blocked the way to the Quay for carts and passengers. After defendant left there, his truck stopped outside the Three Crowns public-house for ten minutes, surrounded by children, and again obstructed the highway. He had cautioned defendant the day before. When he asked him for his name and address he was very abusive and made use of bad language. – Supt. Galloway said defendant had given the police a lot of trouble. He came from Great Yarmouth, and apparently travelled the country with his trained seal. - Fined 10s. and 4s. costs; in default seven days.

On a December evening in 1906, a horse and trap was crossing the Bembridge to Brading railway line near the station at St Helens.* Somehow, the horse was able to turn onto the line and then, complete with passenger, it bolted along the railway track; just in time to meet an oncoming train …

December 22nd, 1906

SENSATIONAL ACCIDENT AT ST HELENS

Early on Thursday evening, as Mr. Nash, baker, of Brading, accompanied by a soldier, was crossing the railway line in a horse and cart at St Helens, at the railway gates, which were apparently partly closed, the horse suddenly bolted up the railway line. Mr. Nash was thrown out near the station, and after the horse had covered about another 100 yards, the soldier saw a train approaching and immediately sprang out of the trap, alighting in the oyster-beds adjoining the line. The horse, however, continued its mad career, and, being struck by the oncoming engine, was immediately killed, whilst the cart was completely smashed. Mr. Nash was reported to be rather seriously hurt, but the soldier was apparently not much the worse for his exciting experience and thrilling escape from an almost certain death.

A later message states that the soldier's name was Wright. Mr. Callander, the driver of the train, promptly applied the brakes, but the animal dashed into the train and was instantly killed. The remains of the horse and cart had to be removed to allow the train to proceed into the station. Very little of the shock was felt by the train passengers owing to the promptitude with which the brakes were applied. The occupants of the cart were rather badly bruised, but so far as could be gathered they sustained no further serious injury.

THE WEEK'S NEWS

Warning a witness against judging too much by appearances, his humorous Honour Judge Gye remarked at Portsmouth: 'My position might warrant me in getting £3,000 a year, but people don't always get what they deserve'.

---

* The station buildings still exist, at the junction of Embankment and Station Road.

To the Editor of the Isle Of Wight County Press. AN EMPLOYEE'S WAGES.

Sir, - At the St. Helens Council meeting, the Chairman, who was advocating reducing an aged workmen's wages from 10s. to 5s. per week, stated that I looked upon this aged workman in the light of a pensioner .... I was not in favour of the reduction, and during the whole of the time I was Surveyer to the Council I did everything I could to lighten this poor old man's burden, and I am astonished that the Chairman, who at one time was an advocate of every man having a 'living wage', should endeavour by inaccuracies to deprive this old man of 5s. per week. - Faithfully yours, JOHN I. BARTON

PIGEON SHOOTING APPLICATION - Mr. W J. Barr, of the Victors, Cowes, applied for an occasional licence for the purposes of a pigeon-shooting match at Dottens Farm on the 27th of December inst. - The Chairman asked what drinking had to do with pigeon-shooting, and said they would shoot better without it. - The Bench refused to grant the application.

A Central News message Wednesday, states that details of the wild Easter orgie at Coalisland have reached Belfast. Inter-county cock-fights were held, and the crowd consumed 45 cart-loads of liquor. A free fight followed, in which many persons were seriously injured by bludgeons.

1907

Mr. Tross of Northwood was accused of poaching. In court, he was rude and unco-operative. He would make a more sinister court appearance just a few weeks later ...

January 5th, 1907

AN INSOLENT POACHER

Frank Tross, of Northwood, pleaded guilty to a charge of poaching at Ridge Copse, Northwood, belonging to Mr. F.T. Mew. - Mr. H. C. Damant prosecuted. - George Moore, assistant gamekeeper in the employ of Mr. Mew, stated that on December 17th he saw defendant's lurcher dog hunting right through Ridge Copse, Northwood. After watching the dog for some time witness went down through the copse and saw defendant coming along under the hedge of the adjoining field. He asked him what he was doing there and defendant said he did not know ... Asked by the Bench if he wished to say anything, defendant replied 'No; I can talk to a man but not a pig'. - The Chairman: I don't know what he means. Is he drunk? - The Magistrates' Clerk (Mr. John Fardell): I don't think so. It is only a pure insult, Sir. - Supt Galloway (deputy chief constable) put in four previous convictions against defendant, who Mr. Damant said was a regular nuisance in the district. - The Chairman said defendant appeared to be an incurable poacher. He would be fined £1 and 5s. costs; in default 14 days.

The Great Conflagration at Cowes. Marvin's and Lallow's wharves, Cowes, February 1907. (*See page 87.*)

Late one February afternoon, what started as a chimney fire in a house at Medina Road, Cowes, soon turned into one of the largest and most destructive fires that the town had ever seen …

February 23rd, 1907

GREAT CONFLAGRATION AT COWES
IMMENSE DAMAGE TO WATERSIDE PROPERTY
FIREMEN'S FIERCE FIGHT WITH THE FLAMES
SPLENDID HELP FROM BLUEJACKETS
AND NEIGHBOURING FIRE BRIGADES

One of the most destructive fires which Cowes has ever known occurred on Monday evening last, when a considerable range of yacht storage premises and much valuable property were consumed. The scene of the fire was on the wharves and jetties owned by Mr. A.E. Marvin and Mr. S. Lallow, at the town end of Medina-road, just below the Police-station. The entrance to Mr. Lallow's wharf (formerly known as Bannister's) is through a gateway under the familiar archway adjoining the shop of Mr. Croutear, the fisherman, and his wife, who live on the premises. Behind this, on the wharf on the left, were the stores of the Mitcham Motor-boat Company and on the right, other stores rented by Messrs. Marvins. Further on, to the right, were nine yacht stores three storeys high. These were the property of Mr. A.E. Marvin. Mr. Lallow had extensive storage accommodation on the wharf for material of all sorts, mostly wood, used in the building of boats, and other stores were used for the gear of Sir Allen Young's steam-yacht Stella, for the boats and other property belonging to the Cowes Harbour Commissioners, and others. All these stores were built mostly of wood and had been standing many years, occupying practically two quays running out into the Harbour parallel with one another, with a slipway between them.

Somewhere between half past 4 and 5 o'clock the premises occupied by Mr. and Mrs. Croutear were found to be on fire. The alarm was given at the Police-station, and Inspector Bignell at once telephoned to the Fire-station. This is an instance of the good purpose to which the telephone system recently installed in connection with the Fire-brigade may be put. The message brought Captain Billows and the members of the Fire-brigade to the spot in quick time. They at once got to work, but the fire had secured a good hold on the building. Notwithstanding the efforts of the brigade, the flames, fanned by a fresh off-shore breeze, rapidly spread out towards the Harbour; indeed, the rapidity with which the flames spread and devoured all within reach was marvellous. Hardly any time was given to those who were on the wharf to save anything, and even as they were venturing to do it they had to beat a hasty retreat for safety. Fortunately the wind was blowing in the right direction for limiting the area of the fire by driving it seaward. Had the stiff breeze that was then blowing been from the south-east, and the fire had broken out in the night, it is safe to prophesy that the whole of the premises in Birmingham-road which include bonded stores and the well-filled timber-yard of Messrs Sharp and Co., would have fallen prey to the flames … In half an hour from the time of the discovery of the outbreak the wharf was doomed, for the flames had got such a hold that they enveloped a considerable space and rose high into the air. When darkness came on and the fire was at its height the Solent was illumined, and the reflection on the dark sky could be seen at Southampton, Portsmouth, Ryde, and Newport, and practically all over the Island. The Cowes Brigade had not been long upon the spot when assistance reached them ... The Newport Fire-brigade was sent for, and Captain Russell quickly mustered eight men of his Brigade and after some difficulty in horsing the engine, galloped off to Cowes about 6.30 with 750 ft. of hose, reaching the scene in a commendably short time. Later on, the Ryde Brigade dashed up and at once prepared to render any assistance possible with the 1,500 ft. of hose they had brought with them.

There was a large quantity of highly inflammable material in the stores, and explosives in the way of rockets and small cartridges. There were consequently explosions at times, giving an additionally alarming character to the fire, but no personal injury resulted. Fears were entertained as to the quantity of petrol in the Mitcham Motor Company's premises, but Mr. Aitken, the Company's local manager, had pitched overboard all the cans of petrol he had time to lay his hands on, and he also had turned down the slipway into the water a valuable motor-car, which thus escaped the flames, but did not escape damage, of course. The fire burnt furiously for two hours then the combined effects of the firemen began to tell. Supreme efforts were directed to preserve the premises of Messrs. Shepard Bros., which formed a barrier to the flames on the south side. On this Company's wharf is a large bonded store, and as the walls had become hot and there seemed a prospect of further destruction, the locks of the store were forced by the Naval Brigade and some 200 cases of wines and spirits and many casks were removed to a place of safety ... By 8 o'clock the diminution of the mass of the fire became very marked, and two hours later it only remained for the local Brigade to finish the task of extinguishing what remained of the burning rubbish. Mr. Croutear's house had been gutted, and everything else behind it had either been burned to a cinder or else damaged absolutely beyond any repair.

Mr. Aitken, was able to save some of the Company's property, but much that was of considerable value had to be left. He was able to put afloat six motor-boats, but four had to remain, and these, with three valuable motor-engines ready for dispatch to France and Constantinople, were included in the ravages of the fire. In one of the stores was a valuable refrigerating apparatus and in another a considerable amount of gear belonging to the Royal Yacht Squadron, including chairs and rugs for use on the lawn in the summer. All these stores, with their contents, were consumed in half an hour from the commencement of the fire.

While the fire was raging an enormous number of people gathered to watch it. Every position from which a view could be obtained was occupied. On the adjacent jetties and wharves and along the shore at East Cowes spectators were as thick as possible. In Medina-road and at the end of Birmingham-road there was another great crowd. The police force was quickly augmented, with the Deputy Chief Constable in charge. The police duty was light owing to the orderly behaviour of the people, which was partly obtained through the discreet and considerate manner in which the police officers and their subordinates did their duty.

The total damage is estimated at somewhere about £16,000.

AFTER THE FIRE

All day on Tuesday, large numbers of persons who visited the spot witnessed the clearance which had been made from the street right out to the end of the two piers. Those persons who had the privilege of entering the charred gateway of the wharf found much to impress them in the devastation all around them and in the remains of the many burnt-up objects of interest which a few hours before had been very valuable. Among these were the motor-engines of the Mitcham Motor Company. They lay where they had been burned and were now absolutely useless. Shapeless things like stoves could be identified as the once artistic and expensive apparatus used for warming yachts' cabins, and there were many other things about the wet and ash-covered ground indicating how fierce the fire had been. Proving the great heat maintained for a time there was a launch propeller shaft of the hardest nature which had been melted like lead. Several photographers were taking pictures of the ruins from various points of view. We learn on further inquiry that the cause of the fire was probably the overheating or igniting of a chimney in the house of Mr. Croutear, the flames being first observed in the back room upstairs when everything had become ignited. This house, which belongs to Messrs. Lallow, was completely burnt out, and the tenant's loss, which is covered by insurance, is estimated at about £200. Nearly all the owners of property on the wharf were insured.

————————◆————————

TOWN AND COUNTY NOTES

THE AURORA BOREALIS was very vividly seen on Saturday evening last by many of the residents of the Western Wight. By many, the display of the brilliant Northern Lights was mistaken for a fire in the distance.

EXTRAORDINARY BURNING FATALITY. - A VICTIM TO HIS PIPE. - On Wednesday morning of last week, a man named James Westmoor, aged 71, living at Nettlecombe, Whitwell, was severely burned when proceeding to his work. It is supposed that some live ashes fell from his pipe and set fire to his clothing, most of which was consumed. When found he was struggling home with just his overcoat flung around him. Later in the day he was attended by Dr. Woodford, and the burns being of so serious a nature the patient was removed to the infirmary at Parkhurst where he died the following Monday.

At an ordinary general meeting of the shareholders of the I.W. Express Motor Syndicate the directors reported a deficit of £3,323 16s. 4d.

At a meeting of the Channel Tunnel Company on Monday it was stated that the tunnel scheme would cost £16,000,000, and the directors were satisfied that there would be a high percentage of profit on the outlay.

COUNTY ASYLUM. - The Committee of Visitors of the Isle of Wight Asylum reported that the number of patients was 103 males and 163 females, total 266. Although some people had an idea that the percentage of lunacy in the Island was greater than in any other part of the country, that was not the case, and the statistics showed that if the increase in the Island had been equal to the increase in other parts of the country, they would have had 35 more patients at the Asylum than they had at the present time.

THE RAILWAY TIMES, in a leading article deals with the proposed electrification of Island Railways. While no doubt an attractive scheme, our expert contemporary is 'afraid that it will be found impracticable'.

————————◆————————

If only in terms of swearing, shouting and screaming, Mr. and Mrs. Page of Godshill seem to have been an evenly matched couple. Once again the County Press headline is suitably succinct ...

March 9th, 1907
MAKING NIGHT HIDEOUS
James Page, a gypsy, of Oakfield, was charged with using obscene language at a gypsy caravan near Godshill Schools on the previous Saturday night. P.C. Stevens said the defendant was quarrelling with his wife and using most filthy and disgusting language, which could be heard in houses about the village and about which, many complaints were received. - Defendant, against whom there was a previous conviction, was fined 5s. and 9s. costs; in default seven days.

Jane Page, wife of the last defendant, pleaded guilty to a similar offence, committed at the same time and place. - The constable stated that defendant screamed, shouted and swore for half an hour, until she fairly collapsed through exhaustion. - When shown some of the language and asked if she could read defendant said 'No I can't, worse luck. I can't remember it'. She added 'I am the mother of 12 children. I am seven-and-forty and I can't remember it' (laughter). - The Deputy Chief Constable said both defendants were a very great nuisance. - Defendant was fined 5s. and 9s. costs; in default seven days.

————————◆————————

Mr. Williams had the contract to build a new harbour wall at Newport Quay. It was a big contract and a big wall, being five metres high and nearly two metres thick at its base. In the small hours of Thursday morning Mr.Williams dreamt that the wall had collapsed and just a few hours later his dream came true. Perhaps he had inside knowledge ...

April 13th, 1907

COLLAPSE OF NEW QUAY WALL AT NEWPORT
CONTRACTOR'S DREAM FULFILLED

A serious and alarming incident occurred on Thursday afternoon at the Newport Quay extension works, which are being carried out by Mr. W.F. Williams, builder, &c., of Newport, under contract with the Corporation. Early on Thursday morning Mr. Williams awoke from dreaming that the massive concrete wall being erected on the Quay was slipping into the river. When he arrived at the Quay the wall was still intact, but later in the day ominous cracks appeared, and at about 3 p.m. the wall collapsed in the river for a length of over 50 yards, commencing at the termination of the old wall. The wrecked wall was 16ft. high from the foundation, 5ft. in thickness at the base, 4ft. thick in the middle section, and 2½ft. wide at the top, and was constructed in solid concrete. Early this week a steam grab had been busy in transferring large quantities of excavations of clay, with mud, &c., from the river in front of the wall to a large vacant space behind the wall, filling it almost level with the top. It was evidently the pressure of this enormous quantity of wet material placed behind the wall which forced the wall over. Fortunately no one was injured in the accident, which, however, means a serious loss for the contractor, who had been making good progress with the work. The wall broke in various parts as it went over and the huge masses of concrete sticking up out of the mud presented an extraordinary sight, which has attracted many people to the scene. …. £1,661 was the amount of Mr. William's tender accepted by the Corporation early in January for the work, and nearly a third of the specified total length of wall is wrecked.

———————◆———————

Back in January, Frank Tross had appeared in court charged with poaching (see page 85). With an accomplice he was now back in court but this time charged with a cowardly attack on a Porchfield farmer and his family, subjecting them to a nightmare which must have left them terrified …

April 13th, 1907

POACHERS BESIEGE A FARMHOUSE
EXTRAORDINARY BRUTALITY AND TERRORISM

Frank Tross and *James Dunford*, labourers, of Northwood, the latter living at a place known as Sloven's Hole, were charged on three separate summonses with assaulting Harry Taylor and Annie Hayles at Locks Green Farm, and with wilful damage to the extent of 25s. Mr. H. C. Damant prosecuted and Mr. C. S. Hiscock appeared for the defendants who pleaded not guilty.

Mr. Damant said the case was really a very remarkable one, and one would almost have thought that it was impossible that such an occurrence could take place in any Christian country on a Sunday afternoon. Mr. Taylor was the occupier of Locks Green Farm and it appeared that on Easter Sunday afternoon the defendants were sitting on the green outside Taylor's premises drinking out of bottles which apparently contained brandy. After a while one of the defendant's dogs evidently got tired of watching its master drinking, went into the farmyard, and commenced killing fowls, three being killed and two of them nearly eaten up. Mrs. Taylor went out and remonstrated with them for allowing the dogs to worry the fowls, whereupon they both used most disgusting language to her and conducted themselves indecently, although that was not charged against them … Charlotte Taylor, wife of Harry Taylor, said she saw a black dog worrying her fowls, and she went out and asked the defendants, who were outside on the green, whose dog it was. Tross got up and said it was his dog. She told him that the dog had killed three fowls, and he used very bad language towards her. They came inside and asked her whether she was a man or a woman. Her husband came on the scene and asked what was the matter, and told them they had better get off or it would not be so well for them. Dunford then held her husband and Tross beat him. Dunford held him by the muscles of the arms, and Tross hit him in the jaw and on the nose and somewhere about the temple; and Tross beat her daughter down twice. Her husband's face was very much swollen and blood ran from his nose, and his shirt was very much torn. When her daughter came out and told defendants they were killing her father Tross hit her and knocked her down twice and after being hit the second time she was dragged into the house quite unconscious. Defendants then commenced to kick and knock out the doors, and they beat one door right in - the back door next to the kitchen. Tross kicked the milk churn and damaged it and defendants also broke the children's toy horses. The defendants came there at 3 o'clock and left at 10 minutes to 6. They were about there all the time, and kept coming and knocking and kicking at the door and trying to get in. When they knocked the door once her husband asked 'Who's there?' and they said 'Friend'.

Harry Taylor said on Easter Sunday afternoon he was looking after his sheep in the field when he heard a noise, and on returning to the farm he found men lying down within 40 yards of the front door using very bad language. He asked them to go. The men had bottles with them. There were defendants and two others, who ran away. They were using very bad language. After asking them to go away he went on to go indoors, when Dunford said 'Mr. Taylor, I am the —— man for you', and followed him in. He went round to the back door and hung up his jacket and he overheard Tross kicking a milk can. He went to the defendants and said 'Now men, you had better get off'. Dunford then collared him by the throat and held him back against the wall and Tross struck him about the face violently, blackening his eyes, and making his nose and mouth bleed. Tross who also knocked his daughter down when she came out and called to them, hit him with all his force and said 'Let's kill the —— now'. As soon as witness's son arrived, he drew Tross away and Tross struck his daughter and knocked her across the yard. His daughter went right off insensible and he was obliged to have a doctor for her as she could not eat. As soon as they got the women in, the defendants beat one door down and they used very bad language and said they would beat the other —— door down. They beat one door down and got into the kitchen door and there witness and his son, with three bolts on the door, were keeping it from being forced for over an hour, whilst defendants were outside kicking it. When in the dairy they helped themselves to a bottle of vinegar - which they evidently mistook for beer or brandy (laughter) - and some eatables and remained for nearly three hours, knocking the house about and terrifying the besieged occupants, until Mr. Taylor, in desperation, said if they did not go away he would shoot them.

P.C. Herrington, said at 6.35 on Easter Sunday evening he was at Calbourne when he received a complaint and at once proceeded to Locks Green Farm, where he saw Taylor in a very frightened state. The front of his face was covered with blood and the right side of the jaw was very much discoloured. The daughter was in a state of collapse looking very ill, her mouth was swollen and underneath the top lip the skin was broken and bleeding and it was very black. The backyard and the floor of the house was covered with blood, and the kitchen door was knocked down, the hinges being torn off and the plastering being knocked down. The door of the living-room had its hinges almost twisted off, and it was very much damaged, there being scores of toe marks in the door, where the defendants had evidently kicked the door. There were generally about the premises signs of very great disorder. The estimate of 25s. for the damages was a very low one ... Superintendent Galloway, Deputy Chief Constable said that just before noon on the previous Wednesday he arrested the prisoners and charged them with assaulting Harry Taylor. Both replied 'I have nothing to say' ... Mr. Hiscock, defending, said the whole situation was best summed up in the words of Mr. Taylor, who said that on that occasion the defendants were not men, but beasts. It was quite clear that the defendants were very badly drunk; men did not drink from a vinegar bottle unless there was something very wrong with them. Whilst it would be said that the question of drink was no excuse for the defendants and that nothing would justify their conduct, yet he most respectfully pointed out that had they been sober such a thing as that would never have occurred. His clients wished him to express their regret that such a thing should have occurred, and if they were given the opportunity they were quite willing that some compensation should be paid to prosecutor, not only for the injuries he might have sustained, but for the damages ... Superintendent Galloway said Tross had been convicted five times previously - for assault, refusing to quit licensed premises, and poaching - and Dunford for refusing to quit licensed premises and poaching. Both, he said, were labourers and poachers. Dunford when first interviewed, expressed his regret and was inclined to surrender himself to the police. The Bench retired to consider their decision and on returning into Court the Chairman said they had found Tross guilty of all three charges. The sentence of the court was that Tross be imprisoned for six months with hard labour for the aggravated assault on the young woman, to two months' hard labour for the assault on Taylor, and to one month's hard labour for wilful damage. Addressing Dunford, he said his conduct was disgraceful and the sentence of the court was that he be imprisoned for two months' hard labour for the assault on Taylor and one month with hard labour for the wilful damage, making three months imprisonment altogether. - The sentences on Tross for assault will run concurrently .

*The Rolf family lived and worked on Bleakdown, just outside Rookley. In 1907 their
remote cottage was hit by a powerful lightning strike, practically demolishing half of it.
Their misfortune caught the popular imagination and became the subject of many local
postcards ...*

May 4th, 1907

THUNDERSTORM IN THE ISLAND
A BRIEF BUT TERRIFIC VISITATION
A HOUSE PRACTICALLY WRECKED AT BLEAKDOWN
LIGHTNING'S EXTRAORDINARY FREAKS
SOME MIRACULOUS PERSONAL ESCAPES

A terrific thunderstorm, with unusually vivid lightning, occurred on
Monday, just before 1 o'clock and again at 3 o'clock in the afternoon. The
accompanying rainstorm was very dense, and as it approached Cowes on the
water it completely blotted out vessels from view.

The effects of the storm were felt with exceptional severity in the central part
of the Island, the most serious damage being done to a house at Bleakdown, in the
occupation of Mr. Jesse Rolf, gravel contractor, the house being struck by
lightning and practically wrecked ... Mr. and Mrs. Rolf, their youngest son,
George, and Mrs. Rolf's sister, Mrs. Attrill were at dinner in the kitchen when the
alarming occurrence happened, and all excepting Mr. George Rolf who was
tapping the kitchen window to a relative outside, were found on the floor terrified
and partially stunned. The dwelling was struck at the south-west corner, the
chimney being knocked over, whilst the slated roof at that end of the house was
demolished. Apparently the lightning descended the chimney, hurling the bed-
room stove out from the fire-place, knocking down a wooden partition, and
practically damaging the whole furniture. Continuing its course, the current cast
down into the kitchen, tearing off the mantelpiece and working much havoc with
the contents of this room. Every room suffered, plaster being torn from the
ceilings and two bed-room doors and the sitting-room doors were forced off their
hinges ... Most singular is the fact that the pane of glass Mr. George Rolf was
tapping when the house was struck by lightning was left intact, whilst all the
others were shattered, and with the exception of one in the sitting-room most of
the windows were completely smashed. The lightning also brought down the
spouting in front of the house, snapped the stackpipe in two, and tore up the
drain leading to an old well into which the water emptied. The out-buildings
suffered slightly, and pieces of bricks were found quite 100 yards from the scene,
one piece being embedded 10 in. in the ground. The front door key was found in
the yard, and a gold bracelet was moved off the dressing table ... A pendulum
was taken clean out of a clock in a case, and a cash box was twisted and bent
badly, and the gold coins it had contained were missing. A sauce-pan on the grate
was broken and the poker was bent and twisted ... It is miraculous that no one
was killed and that the three horses in the stable escaped. A young horse
harnessed to a cart, left standing outside, bolted and got some little distance
before being stopped. A dog on the spot was seen to turnover on its back as if
shot, and was not seen again by those at Bleakdown till the next morning ...
Hundreds have since visited the scene, including a number of photographers.

Interviewed by a County Press correspondent from the central office, Mr. Jesse Rolf, who was naturally much perturbed, spoke of the terrifying experience which he and other members of his family had passed through, and acknowledged with relief that their escape was nothing short of miraculous. What was a short time before a comfortably furnished little dining-room was now a scene of wreckage ... An antimacassar on the back of the chair in which Mrs. Rolf was sitting was partly burnt by the lightning, as was the table-cloth immediately in front of Mr. Rolf ... In the words of Mr. Rolf, the room seemed filled with lightning and the sensation was that of a tremendous explosion all around them, accompanied by an almost suffocating smell of what those present described as sulphurous fumes. It seemed to be nothing but fire and smoke for an instant. Suddenly a large mass of ceiling plaster smashed down on the dinner table and on those sitting around it, whilst the mantle shelf was driven out from the chimney, which was swept clean of soot by the lightning, adding variety to the colour of the debris. The large overmantle mirror and ornaments on the shelves were smashed into fragments, which flew across the room, fortunately mostly above the heads of the occupants.

Mr. George Rolf said: 'Everything seemed dark as a dungeon after the flash, but I found father, who had fallen close to me, and mother, and somehow I got them out from the debris to the door, whilst my aunt crawled out behind' ... The door of the front sitting-room was blown in, a lot of furniture broken, the top of the backs of chairs being cut clean off, and the window at the east end was blown out ... Much of the brickwork was completely broken up and the garden was strewn with red brick splinters whilst large pieces of brick and slates from the roof were hurled in all directions and were found quite 100 yards from the house. Some of these were carried away by visitors as mementos, as were pieces of debris at the house. Many visitors have been admitted to view the interior of the house on payment of a small fee ... The escape of men taking shelter in the stable was no less miraculous than that of those in the house. Mr. Fred Rolf, who was sitting on some hay by the wall near, was struck on the left side by the lightning, which stripped off part of his jacket sleeve, his trouser leg, and his boot. His leg was somewhat badly burnt by lightning. Some silver and copper coins which were in his trousers pocket were cut out of the leather purse and were found outside in the yard, bent and partly melted ... Mr. Rolf's damaged boot, which had a piece of leather cut clean off the side by the lightning, has been exhibited in the Central Office window of the County Press during the past week and has been the centre of much interest, as also have photographs of the wrecked house, which have been on view and also published in the London illustrated papers.

The house belongs to Mr. Athur Atherley, J.P., of Shanklin, and will have to be rebuilt to a large extent as the walls are cracked in addition to the other damage described above. The tenant, like the owner, is insured and Mr. Rolf's damage is estimated at about £100.

There appears to be something specially attractive to lightning in the Godshill district – it is suggested that it is a mineral in the soil – as this district has suffered severely in recent years. Godshill Church was struck and seriously damaged by lightning a few years ago, and it will also be remembered that a number of cattle belonging to Mr. Frank Creeth, of Godshill, were killed by lightning in a field in an exposed position.

The following Sunday was a busy time for the Rolf family ...

The lightning-struck house of Mr. Jesse Rolf, at Bleakdown, was simply besieged by visitors from all parts of the Island throughout Sunday last, it being estimated that quite 3,000 were present during the day.* As a charge for admission was made to view the wrecked premises, a substantial sum must have been netted for the benefit of the sufferers from the visitation.

———————◆———————

On a summer's day morning in Cowes, a Mrs. Chambers was arrested by a policeman who found her lying on the ground drunk, and according to him she was using the most disgusting language he had ever heard. Whether that was likely or not, she was certainly very vocal in court ...

July 27th, 1907

'BIGGEST NUISANCE IN COWES'

Margaret Chambers, married woman, of Cowes, was charged with being drunk and disorderly. - Defendant, in reply to the charge, said 'I dare say it is right, sir. I take fits now and then. I plead whatever you like me to do'. - The Chairman reminded defendant that it was not what the Bench wished. It was for her to plead guilty or not guilty. Which was it? – P.S. Evans: She says she does not know. - Defendant: No, I take fits. – P.C. Chisholm said that on the 17th inst., at 10 a.m., he was at Market-hill, Cowes, where he saw the defendant drunk. When spoken to she became very disorderly, and lying on the ground for 20 minutes, used the most disgusting language he had ever heard. Eventually he had to lock her up, and she was kept at the Police-station till she was sober. - Defendant interrupted the witness whilst he was giving evidence, and when told by the police officer to be silent she said she had four sons in the Army and Navy, and she was not going to have her life sworn away by a policeman. She added that she had had fits - fits of drunkenness (laughter). - Inspector Bignell said the defendant was very drunk and used very bad language. She was released from the Police-station when sober, about 11.30 on the night of the 17th inst. - Defendant now said she had fits now and then, and people put it down to drunkenness, but she was not drunk. She always had fits. She had a sunstroke when she was in India. She was a respectable married woman and took a fit through the heat now and then. - The Chairman: You have got a fit now (laughter). - Supt Galloway (Deputy Chief Constable), in reply to the Bench said the defendant was the biggest nuisance in Cowes. - Whilst the Chairman was conferring with his colleagues the defendant shouted out 'Come on, guv'nor; shove it on as hard as you can. I am only a woman. - Court Officer: Silence. – Defendant: Silence! I am a prisoner and you are an officer, and I can do as I like. Swear a poor woman's life away! Go on, guv'nor. Shove it on'. - The Chairman: Margaret Chambers, the Bench sentence you to be imprisoned with hard labour for seven days. - Defendant: A good job. Ain't I glad. How much to pay? - Defendant refused to leave the dock and was forcibly removed by several police, who carried her out of the Court screaming.

---

* If a charge of 6d. was made for each of the 3,000 sightseers, a total of £75 would have been raised, well over a year's wages for a lot of people.

Britain's prisons did not see themselves as places of reform; they were places of confinement and punishment. Their regimes were harsh, unforgiving and soulless - but they did keep good records ...

October 19th, 1907

PARKHURST CONVICT PRISON

The report of the Commissioners of Prisons for the year ended March 31st last has been published. From this we learn that in Parkhurst Convict Prison there are 817 cells. The total number of prisoners during the year was 1,141. The daily average was 770, greatest number at one time 795, least 739. Not every prisoner conducts himself with regard to regulations. Thus 195 prisoners were guilty of violence, 3 attempted escapes, 61 indulged in idleness, and there were 421 other breaches of regulations. For these offences 31 prisoners were restrained by irons or handcuffs, 10 were placed in close confinement in special cells for refractory prisoners, 2 underwent flogging, 463 were put in close confinement in ordinary cells, 326 were subjected to dietary punishment, and 481 lost stage or privilege. The total number punished was 533 ... The two prisoners flogged were guilty of gross personal violence to officers of the Prison, and for the due preservation of discipline corporal punishment was considered necessary. One prisoner received 24 strokes with the birch, the other 36. The staff, which is 169 strong, cost £18,683. Maintenance of prisoners, including, besides food, what may be described as housekeeping expenses, £11,235. From the Governor's report it appears that the state and discipline of the Prison during the year were satisfactory. Two cases of suicide and two attempts were recorded. The prisoners have been employed at making projectile bags, boat-fenders, grommets, potato nets, and counter stamp cases, bed cases made and filled, beds remade, kit boxes repaired, uniform, clothing, and boots for officers; for prisoners, outer and underclothing, boots, bedding, and furniture as well as bookbinding and printing for the Home Office and all the civil prisons in England and Wales. The total earnings of the prisoners are put at £12,146. Of this sum, £4,163 was earned in manufactures, the most prominent items being – printers £1,598, book binding £877, ship fender making £526, tailoring £406, net making £334. Earnings on the farm are stated to have been £2,291, on buildings £2,773.... The medical officer says the general health of the inmates has been satisfactory, and the mortality (20 deaths) moderate, taking into consideration the number of invalids, weakminded, and insane prisoners received. 381 prisoners were received during the year, an increase of 91 upon the previous year. Weakminded convicts continue to be collected here, and in addition others whose mental state is doubtful after their observations in the infirmary are placed in the weakminded parties for further observation. The weakminded continue to be employed at market garden work chiefly, but some at roadsweeping, coir picking, &c. The total number of reports for misconduct by the weakminded and further mental observation cases was 174, this very favourable result being due largely to the tact with which this intractable type of prisoner is dealt with by the officers specially appointed to look after them.

THE WEEK'S NEWS

VENTNOR - ACCIDENT - On Sunday morning some consternation was caused in the upper part of the High-street owing to the noise occasioned by the smashing of plate glass. The side window of Mr. Osborne's premises had been smashed, together with the glass in the door, by a pony, which was found inside the shop amongst the fragments of glass. It appears that Mr. W. Dore was delivering milk in Steephill-road, the horse and float standing on the hill. The animal started off down the hill, but failed to turn into the High-street satisfactorily, and dashed into Mr. Osborne's window opposite. The driver came on the scene within a few seconds, he being in the act of returning from one of the houses, after delivering milk, when the animal started. The horse was cut a little, but the injuries were not serious.

YARMOUTH - PIG OVERBOARD! - There was a little excitement at the Town Quay on Monday when some pigs were being shipped on the cargo boat and one of their number jumped overboard. The pig swam round by the Castle and an exciting chase ensued for its recapture, which was ultimately accomplished by Messrs. Doe and Travers, who had put off in a boat and secured the animal, which was then in a very exhausted condition, but the application of artificial means of respiration soon had the desired effect of securing the pig' s recovery.

YARMOUTH - LARGE SUNFISH* CAUGHT OFF YARMOUTH - Whilst fishing off the Needles on Monday Mr. Charles Calloway, a well-known fisherman of Yarmouth, captured a huge sunfish some 4½ft. in length and weighing over three cwt., and with some assistance got it into his boat after some excitement. A much smaller sunfish was caught off Sandown some two years ago. The latest catch, which aroused much curious interest when brought ashore, has since been exhibited at Newport. The last exhibition of this catch takes place today at the Castle-yard, High-street, Newport, instead of the Plough Inn yard.

SHANKLIN - BIG MACKEREL CATCH - An unusually big haul of mackerel - especially at this time of year - was made by Messrs. Loosemore and Kemp yesterday (Friday) morning in the Shanklin Bay. The draught of fishes was so great that other boats from the shore had to go out in order to bring the nets in. The catch numbers between six and seven thousand.

1908

A letter had recently appeared from the relatives of a patient who had been admitted to the Workhouse infirmary, complaining of their treatment there. Complaints about the Workhouse were now a comparative rarity and unlike years before, there were now members of the public only too happy to speak up and defend it ...

---

* Weighing up to 1½ tonnes, they are still occasionally seen off the British coast in the summer where they 'sunbathe' by floating on their side.

January 25th, 1908
A FORMER INMATE'S TRIBUTE TO THE ISLAND WORKHOUSE
To the Editor of the Isle Of Wight County Press.

Sir, - I have noticed with sorrow the remarks about the Workhouse. I should like to say a few words on the other side. It may seem very astonishing, but I want to say that the happiest three years in my life were spent as an inmate of the Workhouse. I went there out of health, but left it with a good, sound constitution. It is true that the butter was not the best 'fresh', but when I remembered that often when living at home I had had dry bread or bread and dripping, I ate it and was thankful. The same regarding the meat; it was not always of the best quality, but there - before going there, many a day I had had none. As a family, we had had only two-pennyworth of liver in a week among us. The regular living and plain diet built me up, and I am now a strong woman. I never met with anything but kindness from the Guardians nor anyone else. I am quite sure there are many there who could say the same. I have not mentioned that I am writing this to anyone save to you, but in fairness to those who work so hard for the good of the poor I ask you to insert it, - Yours obediently, FAIR PLAY.

———————◆———————

Mr. Salter was a Newport councillor who was of the opinion that the council was run by self-serving cliques who took important decisions behind closed doors, paying little attention to public opinion. He eventually resigned from the sanitary committee in protest and at the last meeting he was to attend, heated words were exchanged …

April 4th, 1908
NEWPORT TOWN COUNCIL
ALD. CLARK AND MR. SALTER - EXCITING SCENE. - Mr. Salter wrote resigning membership of the sanitary committee … In the course of some discussion, Mr. Salter proceeded to explain his reason for resigning and was referring to the control of the committee by a minority of the Council, when Ald. Clark rose to a point of order, saying if Mr. Salter persisted in criticising the action of the committee he (Ald. Clark) should reply warmly.

Mr. Salter, snapping his fingers, said he did not care that for Ald. Clark's threat. The manner in which he (Ald. Clark) treated him and his proposition was something cruel. Mr. Salter said he knew the committee were all one man and he declined to serve on it … Ald. Clark said to talk about the minority having control of the committee was simply ridiculous. This had all arisen because Mr. Salter could not have his own way in regard to the time of the meeting of the committee. It was the only meeting held in the evening and Mr. Salter wanted it held in the morning. Other members were entitled to consideration besides Mr. Salter.

Mr. Salter: You have no right to stand there and blackguard me. Who are you?

Ald. Clark: Perhaps a little better than you.

Mr. Salter said … Ald. Clark had no right to abuse him …

Ald. Clark: I am not abusing you.

Mr. Salter: Yes, you are; you are always doing it.

Mr. Salter then used an expression which was not heard at the reporters' table, towards the Alderman, who was standing by his side.

Ald. Clark: What did you call me? You called me a (an uncomplimentary expression was given).

Ald. Clark, with some heat and wringing his clenched fist in the face of Mr. Salter, said 'If you weren't such an old man I would give you —— (repeating the expression alleged to have been used by Mr. Salter).

Mr. Salter: I did not say ——. If I were a younger man I would take up your challenge pretty sharply. To come here and blackguard me at every opportunity you have ——.

Ald. Clark: Who are you?

Mr. Salter: A better man than you.

Ald. Clark: Perhaps a little better.

Mr. Salter: Yes.

The Mayor, who had vainly endeavoured to restore peace, then poured oil on the troubled waters and the Alderman and Councillor resumed their seats, the Mayor saying they had no wish to take any notice of the personalities introduced. The proposition was carried.

———————◆———————

THE WEEK'S NEWS

The usual stock of pipe tobacco kept at the Victoria Docks, London, weighs 20,000 tons and is worth nine million pounds.

Local Oracle: 'Well, gents, it's like this 'ere. There's things as is, and there's things as isn't; and there's some things as neither is nor isn't. And to my thinking, this 'ere new regulation of the Parish Council comes somewhere between the last two'.

EAST COWES. - CORRECTION. - In order to avoid creating any wrong impression we are asked to state that there was no dancing at the Congregational tennis social reported last week.

PROFANE LANGUAGE. - *Charles Atrill*, Elbow-place, Warwick-street, labourer, was summoned for the use of profane language at the Esplanade. - John Rogers, lavatory attendant, explained the case. Defendant's conduct was of the most disgusting character, and when remonstrated with he asked 'What the —— he had to do with it'. Defendant also said that he 'Helped to pay for the —— place', and witness 'Was —— well paid to clean it'. – Fined 10s. and 10s.6d. Costs.

NEWPORT. - SNOOKS HILL. - Miss S. Snook, daughter of the late Mr. George Snook (the former owner of the smithy on the hill), is now on a visit to her old home. She states with reference to the recent discussion in these pages on on the origin of the name 'Snook's Hill',* that the late Mr. Snook's family had

---

* Over previous weeks discussions had taken place on the letters page regarding the origin of the word 'Snooks'. None of the writers seem to have considered that someone named Snook may have been involved. One suggestion had been that it was a corruption of 'seven oaks'.

carried on the business there for years, and that her father was the first of his name to own the smithy and reside there … The name was given to the hill on the naming of the streets some years after the close of Mr. Snook's half a century residence there, and in consequence of the long residence.

A BIG CATCH. - On Friday morning, Mr. Sheppard, of the barge Ellen, caught a conger eel measuring over 4 ft. at Newport Quay.

———————◆———————

For some horses the age of the motor-car came just a little too late to save them from their suffering, while for others, it could have waited just a little longer…

July 25th, 1908

HORSE'S BROKEN LEG

On Tuesday evening one of a pair of brake horses, when passing through Newport Market, slipped and fell after shying at the reflection of a public lamp on the freshly washed surface of the Market, with the result that its leg was broken. The valuable animal was dispatched as it lay in the Market by veterinary surgeon, Mr. J. Cowper Blake, who used one of the new RSPCA humane killers. The incident caused a good deal of excitement and a large crowd assembled. The lady passenger in the brake, who fainted in the excitement, had 'first-aid' rendered.

ALARMING MOTOR ACCIDENT

On Saturday evening, at about 8.30, as Mr. and Mrs. Leaver, of Northwood, were coming home from Newport in their pony trap, Mrs. Leaver's hat blew off near the gravel-pits. The pony was sharply pulled round across the road, with the object of returning for the hat, when a motor-car, which was coming behind, dashed into the front of the vehicle, knocking the animal down and overturning the van. Mr. and Mrs. Leaver, who are elderly people were thrown out into the road, but luckily escaped serious injury, although they have since been suffering much from shock. The pony, however, fared badly, having one of its legs broken and had to be shot.

Once again court defendants rise above it all and give everyone, or nearly everyone, a laugh … (The indecent behaviour the first defendant is charged with is almost certainly a case of relieving himself in public, a charge which from time to time accompanied that of drunken behaviour.) …

August 29th, 1908

ECCENTRIC DEFENDANTS

Frank Dore, Elmfield, was summoned for indecent behaviour near St John's Church on the 12th inst. - When defendant's name was called he shouted from the back of the Court 'I am here, but I can't get up to the box'. He was brought up by a constable, and shouted 'Not guilty' in a loud voice. He was told that he must behave himself. – P.C. Broome proved the offence … Defendant said he was three parts blind, but swore that he was quite innocent of the crime. - At

this a man at the back of the Court called 'Hear, hear ' and had to be ejected. -
Defendant went on to say that there was another man, named Tutton, whom the
constable accused of being drunk. He (defendant) said 'What if he is? I am here
to take care of him. Do you lock people up for nothing?' - A previous conviction
was put in against defendant, who was fined 5s. and 11s. costs.

William Tutton, St Helens, was summoned for drunkenness and disorderly
behaviour. This was the man who had been ejected from the Court during the
progress of the previous case. He now made his appearance in the prisoner's
dock, smiling and nodding to the magistrates. The Clerk (to P.C. Broome): Is he
drunk? - P.C. Broome: Not yet, Sir (laughter). Defendant was charged with
having being drunk on the 12th inst., and replied 'That's bad, ain't it?' (laughter).
He added 'A drunken man gets sober sometimes, but a fool never gets wise'
(much laughter). P.C. Broome stated that this defendant was in company with the
defendant in the last case. He was drunk and creating a disturbance. - Defendant
kept up a running commentary while the evidence was being given, and said to
the Chairman 'You've knowed me a good many years, ain't you?' (laughter).
When sentenced to pay 2s.6d. and 9s. costs, he observed to one of the magistrates
'Ain't your head going grey; what have you been doing to it?' He was removed
from the dock, and left the Court apparently very well pleased with himself.

THE WEEK'S NEWS

A disastrous colliery explosion occurred at the Maypole Colliery, Wigan, on
Tuesday, 76 workmen being entombed in the mines. Hope of rescuing the men
alive has been abandoned. When the bodies of seven of the men had been got
out, the exploring of the workings was brought to a sudden end on Thursday,
and it is thought that for some weeks the work of the rescue parties will have to
be abandoned. A fire is raging fiercely in the workings, and the working parties
were nearly overwhelmed with the dense smoke and poisonous fumes. It has
now been decided to flood the workings.

A DESERVING CASE - A collecting box has been placed at the Newport
Railway-station for contributions on behalf of a relief fund for Guard Percy
Peach, a much respected and very deserving servant of the I.W. Central Railway
Company for about 14 years, who has been laid aside for some time and is now
dangerously ill. Guard Peach has a wife and young family, and the case is a very
deserving one.

---

*In late April 1908, HMS Gladiator, with 250 men aboard was heading for
Portsmouth, having come from Portland, and had entered the Solent at Yarmouth. At
the same time, the St. Paul, an American liner, had just left Southampton for Cherbourg
and it too was approaching Yarmouth but from the opposite direction. The two ships met
in a blinding snowstorm and the St. Paul smashed amidships into the Gladiator, ripping
a large hole in her side. She drifted, taking in water, and eventually capsized off Sconce
Point, Yarmouth with the loss of 29 men. The acccident itself is well documented
elsewhere, but not so the righting of the ship some months later ...*

The wreck of HMS *Gladiator* off Fort Victoria, Yarmouth, April 1908. (*See page 105.*)

September 12th, 1908

RAISING THE GLADIATOR
SUCCESSFUL OPERATIONS

The final operations connected with the raising of the cruiser Gladiator, off Fort Victoria, Yarmouth, were commenced on Monday and were naturally the object of considerable interest, large numbers of people going over, both by land and water, to watch the progress of the work by the Liverpool Salvage Association. On Saturday and Sunday the salvage employees were busy getting everything in readiness for the great effort of placing the ship on an even keel. Working parties boarded the wreck, and placed 250 tons of pig-iron ballast on the Gladiator's port bilge keel. This was placed so that as the vessel listed over to port it would slide into the water, to be afterwards recovered ... Two old coal-barges, fitted with special pumping appliances, were moored to the wreck, their duty being to force out the water and charge with compressed air the four huge camels or cylinders which had been sunk and attached to the submerged starboard side of the Gladiator, giving a buoyancy power of something like 800 tons ... The many people who visited the scene of the wreck on Sunday in the hope of seeing something done were disappointed. The work commenced early Monday morning in perfect weather conditions ... Tugs attached 2in. steel hawsers to the wreck and shortly before noon the pumping commenced, volumes of water drawn from the hold of the Gladiator being poured over the sides, and simultaneously pumps were engaged in emptying the sunken camels and filling them with air ... Within an hour it was reported that the ship was rising, and by two o'clock the lift was perceptible from shore ... As the tide began to flow, so the work of the air cylinders and the hauling by the tugs began to take effect. The Gladiator's masts began to rise, and by three o'clock the ship had lifted quite 20 ft. All hands were then ordered off the wreck ... By 8 o'clock it was reported that the ship was within about 20 degrees of the vertical ... By 8 o'clock the following morning, her masts were almost perpendicular ... Gales halted work for the next two days but on Thursday the weather was much calmer, and permitted the resumption of work. The task of patching up the 38ft. rent in the vessel's starboard side will be early undertaken, and after this has been done the pumps will be set to work and the ship refloated.*

———————◆———————

History was about to be made. The introduction of the state pension was just a few weeks away ...

September 26th, 1908

OLD AGE PENSIONS
APPLICATIONS OF ISLAND CLAIMANTS
ISLAND CLAIMANT FIRST IN THE KINGDOM

Island claimants, in common with those eligible the country over, took their first step towards securing an old-age pension on Thursday last, when the application forms for old-age pensions were issued from the 25,000 Post-offices throughout the Kingdom. The pensions, of course, will not become due until January 1st next, but the authorities, in view of the widespread inquiries which will be necessary by the pension officers are anxious to encourage claimants to send in their applications as soon as possible.

* The operation to raise the *Gladiator* cost £50,000 but the ship never sailed again. It was found to be beyond economic repair and was eventually sold for scrap for £15,000.

Those who may claim the pension are all those with a less income than £31.10s. a year or 12s.1d. a week, who are now 70 years of age or over or will be 70 on or before January 1st next ... The number of claimants for application forms in the Island have so far been well up to the average of the country in the matter of promptitude for claiming, for it is believed that an elderly lady of East Cowes was the first claimant in the country to send in her application ... In Newport there has been a steady demand for application forms, about 30 having been issued at the Central Post-office ... There has been a similar demand at most of the other principal Post-offices in the Island.

A couple living in the open air on Bowcombe Down with their five children were prosecuted for neglect by the NSPCC. Despite the charge and all it implies, the Medical Officer for Newport describes the children not just as 'well nourished' but 'very well nourished' a claim that might reflect well on the parents and certainly a claim that could not be made for all the children who had roofs over their heads ...

October 3rd, 1908
EXTRAORDINARY EXPOSURE OF CHILDREN
FAMILY'S OPEN AIR LIFE
Harry Cross, labourer, of no fixed abode, and *Helen Cross*, his wife, were brought up on remand charged with having neglected and exposed their five children in a manner likely to cause them unnecessary suffering and injury to health. The male prisoner pleaded 'I am guilty of exposing the children for a couple of nights, but they had plenty to eat and drink'. The female prisoner also said the children had plenty to eat and drink, and they had money to get more food with. They could not get into the Workhouse whilst they had means to get food.

Mr. Damant, who prosecuted on behalf of the NSPCC, said that the children were between the ages of 15 years and 12 months old. The male prisoner, apparently, would do no work, and he found difficulty in getting a house, as he had been ejected some seven times this year at Newport because he would earn no money and pay no rent. On September 6th prisoners appeared to have left their last house at Newport and to have taken the children up on the downs, where they had been living without any covering or proper clothing. - The Chairman: Just in the open-air! - Mr. Damant: Yes sir, in the open air. – Cross: It is all lies.

Mr. Damant said on the day they were found it was raining hard and the children were soaked through to the skin and most of them were in a very verminous condition. When the prisoners were apprehended the children were taken to the Workhouse where they had remained.

P.C. Harris said that on 14th September he went to Limerstone-down where he saw the five children of prisoners lying on the ground, with nothing but a piece of old blanket to lie on. They were in a more or less filthy and verminous condition, their hair being matted together and the scalp of the baby was filthy. The baby was crying. Prisoners were not present, and he asked where they were. The ground was wet, and the vapour was rising from it. The children were scantily clad and their clothes were little more than rags. On the 20th inst., he searched Bowcombe-down for the prisoners and ultimately found them in the vicinity of Coleman's Farm, Porchield, in a shepherd's hut with their family. Witness said 'Cross, you and your family will have to go with me as you have neglected to provide a home for your children'. Cross replied 'I thought it would come to this. I suppose they will charge me with neglecting my children and will put them and the 'missus' in the Union' ... The prisoners were a week on Limerstone-down. – Cross: No, only two nights. We slept in a shed before that. Witness said the prisoner's daughter admitted in the prisoner's presence that they had been in the open for the time stated.

Inspector John Marsham, NSPCC, said in consequence of complaints he received about this family he went to Bowcombe-down on the 15th of September. On his way out through Carisbrooke he met the female prisoner coming down with a basket containing a few blackberries. In reply to his questions she said the family had got a house at Shorwell and they were comfortable there. Not believing her statement, he proceeded to Bowcombe-down and eventually found the male prisoner and four of the children lying under the hedge on top of the down on a piece of wet blanket. The children were huddled together, and their little clothing was saturated by the rain, which was still falling. The rain was running from their matted hair down their necks. They had no covering except two dirty old jackets. The children were in a deplorable condition, their hair being matted and swarming with vermin. – Cross: I wonder they did not eat you....Witness said he knew Cross had been turned out of six or seven different houses during the past year for non-payment of rent. – Cross: That is why we kept the children so well. We bought food instead of paying rent. Witness said, with the exception of the baby, the children looked fairly well nourished. Prisoners repeatedly interposed impertinent remarks and the Chairman told them to hold their tongues. As witness left the box Cross shouted 'I hope I shall be singing when he is burning. It won't be long by the look of his hair' ... Dr Coombs, medical officer for the borough of Newport, said he examined the children and described in detail their dirty, verminous, and poorly clad condition, but said the children were all very well nourished ... The Chairman (to the female prisoner): If the Bench dismissed the case against you, would you go to the Workhouse? - Female Prisoner: Yes, sir; if I can go with my children. - The Chairman: Your children are there. - The prisoner then replied in the affirmative. The Chairman: Then your case will be dismissed. - Addressing the male prisoner, the Chairman said: The sentence on you is that you be imprisoned with hard labour for one month. – Cross: Thank you, sir. I will put my concertina ribs on.

1909

The first state pensions were about to be paid. The sums involved were modest, the full pension amounting to a maximum weekly payment of five shillings. In the same issue in which this report appeared, five shillings could purchase one vest from Godwins the outfitters, or one bottle of whisky. Surprisingly, it was also the weekly rent for a two-bedroom cottage in Gunville or a six-roomed house in Wroxall ...

January 2nd, 1909
THE ISLAND AND OLD AGE PENSIONS
FIRST PAYMENTS YESTERDAY

Yesterday will be memorable for the payment of the first State old-age pensions ever paid in this country. Officials at the principal Island Post-offices were busy on New Year's-day cashing the money orders presented by or on behalf of the pensioners ... The Isle of Wight supplies over 1,500 pensions, which in proportion to population is claimed to be the largest percentage of pensioners of any district in the United Kingdom ... Though there are no centenarian pensioners in the Island, there are two who will attain their hundredth year in a few weeks time, one being an old lady at Wootton, whose 75 year-old daughter is also a pensioner, and the other lives at Ryde ... Most of the pensioners have been granted the full amount of 5s., and the greater number of these claimed their first weekly pension yesterday. Some in their eagerness to obtain this much appreciated help were seen outside Island Post-offices yesterday morning waiting for the opening hour, and many were the expressions of gratitude from the recipients.

———◆———

One January night, a man walked into the hall of the Crown Hotel at Ryde, approached the heavily pregnant landlady who was in conversation with another man, and drawing a revolver, shot her at point-blank range. She collapsed into the arms of the man she had been talking to, who happened to be a plain-clothes policeman who had come to discuss her husband's arrest earlier that afternoon.

The County Press clearly knew more than it was able to reveal and readers, both then and now, were left to read between the lines, and quite odd lines some of them were ...

January 9th, 1909
RYDE SHOOTING SENSATION
HOTEL LANDLADY WOUNDED
ASSAILANT IN CUSTODY
VICTIM'S HUSBAND CHARGED WITH THREATENING ASSAILANT

A serious case of shooting occurred at Ryde on Wednesday evening, which resulted in the arrest of Warrant Officer William Bradley, of the 12th Howitzer Brigade, Aldershot, and the removal to the Isle of Wight County Hospital, in a critical condition, of Mrs. King, wife of the proprietor of the Crown Hotel. We understand that in the afternoon of Wednesday, James King, the proprietor of the Crown Hotel, was arrested on a warrant charged with threatening the life of Warrant Officer Bradley. At about 7 o'clock Bradley appears to have rushed into the Crown Hotel. At that moment P.C. Fewtrell was speaking to Mrs. King about her husband, and they were standing in the hall. Bradley, without warning, drew a revolver and fired at least one shot, which struck Mrs. King in the centre of the body. She fell into the arms of the constable, Bradley being at once seized by persons who had rushed into the hall on hearing the shot. Mrs. King was taken to the Isle of Wight County Hospital in a very serious condition … The occurrence caused a great sensation in the town on Wednesday evening, and for some time St Thomas's-square and the neighbourhood of the hotel was packed with a dense crowd. The attitude of the crowd was at first decidedly hostile to Bradley, and when he was removed from the hotel to an omnibus for conveyance to the Police-station there was a good deal of booing and hissing. The contradictory rumours with regard to the case, however, and the remarkable evidence brought forward at magisterial proceedings no doubt made the popular opinion more undecided, and although the Police-court was packed to suffocation there was no demonstration for or against Bradley.

We understand that the bullet entered the centre of Mrs. King's body, and was probably deflected by one of the ribs, which was broken. It was extracted on Wednesday evening without serious trouble. To add to the complications of the case, Mrs. King at the time of the shooting was in daily expectation of the birth of a child, and a female child was born on Thursday evening. We believe that the birth was quite normal and the child is progressing well … As usual in all such cases, many sensational rumours are current in the town. Most of these deal with matters which it would not be proper to discuss here …

MAGISTERIAL PROCEEDINGS.

The charges were as follows:

William Bradley, aged 40, of Aldershot, was charged with feloniously shooting one Annie King with intent to murder her. The charge-sheet showed that there were found on prisoner a £5 note, 9s.11d. in cash, a gun-metal watch, a ladies gold wristlet watch, and a gold ring.

James King, Crown Hotel, licensed victualler aged 38, was charged with having, on December 29, feloniously sent to one William Bradley a certain letter threatening to kill and murder the said William Bradley.

P.C. Fewtrell said that at about 6.15 on Wednesday he was at the Police-station in plain clothes, when he was asked by Mr. King, landlord of the Crown Hotel, to go to his house and convey a message to his wife. Witness went to her and asked the maid for Mrs. King. She came along the passage into the front hall and was showing witness into the front room when the prisoner came in through the front swing doors from the street. He stepped towards Mrs. King, and thinking he wanted to speak to her, witness stepped back a pace. At the same time he nodded and said 'Good evening, Mr. Bradley'. Prisoner immediately took a revolver from his right-hand overcoat pocket, took aim and fired at Mrs. King. Mrs. King threw her arms out. The Magistrate's Clerk (Mr. J. Fardell): Did she say anything as he fired'. - I think she made some remark like 'Oh God!' - Q. Did he say anything? - He said 'There!' … I caught Mrs. King before she fell. - Q. What did you say? - I turned to Bradley and said 'Stop! That is enough, Mr. Bradley'. I then laid Mrs. King on the floor in the passage and someone went and took the prisoner … I immediately telephoned for Dr.

Turner and then took prisoner into custody. I cautioned him and took him into a back room. He said 'Oh God! What made me do it? I had no intention of doing it when I came to Ryde this morning'. He kept muttering about the Crown Hotel - the Crown Hotel had ruined him' ... A remand was granted.

The case against King was then gone into. The Chief Constable said the warrant for his arrest was granted on the following letters, which were read by the Magistrates' Clerk:-

Crown Hotel, Ryde, I.W.

Please pass the word onto Liverpool and anywhere else also. I trust in your kindness to him that he has not betrayed you, the ——. God have mercy upon ourselves when we meet face-to-face, man to man. I will either shoot him dead like a dog or crush him to pulp. I will damn him to the whole regiment, to his comrades, to his wife, to his children, to his officers, to his officers' wives, to his battery comrades, to his battery comrades' wives, to the Aldershot command. If he lives to go to India I will damn him there, and to his children in years to come. I cannot even spare in my wrath even the grave of his departed child shall crumble his feet at my mercy (sic). He is the most deceitful and detestful man in the regiment, despised by officers, by NCO's, and by his men, known through the regiment as a dirty cur. What price his bones when I have finished with him in the Barracks at Aldershot - the Barracks I love so well, the men I love so well and have their respect. There is one I hope to spare, his wife, in the drama, or is it comedy, or farce, or tragedy. I am sure I do not know, but the sins of the father shall be born unto the children, even unto the third and fourth generation. Vengeance is mine, I will repay, sayeth the Lord.

My brain is dizzy. I have this pen in hand. I was elsewhere 22 years ago; I enlisted as a private soldier, penniless. Since that I have had to keep my father and mother, my wife, my five children and Bradley's —— and I have saved sufficient money to come into the smartest house in the Isle of Wight - a free house, and the customers love me, but I am dead to them - dead to the world. I have no wife, no children, nothing but death for me, thanks to Bradley's lust and his love for another woman and entirely forgetting his own lady, God bless her! God have mercy on his soul. My brain is dizzy. What will you give for his broken bones when I have finished with him ... After you receive this drop me a line of sympathy. I have one ambition in life and that is to be a man and a gentleman, though once a private soldier. Death where is thy sting. If your wife has escaped from his penance you have something to be thankful for, for he is ashamed of his wife and her family.

The Magistrates' Clerk said the letters were addressed to the prisoner. This was one of a series of letters produced to him (Mr. Fardell) and in the same handwriting. The allegation was that the prisoner (King) wrote the letters and that they were intended for the other prisoner. Prisoners were remanded in custody.

(The relationships between those involved and what lay behind the unusual letter became clearer when the men went for trial months later, see page 112.)

TOWN AND COUNTY NOTES

SHANKLIN. SEASONABLE SOUP. - In order to alleviate the distress which has been especially occasioned by the snow, a committee, hastily convened, met on Thursday evening and forthwith made arrangements for the provision of soup at Mrs. Jones's Restaurant, Regent-street. Tradespeople assisted the committee most generously.

SEASONAL CAPERS. - 'When I bought this automobile from you a few weeks ago', cried the irate purchaser, 'you said you would be willing to supply a new part if it broke anything!' 'Certainly, sir!' agreed the manufacturer. 'What can I have the pleasure of providing you with?' 'Well', replied the purchaser, 'I want a pair of new ankles, a left eye, three yards of cuticle, a box of assorted fingernails, four front teeth and a funny-bone'.

ROYAL ISLE OF WIGHT COUNTY HOSPITAL. - Report for the week ending on Wednesday February 3rd, 1909: Patients admitted, 9; patients discharged, 8; patients died, 1; remaining in the house, 49; waiting for admission, 4; out-patients on the books, 216; casualties and attendances 81.

Ventnor is top of the Daily Mirror sunshine records.

EXTRAORDINARY GOLF COINCIDENCE AT ST HELENS. - An extraordinary coincidence occurred during the course of a foursome, played on the links of the Royal I.W. Golf Club at St Helens on Saturday. In the driving off from the third tee it was found that both players had driven exactly the same distance, and both balls were actually touching. One player, of course, had to lift whilst the other player played his stroke, and on driving the fifth green the same thing happened again.

———————◆———————

The case of Mr. King's threatening letters and Mr. Bradley's intent to murder both came to trial on the same day. The judge wanted to hear the jury's verdict on the first case before he pronounced sentence in the other ...

March 20th, 1909
THE RYDE HOTEL SENSATION

At the Hants Assizes yesterday, *James King*, late landlord of the Crown Hotel, Ryde, was charged with sending a letter threatening to murder William Bradley ... Mr. Du Parcq, defending, in addressing the jury, said the case was bound up with some of the saddest circumstances, one of the most terrible human dramas the Court had had to deal with. He was going to ask the jury to say that when the prisoner wrote those wild, incoherent letters he was suffering from one of the greatest mental shocks a man could have experienced ... He and Bradley had been comrades in the same battery. They were stationed together at Aldershot five or six years ago. His wife and Mr. and Mrs. Bradley were great friends but witness was always very reserved. - Q. Had you any reason for that?

- On account of Bradley's marked affection for my wife. - Q. Your wife had a child in 1904? - Yes. - Q. About the time you are speaking of? -Yes. - Q. What did you christen the child? - Maisie. - Q. Did you have any idea in your head about the child? - From the moment of its birth. The Judge: Do you mean as to its paternity? - Yes. Q. When the child was born you thought your wife had been unfaithful? -Yes ...

Witness went on to describe the receipt of a Christmas card ... which bore the usual greetings, and contained photographs of Bradley and his wife and children. Q. When you saw that photograph did something strike you? - Instantly. There was a waitress standing alongside and I said to her 'Who is that child like?' She replied 'Maisie'. - Q. How did you spend that night? I went to bed but did not sleep. I lay awake all night thinking. - Q. Your wife heard the remark, did she make a statement? - Yes ... Q. What was the effect on you? - Broken hearted, downhearted, nothing else in the world to live for, when I found my wife had been betrayed by a comrade ... I took to drink ... Until I had the letters I wrote read back to me to at the Police-court I had no idea of what was in them. Q. Did you write 'I will either shoot him like a dog or crush him to pulp? - It says so ... The jury considered their verdict, and after a short discussion brought in a verdict of 'Not guilty'. There was some applause in Court.

William Bradley was next charged with shooting Annie King, wife of the licensee of the Crown Hotel, with intent to murder her. Mr. Temple Cooke, prosecuting, outlined the case... On December 23rd Mrs. King received a card from Mrs. Bradley enclosing a photograph of her family, and that gave rise to trouble between Mr. and Mrs. King. Mr. King had sent eight threatening letters to Mr. Bradley who applied for a warrant against King. King surrendered himself to the police and was detained, and Bradley knew this ... when he called at the Crown Hotel, and meeting Mrs. King in the hall, who was talking to Constable Fewtrell, he pulled a revolver out of his pocket and shot her, remarking 'There, you ——' ... The prisoner then gave evidence. He carried a pistol for his own protection in consequence of receiving the threatening letters ... I travelled to Ryde and went into the Hotel. I saw P.C. Fewtrell, in plain clothes. In my upset state I confused the idea of the constable being there with King being there. I had the revolver in my right-inside coat pocket ... I took out the pistol and was going to put it in the outside-right pocket but to my horror it went off. Q. Did you deliberately shoot that pistol at Mrs. King? - I did not. - Q. Is it true that you called her a ——? - I certainly did not do that; I could never use that expression to any woman, especially to Mrs. King ... Prisoner said the letter he wanted to get from Mrs. King was a refutation of the charges against him, which were not true. He was angry at their being made. He had another letter from King in which he made a similar accusation about one of his children. Mrs. King told him some years ago that King had previously made the same accusation against her and had compelled her to admit it almost by force ... The jury retired to consider their verdict and were absent half an hour. On their return the Foreman announced that they had found the prisoner guilty of the charge.... His Lordship said he knew what prisoner's feelings must be. It was one of the most painful cases to him because he had heard of the prisoner's good character but a judge had no feelings, at least he was supposed not to have any ... You will go to penal servitude for ten years'.

The Floating Bridge from Bridge Square, East Cowes, 1906. (*See page 115.*) Photograph by Alfred Arnold.

From time to time, the plans for the proposed Medina Subway linking East and West Cowes were dusted off but were never to come to anything. Eventually the Cowes Ferry Committee bit the bullet and decided to spend £3,000 on a new floating bridge to cope with what they described in 1909 as 'the greatly increased traffic'. If only they could have seen 100 years into the future ...

May 29th, 1909

NEW COWES FLOATING BRIDGE

Last (Friday) night the new floating-bridge, constructed by Messrs. White and Sons at their Vectis Works, Cowes, was placed upon the chains. It has been built at considerable cost to cope with the greatly increased traffic between Cowes & East Cowes, especially during the season, and it will supersede the old and somewhat dilapidated bridge, which for many years has done splendid service. Providing everything goes well and the running is satisfactory the new bridge will be in use today (Saturday) ... Whilst there were some who advocated the construction of an overhead bridge and others a tunnel under the Medina - schemes involving tremendous cost - the Ferry Committee favoured a continuance of the old and less expensive system by the provision of a fine new floating bridge of an up-to-date pattern. The new bridge is built of steel throughout and it will readily be seen that it is a great improvement in every way on the old bridge, which looks small by comparison. The total available floorspace has been increased ... being ample to enable two horse vehicles to be drawn up abreast, which was an impossibility on the old bridge. The extra width on the north side, on which the engine room is situated has been utilised in making a passageway, lighted by windows with an opening midway affording an excellent view of the river whilst crossing. Through this passage one may pass from end to end of the bridge without encountering the carriage traffic. On the south side a similar passage 4ft. 6in. wide has been made enabling small-wheel traffic, such as perambulators, &c., to obtain shelter and at the same time to avoid horses and other traffic. A ladies' cabin has been fitted, provided with cushioned seats. There is ample seating accommodation under cover at both ends. The greatest improvement made on the bridge is the utilisation of the upper deck as a promenade provided with comfortable garden seats. Access to the upper deck is gained by means of spiral staircases. The main machinery is of similar design to that of the old bridge but with slightly increased power. Another feature, which is believed to be a new departure, is the employment of steam power for raising and lowering the prows instead of hand power, which can, however, be used if necessary. The contract price for the new bridge was £2,762. The building of this handsome bridge reflects the greatest credit upon the well-known Cowes firm of White and Sons, who were not only successful in constructing in competition with mainland firms, but in every detail have splendidly discharged their important commission.

THE WEEK'S NEWS

A man's manacled body found in women's' clothing at the bottom of a cliff in Penzance was identified as Mr. Douglas Panton, a London solicitor, who was found to have committed suicide by throwing himself over the cliff.

NEWCHURCH. FIVE LEGGED CALF. – Mr. H.R. Hills of Knighton Farm has in his possession a calf who was born with five legs and who is doing well. The extra leg has grown out from between the shoulders and is about the usual length.

TWO DEATH SENTENCES. - At the Old Bailey yesterday afternoon Mark Reubens and Maurice Reubens were found guilty of the murder of William Stroull, steamship engineer, at Whitechapel, and both were sentenced to death. When sentence was announced the prisoners commenced shrieking and sobbing, one cursing everyone in Court, while the other moaned 'Oh, mother! Mother, dear! Help me'.

NEWPORT. OBSCENE DRAWINGS. – At the Borough Police-station yesterday, an elderly man named William Gauntlett, described as a butler, and an occasional visitor to Newport, where he has relatives, was charged with making obscene drawings in the public convenience in Watchbell-lane. In consequence of complaints P.C. Collins was instructed to watch the convenience, and he saw defendant making the drawings with a piece of pencil on the previous day. When the prisoner left he followed and arrested him. Pieces of pencil and chalk were found upon defendant, who now denied the charge. Fined 15s. and costs.

———————◆———————

Thomas Corney died in Winchester Prison where he was serving a 12 month sentence for theft on the Island. He was no stranger to prison and was well known locally, being described as 'notorious in the Island' ...

July 17th, 1909

NOTORIOUS ISLAND PRISONER'S DEATH

The Winchester Coroner held an inquest at the County Prison on the body of Thomas Corney, 65, who died there while undergoing sentence imposed at Newport earlier this year ... He was convicted in April of stealing a small clock at West Hill House, Cowes, and was sentenced to 12 months hard labour. He had, however, done no hard labour ... Deceased, who was also known by the aliases of Newbury and Taylor, had been notorious in the Island during the greater part of the last half-century, during which he had served nearly 30 years in prison, and the principal part of the remaining period was spent by him in the workhouse. His first conviction dated back to 1864, and his sentences had varied from one day's imprisonment for drunkenness to seven years penal servitude for stealing, arson, &c. When liberated on ticket-of-leave he would contravene the conditions of his licence in order to be sent back to the prison, which he often declared he preferred to the workhouse. He had been known to smash a shop window in the presence of a policeman and to steal goods and take them to the police-station in order to get back to gaol. He evidently regarded prison as his home, and much of his crime was committed with the sole object of keeping in prison as much as possible. An uncontrollable temper led him into much trouble. He committed several acts of violence in the Island Workhouse, on one occasion indulging in considerable window smashing. When brought before the justices he generally indulged in violent language, and sometimes threatened the Bench, though latterly he was much quieter. In his early days he belonged to the Army, from which he deserted three times, and the letter 'D' had been tattooed over his left ribs three times, in accordance with the usual custom in vogue in bygone days of branding a deserter.

A travelling farm labourer died on St. Catherine's Down in curious circumstances. The subsequent Coroner's Inquest, apart from one member of the jury, were apparently satisfied with the odd circumstances of the death. Although there is no evidence of wrong-doing, the dead man's companion might face more rigorous questioning today...

September 4th, 1909
FARM LABOURER'S LONELY DEATH
The death of a tramping farm labourer named Robert Groves, a native of Yarmouth, took place at Chale on Tuesday under particularly strange and painful circumstances. Last Friday evening Mr. David Talbot who is a cowman at Chale Abbey Farm, whilst on the downs near Cowlease, noticed a man sitting by the side of the footpath and spoke to him. Getting no reply, Talbot made a closer inspection and came to the conclusion that the man was drunk. He left him there to get over his intoxication as he thought, and the matter was dismissed from his memory until four days later, early Tuesday morning, when his little boy told him that the man was still there. On going to the spot Talbot found the man in exactly the same position as when he left him the previous Friday, and could at once see that he was seriously ill. He immediately informed P.C. Simmonds, who procured a stretcher and also sent for Dr. Armstrong. Before the doctor's arrival the constable got some whiskey down the man's throat and he seemed to revive somewhat and was taken to the barn at Chale Farm. Mr. T. Roberts kindly prepared some bovril which the doctor prescribed, but the unfortunate man expired before it could be administered. The circumstances of the death are somewhat mysterious, and it seems incredible that the man should have been lying on the down for four or five days without being noticed.

The inquest was held at the Clarendon Hotel, Chale, on Thursday ... George Cassford, farm labourer, giving his address as the Workhouse, said he had been in the deceased's company during the summer. They had been going round to different farms doing hoeing, &c. ... They left Niton Farm together on Thursday last, after having had eight or nine days' work at turnip hoeing. They went to the Star Inn at Niton, where deceased had a cup of tea and he (witness) had a pint of beer, and then started over St. Catherine's-down towards Chale. When on the top of the down they agreed to part to look for work in different directions, and arranged to meet again that evening at Chale-green … He (witness) came down into Chale and had a pint of beer, and then went back on to the down to see if deceased had gone, but found him in the same place. Groves said he would start directly, and that he need not worry about him, so he went off towards Kingston. That was the last he saw of him … David Talbot, cowman at Chale Abbey Farm, in the employ of Mr.Harvey, said deceased was a stranger to him. He saw him on Friday last at about 8.30 p.m. sitting by the cart-road on the Chale side of the down. He had his stick on the ground with his hands on the top and his head was resting on his hands. Witness spoke to him, saying 'Hello, mate, what are you up to here?' but received no reply. He then took hold of him by the shoulders, lifted him up, and shook him a bit, and deceased then told him his name. He asked him if he was unwell or whether he was drunk, but got no reply except a mumble about having had a pint of beer, and concluding that the man was under the influence of drink he left him there, thinking he would be all right when he got sober. He lifted him up several times, but he was quite helpless.

The Coroner: You thought he was drunk and that was your reason for leaving him there. Witness: Exactly. He appeared to be drunk.

Continuing, Witness said he did not think anything more of the matter until Tuesday morning at about 5.30, when he and his little boy were fetching the cows, when the boy told him that the man was still there. When he had finished his work at about seven o'clock he went up and found the deceased lying in exactly the same position as when he last saw him … Dr. Armstrong stated there were no signs of excessive drinking. All his organs were healthy. His stomach and intestines were quite empty … Mr.Hobbs, a juror, asked the witness Cassford what his object was in going back to the down to see Groves when an hour previously they had agreed to part to seek for work.

Cassford: I went back to see if he was gone. I don't know why, except that I was wondering whether deceased had gone. Deceased was a very contrary man at times.

Mr. Hobbs: It seems very strange.

… The Foreman of the jury announced that they were agreed that the deceased died from exposure and want of food. They wished to add that they considered that no blame whatever could be attached to Talbot.

Mr. Harvey, of Chale Farm, said as Talbot was in his employ, and they were particularly busy, he should like to point out that he should have objected to him running about looking after a man supposed to be drunk. The Coroner said he could not discuss that. They must not let business interfere with their humanity.

———————◆———————

Harry Blow was on his way to remove a cart full of flint from the Cement Mills at Stag Lane. In order to do this, he and his horse and cart would have to cross the busy Cowes to Newport railway line at the entrance to the Cement Mills. What happened at the crossing would have made even Buster Keaton's jaw drop with admiration. What the horse must have thought is another matter …

October 23rd, 1909
ALARMING ACCIDENT

A hairbreadth escape was experienced by Mr. Harry Blow, a young carter of Shide, in the employ of Messrs. H. Westmore and Son, carrying contractors, &c., of Newport, on Saturday morning. Blow was in charge of one of the carts removing flints from the West Medina Cement Mills for rural highway purposes, and was driving down to the Mills between 11 and 12 o'clock. In order to reach the Mills it was necessary to cross the railway line. It was raining and blowing hard from the south-west at the time, and this may account for the fact that Blow did not hear the approach from the opposite direction of the 11.45 through train from Cowes. He states that the gates were open, but before starting to cross the railway he looked up and down the line to make sure that no train was approaching. Not seeing or hearing a train he started to cross the line, but just as the cart was in the middle of the railway track he was horrified to see the Cowes train coming at full speed close upon him. Without a moment's hesitation Blow jumped from the front of the cart into the hedge and the train immediately crashed into the cart, smashing it to splinters and scattering pieces of the wrecked vehicle in all directions, some being thrown 20 yards. Fortunately no serious injury resulted to the train, and very little damage was done to the horse, which bolted towards the Mill with the shafts of the cart still attached to it. Blow's presence of mind in jumping from the cart no doubt to save him from serious injury, if not instant death, and he is to be congratulated on his miraculous escape ...

1910

Assuming the County Press faithfully recorded each and every court case, and there is no reason to suppose they didn't, instances of cruelty to animals definitely declined for some reason during these years, both in numbers and severity and cases like the following one were becoming rarer.

Mr. Spartali, the defendant, had been the Greek Consul to London at one point and had subsequently made a fortune as a grain dealer and merchant banker before retiring to the Island. He was now 91, but age had obviously not mellowed him. He appears to have been what might be known as a 'difficult' man. Self-centred and outspoken, he was clearly not a man to let the truth get in the way of a good story ...

January 15th, 1910
SERIOUS CHARGE OF CRUELTY

Michael Spartali, described as a gentleman of considerable means, aged 91, of Sandford House, Godshill, was charged with causing his horse to be ill treated by starving it. Mr. C.F. Hiscock prosecuted for the RSPCA and said it was one of the worst cases of cruelty which could be brought before the Court. Mr. Arthur Batt, veterinary surgeon, of Shanklin, said that on the 22nd he went to defendant's place and examined an aged black mare, which was lying in an extremely emaciated condition in the stable and was starving. It was unable to move any part of its body except its head. He told defendant that the mare was starving and should be destroyed at once, and it was agonising to see it lying there. Defendant

replied 'Starving be d—d'. Witness said 'You know very well it is starving', and defendant said 'Nothing of the kind'. The mare ravenously ate some mouldy hay which was put up to its mouth. Defendant asked him to send for some medicine for the mare but witness replied 'It does not want medicine; it wants food and the only thing to do with it is to have it destroyed'. The hay in the stable was in a filthy condition, not fit for litter, and the corn shown to him was stinking. No animal, except one starving, would eat it. There was no doubt the animal was starving; it was simply a bag of bones. - Defendant's coachman wanted to ask a question, but Mr. Hiscock objected, saying defendant could have been present or he could have been represented, and the Clerk (Mr. John Fardell) agreed, saying it was not the case of a poor man ... Inspector John Lambert, RSPCA, said that on the 23rd he went to defendant's stable and saw the mare as described by the last witness ... From what the coachman (Robbins) said, witness went to the saddle-room and saw some hay which was quite unfit for food, and some oats which were stinking. Whilst he was examining the hay and corn, Spartali, defendant, came in and said 'What are you doing here? Have you come about the old mare? There is nothing wrong, is there?' He told defendant that from what he could see, and from what the coachman said, he was of the opinion that the mare had been slowly starved. Defendant said 'What nonsense! What has Robbins said?' Witness replied that Robbins said that the mare was down in the field on Monday, and with assistance he got it to the stable, where it went down again, and he informed defendant the same day and asked him to have it shot, as it was then in a dying condition. He told defendant that Robbins further said that the food had been bad and that the mare had not had sufficient to eat, and the seven month-old colt with the mare had eaten the food which the mare should have had. Defendant said 'It is a pack of nonsense'. Robbins replied 'It is true. I have told you several times that the old mare was being starved, as the food was bad, and you know you gave me notice six weeks ago because I told you there was not sufficient food for the mare and colt, and again told you last week'. Defendant said 'Well, that is so, but the mare had not been starved'. Inspector Lambert said 'You are prolonging its sufferings. Surely such a faithful friend, as you say the animal has been, merits a more painless death'. After further conversation defendant instructed Robbins to have the animal shot, and it was shot. Witness asked defendant to allow a post-mortem examination to be made. Defendant asked 'Am I compelled by law to have a post-mortem examination?' Witness said 'No', and defendant then said he should most certainly not allow witness to have one ... The Chairman said defendant would be fined the full penalty of £5 and the costs of the Court, 13s., and he would also have to pay a guinea towards the Society's solicitors fee and half a guinea for the veterinary surgeon; in default, 14 days without hard labour.

———————◆———————

As an important man in the past Mr. Spartali may well have been used to having his own way and the last word; he was certainly determined to have it here. To make sure the world heard the story his way, with no interference, he placed an advert, masquerading as a letter, in the next issue. It was printed in exactly the same style as a letter to the Editor, apart from the word 'Advertisement' at the top, and to the casual observer it looked for all the world as if it was a genuine letter. It was littered with untruths ...

January 22nd, 1910

[Advertisement]

RE HORSE CASE REPORTED LAST SATURDAY

To the Editor of the Isle of Wight County Press.

Dear Sir, - I am reluctantly obliged to trespass on your valuable space to vindicate my coachman Robbins, who is unjustly accused of starving a mare on incorrect charges* and fanciful conversation brought forward in ignorance of the facts.

As I was not able to attend the Court through old age and indisposition, I sent the coachman to state the facts and be cross-examined by the Court. For some technical reason or other Court refused to hear the defence ... I am therefore obliged unwillingly to state the facts in fairness and justice to an innocent coachman ... *(Mr. Spartali then explained how the mare had access to large amounts of turnips, cabbages, celery, grass, oats and hay 'of the finest quality')* ... If a horse can starve on such fare, I leave others to judge. As regards the 'poor mare', she collapsed whilst grazing in the turnip field and was brought home and stretched on a large airy stable. We immediately sent for the doctor, but unfortunately he only came some days afterwards.† During this time the mare got much worse and thinner ... She was given by the coachman, warm gruel, hay, and corn, often daily, but she ate very little and oftener refused them. When the doctor at last came one afternoon ... his opinion was that she would die in a few hours, and he refused giving any medicines and advised shooting her. But I suggested as her end was so near I would prefer her dying a natural death (in accordance with my principles, not to kill any of God's creatures, not even a bird or rabbit), to which the doctor made no objection. The next day I met the Inspector at the stable and at his wish she was shot in his presence. Of course, she then and there looked a pitiable sight (after several days' prostration down and most times refusing food), as all animals and human beings look, and we shall all look, on our death-beds, at our very worst.

As regards the conversations, &c., reported at the trial, my coachman solemnly declares they are entirely inaccurate. In conclusion, for the facts and reasons above stated (which can be verified and confirmed on oath), any unprejudiced or unbiased person must admit that the charge of 'starvation' is 'not proven', and that my coachman has done his duty.

Yours very truly, M. Spartali.

PS - Several days before the mare died we ordered some oats from Messrs. Roach and some hay from Luccombe Farm, Mr. Guy's, but through the Christmas holidays they were delayed. I cannot understand that if it is 'a mercy' to shoot a suffering, incurable animal, why the same 'mercy' should not be resorted to for all suffering or incurable human beings, &c.

---

* This is untrue; Mr. Robbins was not charged with anything. As Mr. Spartali well knew, it was he himself who had been charged and found guilty.

† This was also untrue. Annoyed by the slur on his professionalism, the doctor wrote to the *County Press* the next week, declaring 'I received a message from Mr. Spartali at 8 o'clock on Tuesday evening and I attended not 'some days afterwards', but early the very next morning'.

Up until 1866, executions had been carried out in public. They took place in a festival atmosphere and attracted large crowds of onlookers. On the Island, however, there were no such 'hanging days' as they were known, since capital offences were not tried at Newport but at Winchester where any subsequent execution also took place. A newspaper of 1794 had just come into the hands of the County Press shedding some light on the few military executions that had taken place on the Island in days gone by …

April 23rd, 1910
EXECUTIONS AT PARKHURST A CENTURY AGO

Unpleasant reminders of old-time superstition and of the terrible severity of the law a century ago, when sentences of death were carried out in the Island, are contained in the Star newspaper, of London, dated August 21, 1794, a copy of which has been brought to our notice by Ald G. Fellows, JP. This interesting old record shows that considerable prominence was given to Isle of Wight news in the London press of 116 years ago, Cowes being honoured with a special heading. This particular edition contains an account of an execution which took place at Parkhurst Forest, probably near the site of the present Prison. The men executed were Patrick Quire and Patrick Corne, two soldiers belonging to the 87th or Prince of Wales's Irish Regiment of Foot, presumably stationed at Parkhurst, who had been convicted at Winchester Assizes of burglary in the house of Benjamin Calcott, of Northwood, and of ill-treating him and his wife. The report goes on to say 'They were taken from the condemned cell at 3 o'clock in the morning and reached the fatal tree in the Forest of Parkhurst, between Cowes and Newport, about noon, and after demeaning themselves in penitence for an hour were launched into eternity in the sight of the most numerous body of spectators remembered to be assembled at one time in this part of the kingdom, the majority of whom, it is believed, were attracted by the novel curiosity, it being more than 60 years since a similar scene was exhibited in the Isle of Wight. They were both young men and Roman Catholics and were attended by a priest of that persuasion. When their bodies were cut down a mother requested that a dead man's hand might be placed on her child's neck, afflicted with the King's evil, which was accordingly done'.

———————◆———————

Mr. Vibert, a Newport grocer, arrived at his shop one morning to find the air full of gas fumes. He opened the windows to clear the air and after a while lit a match. As you do …

February 12th, 1910
GAS EXPLOSION AT NEWPORT

An alarming gas explosion occurred on Wednesday morning in the shop premises of Messrs. Vibert and Son, grocers and wine merchants, at the corner of Lower St James's-street, Newport. When the shop was entered it was found that gas had been escaping from a chandelier in the room at the back, and the doors were thrown open to get rid of the gas. This apparently did not result, for when a match was lighted later on an explosion occurred, which blew the rounded plate glass panels out of the folding-doors at the front of the shop, pieces of glass being driven right across the street, which fortunately happened to be clear at that moment. Bottles of wine and spirits were thrown down and some were broken. Mr. A. Vibert, who smothered with a mat a slight outbreak of fire, was knocked backwards by the force of the explosion and was slightly singed about the face and head.

Advertisment: WARNING. - To those consumers who use water-slide chandeliers.* Care should be taken that a little water is periodically added to obviate all risk of escapes. Those old-fashioned chandeliers can be easily converted into fixed pendants by the Gas Company, thereby avoiding all risk of accident. Do not search for leaks with a light, but in event of escape turn off gas at meter, open windows, and send immediately to the gas-works, when the same will be at once remedied.

———————◆———————

THE WEEK'S NEWS

Mark Twain, who died last week, has left a fortune estimated at £200,000.

W. Barret, stated to be the heaviest man in America, died at Locust Valley, Long Island, on Sunday. He weighed just over 40 stone.

ISLAND CENTENARIAN'S DEATH. - The death occurred at Lewisham Infirmary on Wednesday, of William Maber, at the age of 100. He was born at Colwell Bay in 1809, and would have been 101 on March 31st. His father, who was born in 1773, kept the Colwell Bay Inn at the time of the Battle of Waterloo. In April last, Maber entered the infirmary, and up to six months ago he used to take a daily walk. He was a great smoker, consuming a quarter of a pound of tobacco a week.

WHITCOMBE CROSS IMPROVEMENT - AN INTERESTING FIND. - The work of cutting away the high bank and rounding off the corner at Whitcombe Cross on the Newport-Chillerton Road, which is nearing completion, is likely to be a very great improvement. A good deal of the material removed consisted of hard stone, which has been conveyed by train to Yarmouth, where it has been utilised in the sea wall by the road over the Common. In the course of the work, a cannonball of 6in. diameter was found 18in. below the surface and some 10ft. in the bank facing Carisbrooke Castle.... We hear that two cannonballs of similar description have been ploughed up in recent years in a field above Clatterford Farm.

THE ISLANDS OLDEST INHABITANT. - 103 ON MONDAY LAST. - His Majesty the King on Tuesday sent a telegram of congratulations to Mrs. Burke, The Lodge, St Lawrence (mother of Mrs. Truslove, wife of Mr. W. Truslove, late of Bank End Farm), who on August 1st attained the great age of 103 years.

Edward Woodcock, 45, who was reprieved after being sentenced to death, hanged himself in Armley Gaol, Leeds, on Thursday.

---

* A wall mounted gas light, obsolete even then, which relied on water to make an an airtight seal in one of its joints. The contemporary 'Manual of Domestic Economy' wrote, 'The water evaporates in use, and requires occasional replenishing, which may be known by the smell of gas in the room'.

The King had been in ill-health during the early part of the year and on Friday, May 6th, at a quarter to midnight, he breathed his last after a series of heart attacks. For the County Press, the King couldn't have died at a more inconvenient time, for at the precise moment the news reached their office that week's issue had already been set and was just about to start rolling from the presses. The process was brought to a halt and in what must have been a logistical nightmare for both journalists and printers, a whole page was removed from the press to be hurriedly replaced with a new one written and set in the small hours ...

May 14th, 1910
THE 'COUNTY PRESS' AND THE KING'S DEATH
A statement having been made by the *Daily Mail* to the effect that it was first to publish in the Isle of Wight the sad news of the King's death, we deem it to be due to the London correspondents of the *County Press* and ourselves to say that this was not the case. A message conveying the distressing intelligence was received by the *County Press* shortly before 1 o'clock on Saturday morning, just as the paper was going to machine, and a brief intimation was at once made in a stop press column, sufficient copies being printed for the night mails. Meanwhile another page was prepared containing full details, and by this means our readers in all parts of the Island were comprised of the melancholy event in the early hours of Saturday morning, a considerable time before the London papers arrived.

The first plane ever to land on the Isle of Wight touched down on the Needles golf course in July 1910. The County Press discreetly glossed over the fact that the landing, although very skilled and daring, had in fact been entirely unintentional. The pilot had taken off from an air show at Bournemouth and soon found himself in a rain storm and bad visibility. Disorientated, he was actually heading out to open sea, rapidly running out of fuel, when in a stroke of good luck he saw Freshwater cliffs behind him and swiftly turned back to land on the golf green ...

July 23rd, 1910
AVIATOR'S DARING FLIGHT TO THE ISLAND
What was undoubtedly the most daring flight of the Bournemouth Week took place on Saturday afternoon, when Mr. Robert Loraine, the actor-aviator,* who flies under the name of Jones, descended on the Needles golf links in his Farman biplane after a thrilling over-sea flight in pouring rain and high wind. The few people who had braved the elements to keep watch on the Needles Cliffs had taken shelter under the walls of the Coastguards' observation-house, when at about a quarter to 4 a lady ran up from the cliff edge, pointed out to sea, and shouted the surprising message that a biplane was crossing the Channel about a mile out. Every eye was at once turned in the direction indicated by the lady and by the hum of the propellers, and the aeroplane could be seen just about due south of the Lighthouse, heading for St. Catherine's ... The pilot no doubt caught a glimpse of the high downs near the Tennyson Beacon, and bearing inwards, he was seen to plane down and alight on the golf

---
* Loraine is said to have invented the word 'joystick'.

The first plane to land on the Island, July 1910. (*See page 127*). Loraine's plane under guard.

Crowds watching Loraine's take-off.

links, about 2 miles from the Coastguard-station. Our representative was amongst the watchers at the station, and, after a hard run along the top of the downs, was one of the first to reach the aviator at five minutes to 4. Mr. Loraine was then standing some little distance from his machine and was being helped to remove his cork jacket by a gentleman who had been the first to reach him. Soon the whole of the little band of people, including the Coastguards, arrived and everyone was eager to greet Mr. 'Jones' as the first pilot of a heavier-than-air machine to land in the Isle of Wight. Whilst awaiting the arrival of the Coastguards the brave aviator, though drenched to the skin and numbed with cold, calmly smoked a cigarette, and told our representative that he had had a very rough time. He said he started from Bournemouth about three o'clock and when about five minutes out from the shore ran into a terrific rain storm, which completely blotted out all signs of land. He groped his way along by pure guesswork, the rain half blinding him and making him very cold. For three-quarters of an hour he battled on, his engine, fortunately, working beautifully. He knew his petrol was becoming exhausted, but was afraid to descend lower than about 1500 ft. for fear of striking the cliffs. 'I was very thankful indeed to see these downs and descended at once. I don't know how much longer I should have been able to keep up. This is a fine landing place. It could not have been better if specially made for me', said Mr. Loraine as he hurried away with the Coastguards, who kindly provided him with clothing and food ... Mr. Loraine said he would make the return journey on Tuesday afternoon, between 4 and 6 o'clock ... On Tuesday, there were, roughly, about 1000 people gathered round the edge of the chalk pit where the plane had spent the weekend undercover, when at about 4.30, Mr. Loraine put in an appearance and ordered his machine to be taken up to the level stretch in about the centre of the golf links ... While Mr. Loraine had tea at Alum Bay House the aeroplane was got in position, facing inland, towards the Tennyson Beacon, so that the start could be made with the wind. The crowd, which by this time must have numbered about 2000, waited patiently and when at 6.15 Mr. Loraine was seen walking towards his machine they cheered lustily. For some minutes the aviator studied the sky, which had become rather overclouded, and he seemed loath to depart upon his journey. Exactly at 6.30, however, after a long talk with his mechanic he suddenly threw off his coat and jacket, and, amidst the applause of the crowd, donned his sweater, his wind jacket, and his cork lifebelt. He climbed to his seat and his mechanic started the engine, the dozen or so artillery men having a hard job to hold the straining machine back. Just at 6.33, with a farewell wave of the hand and a shout to the men to let go from its brave pilot, the biplane darted over the soft down turf and after a run of about 100 yards rose gracefully into the air, amidst the clicking of a hundred cameras and the enthusiastic cheers of the crowd. Flying rather low Mr. Loraine went over the Golf-house, and with a pretty swerve passed directly over Totland and out to sea. Every eye watched him as he headed straight for Southbourne until he disappeared in the haze ... Mr. Loraine, who accomplished his journey in 25 minutes, alighted at the aerodrome where he was heartily cheered. He attained an altitude of 1500 feet.

A vicar writes ...

September 10th, 1910
THE VICAR OF CARISBROOKE ON VISITORS' DRESS AND MOTORISTS

Writing in the current number of his *Parish Magazine*, the Vicar of Carisbrooke (the Rev. W.J. Stobart) says: 'For some weeks past we have enjoyed the presence of the summer visitor. But who devises their clothing? We can remember a time when the English girl was a most attractive creature. Look at Leech's pictures in the old numbers of Punch - pretty, tasteful, and bright, they were a pleasure to look at. But the 1910 female seems either to be wrapped up in a bundle of rags with the least clean one spread over her hat and tied under her chin, or else she discards as much of her clothing as she can, leaves her hat at home and gets her head full of dust, exposes her chest to every wind that blows, displays ankles that show the solidity of her understanding, and runs about the Island half clad, crumpled, and dust-laden. Is it to convey an impression that they have all travelled in motors? Because some of the rushing motors give one a suggestion of a heap of crushed humanity, females and children, lying in a heap. But the motorist deserves a line to himself. He represents the vast arrogance of wealth. He comes hooting, squeaking, bellowing, tinkling, roaring, or whistling with a piercing scream, to tell everybody to get out of the way, because the road belongs to him. He and his rush through the loveliest scenery and the exquisite peeps of land and sea at the pace of a train (not an I.W. Central one) without time to look at anything, he in goggles, his females in folds of material. Why don't they keep to Brooklands? There is a beautiful racecourse, smooth and properly graded, where they could put their heads in bags and fancy themselves in Scotland, or the Isle of Wight, or Devonshire, while circling round and round the course. It may be that we are getting old and do not properly appreciate the spirit of the 20th century. It strikes us that there was more real enjoyment in the days when we had to devise our recreations for ourselves, instead of going to Mr. Cook or Mr. Gamage to find them all ready-made for us.

Mr. Ashby of Newport, understood enough about how the Courts worked to want to make use of their services but he was clearly not so well up on the terminology used ...

December 10th, 1910
LOSER ASKS FOR COSTS

Arthur Ashby, scalemaker, Holyrood-street, Newport, claimed 10s.6d. from George Long, pork butcher, Carisbrooke-road, for repairing scales and weights. Mr. Long said the work had not been done. – His Honour gave judgement for the plaintiff. – Mr. Ashby: I want your Honour to mark your disapproval by allowing me costs. – His Honour: The judgement is against you (laughter).

1911

TOWN AND COUNTY NOTES

The lock out of 4,000 cotton operatives at Padiham, near Burnley, has been settled by the workers returning on the same terms.

THE ANIMATED PICTURES shown by the Animated Picture Company Limited at Medina-hall, Cowes, during the week, have been excellent, the most popular films being 'Back to the Homestead', 'Only Two Little Shoes' and 'Kentucky Pioneer'.

PARKHURST. CORONATION PRISON FARE. - The Home Office has instructed the Prison Governor that the diet on Coronation-day is to be ½lb. bread, ½lb. beef, and ½lb. plum pudding.

NEWPORT. - LARGE FOWL'S EGG. Mrs. Cooke, of Cavendish-place, has shown us an egg laid by one of her hens, which she states is a full ¼lb. in weight.

VENTNOR. - MOTOR IN DISTRESS. The novel sight of a motor carriage being drawn through the town by two horses (tandem) was witnessed on Thursday afternoon, the machinery being evidently disabled. The horses were not seen to smile!

NITON. - Colonel Hobart expressed regret that a Territorial Forces recruitment drive had resulted in their obtaining only one recruit at Niton. He said there must be quite 100 young men in the village who could have joined had they the inclination. One young man in the hall, when asked what he would do if a foreign foe marched up the streets of the village, replied 'Stand by and watch 'em'. The Colonel hoped there were not many Englishmen of that type in the Island.

———————◆———————

During the fox-hunting season the outings of the Isle of Wight foxhounds were reported in a regular weekly column. This is the last report of the 1911 season ...

April 8th, 1911

ISLE OF WIGHT FOXHOUNDS

That the season is drawing to a close is only too plainly to be seen. The sowing operations in evidence, the roller on the seeds, and the spring hedge-making all sound the knell, for the time being, of fox-hunting ... On Tuesday the trysting place was Hardingshute. Hounds were taken across one field to the covert known as Broadlay, where a fox soon unkenneled. In spite of a cold east wind, numbers of people were in evidence, both on foot and wheel, and as a result a good deal of heading took place ere hounds could persuade the fugitive to make his point for Peaked-close-copse. Running this covert, over the railway, and through Whitefield-wood, he took to the open country. Hounds pushed him at a good pace, and I think most of us were congratulating ourselves that

we were in for a good thing when an open drain put an end to further pursuit. Trotting back to Rowborough-copse we again found, but this unfortunate object of the chase was headed in every conceivable direction and was eventually abandoned. Kemphill-moor was the next point of attack, and we had barely heard 'Lieu in there, huic in covert, lads'* when Valiant's well-known voice proclaimed a find. The single voice was but the keynote of the chorus to follow, crashing through the undergrowth and splashing over the muddy rides, hounds could be seen dashing to the cry from all sides. Though this pilot was not of the dwelling sort, it took little persuasion to set him in full flight over the railway and through Rowlands to Ramscroft. It was a woodland hunt in every sense of the word; the rides were deep and boggy, one heard the splash, splash of galloping horses, and saw mud bespattered figures on all sides. Hounds raced and screamed at their fox for 50 minutes, when he then swam the Creek from Firestone above Wootton-bridge. The river was in full tide, and though the pack swam the main stream the marshes were flooded, which completely obliterated every atom of scent. Our first whip was the first to get round by the hunting bridge, and with a 'View, holloa', soon had hounds on the line, but by this time the fugitive had gained some 15 minutes, which, together with a gathering snow-blast saved his life. From the Creek on the Briddlesford side the hunting became slower, and upon nearing Wootton-common the hounds had to admit defeat.

The season's bag ends with a death-roll of 41 foxes, whilst 27 have saved themselves by seeking sanctuary below ground. CURLY WIG.

Almost a year to the day, the second aeroplane ever to land on the Island touched down at St. Lawrence. Unlike the first landing, this one was deliberate and a crowd of several thousand had assembled to watch the almost, but not quite, historic moment. There was no doubt that events the previous year had stolen the aviators' thunder and both dignitaries and the County Press were only able to offer congratulations to the men on the first 'intentional' landing ...

July 3rd, 1911
AEROPLANES IN THE ISLAND
In the presence of thousands of spectators from all parts of the Island three intrepid airmen on Wednesday evening made the first intentional descent from the skies on Vectis ... The descent was made in Lawn-field, St. Lawrence, a charming meadow kindly lent by Mr. John Gell, of Home Farm, and admirably suited for the purpose from the spectators' point of view, because of the mounds and higher land around from which the evolutions could be viewed, but its position on the edge of the cliffs was somewhat alarming to the airmen ... The airmen were expected between 6 and 7, but it was not till 8 o'clock that the report of a bomb sent up by Capt. Pearson of the Ventnor Fire Brigade, from St. Boniface-down, announced that an aeroplane was in sight. Then a speck appeared in the sky directly in a line with St. Boniface-down, and within a minute or so the graceful lines of the aeroplane could be seen with the naked eye ... and shortly it was over the heads of the people, who welcomed the

* Traditional hunting cry.

airmen - for the biplane was seen to contain two persons - with cheers. In two circuits seawards, the airmen gracefully descended to within 50ft. and then dipping downwards the aeroplane took the ground close by the alighting sheet and running swiftly over the turf was pulled up sharply within a few yards of the edge of the cliffs. It was close work and the hearts of many present went up into their mouths in apprehension. However, the airmen coolly descended from their seats and were heartily greeted by the spectators. Members of the Council joined in shaking hands with, and congratulating them on their successful and safe flight, also on being the first airmen to make an intentional landing on the Isle of Wight. Many of the spectators who surrounded the biplane seized the opportunity to write their autographs on its canvas sides, on which were many other names. The first arrivals proved to be Mr. Pixie and Mr. Fleming ... They left Shoreham at 7.15 and the journey had taken exactly one hour. The beacon fire on St Boniface-down proved a great help to them. They could see the smoke from Selsey Bill ... Their machine was a Bristol biplane and this was the 366th time it had been in the air ...

———————————◆———————————

Fishing was still a sizeable industry on the Island and it was an industry that suffered even then from pollution and industrial waste ...

July 3rd, 1911

ISLAND'S SEA-FISHING INDUSTRY
INCREASED CATCHES ROUND THE COAST

The Annual Sea Fisheries District Committee report that in the Isle of Wight, at Alum Bay, there is potting for crabs, lobsters and prawns. At Totland and Colwell Bays similar fishing obtains, also set-net fishing. At Yarmouth the same industries, with dredging, winkle picking and eel spearing are worked. At Newtown there are are set-nets, trammels, stop-nets, trawls, and dredgers. At Gurnard potting. At Cowes and Wootton there are, in addition, eel spearing and winkle picking; and at Ryde push-nets, as well as much hooking. At Seaview and Bembridge the same conditions are found and there is also drifting. At Foreland, Sandown and Shanklin there is also seining. At Ventnor the lobster, crab, and prawn fishery is of chief importance, and trammels are also worked. At Niton, Puckaster-cove, Chale, Brighstone, Brook and Freshwater, potting generally prevails, and there is some tuck-net fishing and also seining along this coast, and at Freshwater trammels and hooking ... Trawling in the East Solent gives occupation to some 90 men, 60 from Portsmouth and 30 from Cowes and Ryde and inclusive of shrimp and prawn trawling, is worth about £5,200 annually. Perhaps the chief injury to the trawling lies in the hampering and destruction of the nets by the obstacles encountered, such as large masses of peat and other dredging material, spilt coal and coal sacks, paint drums sometimes half-full, and other refuse ... The fish are also driven away by the increasing traffic of deep draught ships and by the submarines at practice giving off great volumes of gas. The use of disinfectants in the sewers and the surface water from tar-sprayed roads are also alleged to contribute to this effect.

The year 1911 was the hottest of the 20th century with temperatures not exceeded until 2003. Previously, in the autumn of 1909, severe gales had been followed by an unusually mild winter and a reader's letter told of a thrush laying her eggs in February and asked if the weather was 'going mad'. Two years later, in the blistering August heat of a drought that had so far lasted six weeks, the Island suffered the latest in a series of plagues of wasps. Barely a week passed in the summer without the subject appearing in the news pages or correspondence columns. In the advertising pages of the County Press remedies of all kinds were on sale for destroying wasps. Readers offered their own solutions ...

August 12th, 1911

A PLAGUE OF WASPS

To the Editor of the Isle Of Wight County Press

Sir, - Many of your readers will have been annoyed by the great number of wasps there are this year and may like to know a simple means of destroying their nests. When the entrance to the nest has been located a good plan is to place a piece of paper near so that it can be seen at night. Put a quarter of a pint of spirits of turpentine in a taper-neck bottle and when it is quite dark at night put the neck of the bottle in the entrance to the nest and leave it there. The next day the nest can be taken out by hand, as all the wasps will be dead. I have destroyed 21 nests up to date by the above plan. - I am, Sir, yours faithfully, Charles Morgan, gardener. Bellemead Cottage, Newport.

———————◆———————

Britain was also in the grip of a severe outbreak of swine fever, a highly contagious disease which could kill a pig in a matter of days. The practice of using animal remains for fodder was questioned. What goes around comes around ...

August 12th, 1911

FLESH FED PORK

To the Editor of the Isle Of Wight County Press.

Sir, - Cannot something be done to put a stop to the reprehensible practice now becoming prevalent in the Island of feeding pigs on flesh.* Knackers' carcasses, diseased beasts, and rotten sheep are all considered good enough to boil down for food for animals destined for human consumption. What are the medical officers about that they do not interfere? One would have thought a bye-law could have been passed to put a stop to this abominable modern practice. The smell from the boiling of hounds' food is as nothing compared with the stench from the mess destined for the pig trough. What is our 'dairy-fed pork' coming to? - Percy G. Stone. Merston.

---

* The practice was banned by the EU in 2000, after outbreaks of BSE (mad cow disease).

In 1911 Britain's trades unions came of age in a spectacular manner. A short strike by Liverpool dockers had ended in the desperate employers meeting the workers' demands for higher wages and shorter hours, a first in trade union history. Realising there was something in the air, the unions seized the moment and across the nation one union after another called their members out on strike in support of higher wages. The actions brought much of Britain to a halt in a matter of weeks and the effects were very much felt on the Island ...

August 12, 1911

SERIOUS LONDON DOCK STRIKE

Yesterday morning's news of the London Dock strike, in which some 110,000 men were involved, was of a very serious character and troops, who were stated to have been served out with ball cartridge, were ordered on duty to prevent disturbances which were threatening. Trade and traffic was seriously inconvenienced and large cargoes of food, fruit, &c., were stated to be spoiling ... The local shipping trade has been seriously affected by the strike, as the cargo boat traffic between the Island and London is at a standstill ... The dead meat trade from the Island to London is also paralysed. Inquiries of the leading shipping firms in Newport yesterday showed that the usual trade had been decreased in bulk to the extent of nearly four fifths, with the result that a number of men who help in discharging vessels are thrown out of employ ... News was received yesterday that the 1st. Worcestershire Regiment, of Parkhurst, now at Bulford Camp, had been ordered to proceed to London in connection with the strike and the helmets of the men were sent from Parkhurst yesterday, as they afford better protection for the heads of the men than the caps worn on manoeuvres ...

———————————◆———————————

The following week a national railway strike was called. As is often the case, the Island went its own way but the genie was out of the bottle and the unions' show of strength had taught them the gains that could be won through solidarity. The writing was on the wall and the successes of 1911 led to more strikes throughout the pre-war years ...

August 19th, 1911

THE GREAT RAILWAY STRIKE
200,000 MEN OUT

The general railway strike began on Thursday night. Two thousand telegrams were sent out by the executive of the railway unions in the afternoon calling upon the men throughout the country to cease work at once. The whole of Thursday was spent in fruitless negotiations between the Government and the railwaymen ... Mr. Asquith warned the men that they would put themselves in the wrong with public opinion. He also declared that the Government could not allow the railway system to be paralysed ... Troops are pouring into London and will camp in the parks. Reinforcements are being sent throughout the country to guard the lines. The Home Secretary has instructed police to be ready to enrol special constables. A public warning has been issued that in the event of disturbances a bugle call will proclaim the reading of the Riot Act. This will be followed immediately by the firing of ball cartridges. No blank charges will be used by the soldiers. Col. Seely defended this policy in the House of Commons. The bitterest critics of the railway strike are the men who have remained on duty. 'I shall stay on duty to the last possible moment', declared one man, and another said 'Why should I come out at the bidding of a few lads who have not even got permanent jobs? I have won my position after years of service, and I'm not going to throw it away. I have a wife and children to keep'.

ISLAND RAILWAYMEN AND THE STRIKES.

Yesterday (Friday) all the Island trains were running as usual and there did not appear to be any probability of the Island railwaymen joining the strike. However, on the Central Railway Company's system, where the proportion of Union men is considerably greater than on the Isle of Wight line, it was stated that the men had not yet arrived at a definite decision as to future action and that a meeting will be held on Sunday to discuss the matter. The drivers and firemen of the Central Company were, we understand, yesterday notified that an increase in pay of 6d. and 3d. per day respectively had been granted. The men have been asked whether they will remain loyal to the Company, and all replies have not yet been given.

—◆—

The White Star liner Olympic was the largest ship in the world. Only 12 weeks old, she was starting out on her fifth trip from Southampton to New York when as she sailed past Cowes Parade watched by thousands of sightseers, she was rammed by HMS Hawke, a naval cruiser. The accident caused severe damage to the Olympic and was to have far reaching consequences for her sister ship the Titanic* which was then under construction at the Belfast shipyard of Harland & Wolff, the builder of both ships.

In another link with the Titanic, the captain of the Olympic in Cowes Roads that afternoon and the ship's captain who went down with the Titanic six months later, were one and the same man, Captain E.J. Smith …

September 23rd, 1911

SENSATIONAL SHIPPING COLLISION IN COWES ROADS
THE OLYMPIC RAMMED BY HMS HAWKE
SERIOUS DAMAGE TO BOTH SHIPS
EXCITING SCENES

Cowes Roads was the scene of a very serious collision in broad daylight on Wednesday afternoon, the leviathan White Star liner Olympic, of 45,324 tons, the largest ship in the world, carrying some 3,000 passengers and crew, outward bound from Southampton to New York, being run into by the cruiser HMS Hawke near the Prince Consort buoy, about half a mile from the Cowes Pier and in full view of people on the Cowes Parade. Fortunately, although both ships were very seriously damaged there was no loss of life …

---

* Repairs to the *Olympic* forced Harland and Wolff to delay the completion of the *Titanic* and as a result the *Titanic* left Southampton on her maiden voyage not on March 20th as originally intended, but on the more fateful April 10th, 1912.

SEEN FROM COWES
The fact that the Olympic was on her fifth trip from Southampton to New York was known to many people at Cowes, who had gathered along the Esplanade, and very clearly saw the collision, which caused a great sensation in the town. It was a few minutes before 1 o'clock when the collision occurred. The weather at the time was squally and rain was falling, but there was no fog and nothing to account for two such huge vessels coming into contact. The people at Cowes watched the great Olympic as she came out of Southampton Water and steamed slowly and majestically to the westward, and then rounding the West Bramble buoy off Egypt, headed eastward towards Spithead. The floating palace made a wonderful picture as she glided past the Royal Yacht Squadron Castle towards Old Castle Point. Following a long way astern was the first-class cruiser HMS Hawke, which was coming from the westward, returning from steam trials to Portsmouth. Both ships were going in the same direction. The Hawke, travelling at a fairly good speed, overtook the Olympic near the Prince Consort shoal buoy, nearly off Old Castle Point. The Hawke at first appeared to attempt to pass the Olympic on the starboard side, and then, after getting about level with the liner's foremost funnel, seemed to hang up as if to allow the Olympic to get ahead and steered to port, the supposition being that her course had been changed and that the Hawke was endeavouring to pass under the Olympic's stern. This manoeuvre had

A DISASTROUS RESULT
for, with alarming suddenness the cruiser crashed stem on into the Olympic's starboard quarter, some 50 ft. from the liner's stern. The terrific impact sounded like an explosion. For some minutes the two ships lay together as if out of control, the cruiser's stem being locked into the liner's quarter. Then the Hawke went astern and the terrific damage which had been done was easily visible. The plates of the liner were smashed asunder and scattered in all directions leaving a great gaping hole in her starboard quarter, about 15ft. across at the widest part and tapering off to some distance below the waterline. The water-tight compartments of the Olympic had been promptly closed, and although the ship made a good deal of water there was no danger of her sinking. Naturally the collision caused the greatest alarm amongst the passengers on the Olympic, but the great many who were in the saloons and other parts of the ship were quite unaware until informed that the ship had been rammed by the cruiser. Magnificent order prevailed on board and there was not the least sign of anything like a panic. A number of the passengers had narrow escapes but no one was injured.

THE HAWKE
was seen to take a decided list immediately after the impact. Her bow was completely buckled up and the forward part of the cruiser was indeed a pitiable site. The plating was ripped open and the frame scattered and torn away like paper. When the collision occurred fragments of the cruiser's bow were seen to fly in all directions. The collision mats were put over the shattered bow and the water-tight bulkheads closed. Reports of the collision spread rapidly through Cowes and people flocked to the Esplanade and seafront to catch a glimpse of the badly damaged ships ... The Olympic drifted like a ship out of control

almost into Osborne Bay ... The Hawke, with her shattered bow enveloped by collision mats made a good deal of water, but the bulkheads did their work and the cruiser was able to continue the journey to Portsmouth.

THE DAMAGE TO THE HAWKE

The damaged cruiser was placed in the dock at Portsmouth Dockyard on Thursday morning. Below the water-line the injury appeared to be even worse than above it. The formidable ram was completely shattered, the whole projection being pushed round to starboard and the plates shattered and buckled in all directions ... It is certain that a completely new bow will be necessary before the cruiser will again be ready for sea.

THE OLYMPIC

remained at anchor in Cowes Roads throughout the night. When the huge ship was lit up she presented a brilliant spectacle, the site attracting hundreds of people to the Esplanade. The liner was down several feet in the stern, having made a lot of water, and the pumps had to be constantly kept going. Many people put off in boats to see the damaged ships, the local watermen reaping a rich harvest. Several enterprising photographers were amongst the earliest on the scene, for pictures of such an important event were of considerable value. One of the camera men, Mr. Frank Beken, who had gone off in a motor-boat to photograph the departing gunboat built at Cowes for Cuba was practically on the spot when the collision happened. To an interviewer Mr. Beken said there was a terrific crash and when the vessels drew apart one could see right into the Olympic.

THE OLYMPIC AT SOUTHAMPTON

The crippled Olympic was got safely back to Southampton on Thursday ... Soon after 11 o'clock arrangements were made for the transfer of the passengers to other outward-going liners, and a large number left for London by special train, which also carried the mails. When the liner arrived alongside the quay the gaping rent in her starboard quarter was plainly discerned - a great jagged triangular hole almost down to the water-line, measuring some 15ft. by 10ft., directly in front of the rudder. The plating is forced in 5ft. or 6ft. deep, ironwork bent and twisted, and the interior of two or three compartments smashed by the force of the collision. The more serious damage was below the water-line, and the hole was examined by divers soon after the Olympic was berthed. A quantity of woodwork and other materials from the damaged Olympic was picked up at Cowes, and the mementoes of this eventful collision are highly prized.

(The subsequent naval inquiry cleared the Hawke of all blame. In what was seen by many as an injustice, Captain Smith was declared to have sailed too close to the Hawke, allowing the vast bulk of the Olympic to draw the Hawke into its side by means of suction. Although regarded as an unlikely explanation by most outside the Navy, this phenomenon did actually occur a year later when a tug was pulled from her moorings by suction created by the passing Titanic.)

1912

While wages in Britain had been at a standstill since late-Victorian times, inflation had slowly but surely continued to rise. Hundreds of labourers at the shipyards of J.S. White were paid 20 shillings for a 54 hour week which had been the exact wage earned by the lowest paid labourers 25 years before, men who had generally worked shorter hours. It could not go on; it was not politics so much as mathematics. The successful strike actions of 1911 were still fresh in the minds of the unions who were now firmly resolved never to look back, and a new wave of industrial action swept Britain. The Cowes shipyard workers were called out by their union in pursuit of an extra four shillings a week ...

January 13th, 1912

INDUSTRIAL TROUBLE AT COWES
STRIKE AMONG MESSRS. J.S WHITE AND CO'.S LABOURERS

The wave of industrial discontent which is sweeping over the country has reached Cowes and East Cowes where considerable excitement has prevailed during the week in consequence of a strike among the labourers employed at the shipbuilding yards and marine engineering works of Messrs. John Samuel White and Co. Ltd. For some time past dissatisfaction with the rate of pay has been felt amongst a section of the labourers, of whom some 350 are employed at the two yards* ... It was contended on behalf of the Union that £1 per week of 54 hours was inadequate, especially having regard to the increased cost of living and rents ... The strike commenced on Monday morning when, in fulfilment of their threat, over 300 labourers failed to resume work. Long before daylight the strikers had pickets posted at the entrances to the works on both sides of the Medina, as well as at different points along the roads leading to the works, the Cowes Pontoon, and the Cowes, Mill-Hill and even the Newport Railway-stations. They kept a sharp lookout to persuade men from returning to work and also for others who might be making for Messrs. White's works to secure employment. The picket men did not appear to have a very arduous task ... On Thursday ... the firm offered a starting rate of 21s. to all the labourers actually employed on engineering and shipbuilding work, in addition to an offer of an advance to 22s. at the end of two years service.

The strike has caused distress among a good many families, to whom assistance was given from the funds contributed by the Trade Unionists. We understand that some 50 men were yesterday discharged by Messrs. White on account of temporary slackening of work, mainly owing, we are informed, to the completion of the destroyer Forester.

---

* The *County Press*, anxious to remain impartial, gave both White's management and the workforce space in the paper to each state their case. It was done in polite, even terms with both sides actually thanking each other for their 'courteous, gentlemanly behaviour'.

*Burglars were busy in Cowes. For some it was hungry work while for others it was
so tiring that a little snooze was called for ...*

January 20th, 1912
SHOP BREAKING AT COWES
For the second time in about five weeks, Mr. J. Froud's grocery and provision
stores in Victoria-road, Cowes, were entered during Monday night. Entrance
was effected at the back, where two doors were burst open, one being wrenched
off its hinges ... A 100lb. cheese was hacked to pieces with a chopper and 28lb.
of butter stolen.

HOUSEBREAKING AT COWES
SOLDIERS ARRESTED IN BED
An impudent case of house-breaking was reported at about mid-day on
Wednesday, when Gothic House, Queens-road, belonging to Mrs. Porcelli Cust,
who is away at Torquay, was found to have been forcibly entered by the back door.
The discovery was made by Mr. Augustus, the coachman and caretaker of Cliffside
and Gothic House, which are adjoining properties. Finding the place in disorder,
doors forced open, and burnt paper on one of the floors, he summoned the gardener,
Mr. J. Hart. They searched the house and to their surprise discovered two soldiers,
partly undressed, asleep in one of the beds ... The assistance of a party of painters,
who were working at Cliffside, was secured and they surrounded the house whilst
Hart went to the police. P.C. Smith soon arrived, and going upstairs awoke the
slumberers, who were not a little astonished to find themselves caught red-handed.
They quietly surrendered and were conveyed to the Police-station ... The prisoners'
names were George Windum Hughes and James Grice, both being young privates
in the 1st. Worcestershire Regiment, stationed at Parkhurst Barracks.

------◆------

TOWN AND COUNTY NOTES
RELICS OF THE HAWKE-OLYMPIC COLLISION. - A good deal of interest
and curiosity was aroused by the appearance in Cowes Roads last week of a large
steam salvage vessel near the spot where the cruiser Hawke collided with the
Olympic on September 20th last. Divers were engaged and a large anchor was the
first haul, which was deposited at a local yard. On Monday a large piece of
wreckage was discovered. The 'find' proved to be a portion of the bow plates and
ram of the Hawke, a huge piece of steel weighing about 7½ tons. The metal was
photographed and taken to Portsmouth to the Dockyard stores for examination.

MYSTERIOUS THEFT. - During the progress of the football match at
Steephill between Ventnor and Freshwater on Saturday, Butler, one of the
visiting players, had his watch and ten false teeth stolen from a pocket in his
clothes left in the dressing-room. There was the sum of 30s. in loose silver but
the cash, however, remained untouched.

VENTNOR. - The members of the 'Catch my pal' Union* organised a meeting
on Saturday night in the Methodist Church. The speakers were subjected to
vulgar interruptions. One person signed the temperance pledge. Cat-calls, cries

---

* A temperance society which grew by members recruiting other entrants on the
'pyramid' principle.

of 'Order, order', and imitations of the noise occasioned by the opening of bottles of beer, together with other unseemly conduct which should not be tolerated in a place of worship, quite mediated against what little success the promoters may have achieved.

THE SOUTH POLE EXPEDITION. - The officials of the British Antarctic Expedition in London state that no authoritative news whatever of the success or otherwise of the Scott expedition has yet reached them. It is reported that Amundsen has reached the South Pole.

HALF-TIME FOR ISLAND RAILWAYMEN. - Yesterday most of the employees on the I.W. Central Railway received notice that half-time employment would come into effect next week owing to the coal strike and the consequent curtailment of the railway and boat services.

———————◆———————

For over 30 years Isaac Sheath had lived the eccentric, solitary life of a hermit in a mud hut he had built just outside Chale Green, on the road to Godshill. The previous year he had been moved to the Workhouse Infirmary where he had eventually died. The County Press marked his passing with an obituary ...

February 24th, 1912
DEATH OF THE HERMIT OF CHALE
ECCENTRIC LIFE IN ROADSIDE HUT
The death occurred in the infirmary at Parkhurst on Sunday of Mr. Isaac Sheath, familiar to many Islanders and visitors as 'The hermit of Chale-green'. Deceased, whose age is officially given as 75, but who was believed to be nearly 80,* was of very eccentric habits, which led him to live alone for some 30 years in a mud hut he had built on the waste piece of land at North-grounds, Chale, his occupancy of which came to an end last year, when the Rural District Council, under the new housing legislation, had his primitive dwelling condemned as unfit for human habitation, and Sheath was removed to the Workhouse. He was a native of Chale-green, belonged to a farm labourer's family, and his lack of energy and mental capacity in his youth led to domestic differences at home. After the death of his mother he went into lodgings, but these he eventually deserted for his roadside hut, where he was a familiar figure to passers-by, coaching parties, and others, who took great and often kindly interest in him, and he received many small monetary gifts, but never thought of saving up for the winter, when he had to rely on parish relief and the hospitality of a few friends at Chale-green. With good reason he regarded Mr. John H. Brown, C.C., and Mrs. Brown, of Chale-green, as his best friends, and to Mr. Brown he went with all his troubles, which arose principally from boys tormenting him by pulling off his chimney-pot, throwing stones down the chimney, and otherwise invading his humble abode. The Rector of Chale and his wife were also very good to him and in the winter provided him with coal, evidence of the arrival of which was afforded by his begrimed face and hands. Several years ago two residents in the parish kindly match-boarded his hut

———

* Mr. Sheath gave his date of birth as 1837 to the census on at least two occasions, making him 75.

inside to make it more comfortable, and Sheath showed his appreciation by gradually stripping off the boards to save himself the trouble of collecting firewood; a mattress, table, and chair also given him had a like fate. He was of a very sympathetic disposition and fond of children. He was visited in his last illness by Mrs. Brown and others and stated that he was well cared for and comfortable, though he still had a longing for the free open-air life of bygone years. When the sanitary inspector of the Rural District Council condemned Sheath's hut and told him it must be pulled down, the hermit replied 'Sooner than they should do that I will burn it down', and those who were superintending the removal next day saw the hut in flames on their approach.

———————◆———————

In Victorian times someone in the County Press had an eye for quirky, unusual items resulting in the one-liners which generally appeared in the 'Town and Country Notes' column. They noticably declined in number during the Edwardian years, perhaps connected with the appointment of a new editor in 1908, and the columns of the County Press were arguably the poorer for it. 'Town and Country Notes' became the home to stories of those with double-barrelled names and accounts of their balls and social events and humour, intentional or not, was now more likely to be found in the 'serious' columns of the paper …

March 2nd, 1912
DRUNK AND DISORDERLY IN COURT
Edward Mark Groves, labourer, of East Cowes, was charged with disorderly behaviour. Supt. Galloway said he wished to draw the attention of the Bench to the condition of the defendant, who was apparently drunk. - Defendant (shouting): I am not drunk, sir. I guarantee I am not. Did you ever see a man drunk standing as I am. I can stand on my head (laughter). A drunken man cannot stand the same as a mackerel (laughter). I like a mackerel when he is fresh. I am an honest man. I do not owe any man a penny-piece. - Supt. Galloway: Keep quiet. If I hear any more you will be charged with the offence. – Defendant: Look at my honest blue eyes (laughter). – Supt. Galloway (to the sergeant): Take him out and charge him with being drunk and disorderly. - The case was heard in defendant's absence, P.S. Bennett stating that on the 17th ult. defendant behaved disorderly in Castle-street, East Cowes. - The Chairman: Was he talking and raving as he was doing just now? - P.S. Bennett: Yes, sir. About three times as loudly. - There were stated to be eight previous convictions against defendant, who was now fined 10s. and 9s. costs; in default 14 days.

———————◆———————

The Cowes refuse tip adjacent to Medina Wharf and the Newport livestock market in St. James Square were causing turned-up noses within Newport Council. Councillor Hayles in particular, made no secret of his dislike of either the market or, it seems, those who lived nearby, perhaps a reference to the occupants of the crowded courts and alley-ways of South Street …

March 16th, 1912
NEWPORT MARKET - COWES REFUSE TIP
The council had received a letter from the Rural District Council, referring to swine and other animals being allowed to feed on the refuse-tip near Shamblers Copse, Northwood. They had again written to the Cowes District Council expressing the hope that they would be able to make arrangements to prevent swine and other animals from having access to the tip. - Mr. Alexander hoped they and the Cowes Council would use their influence to prevent animals from feeding on the Cowes refuse-tip, which was very undesirable from a health point of view; it was rather hard on the Rural District Council that those tips from the towns should be allowed in the district. – Ald. Fellows said as to the Cowes refuse-tip, there was no place where a tip might be less offensive than it was there ... One side of the tip was open to the sea and the other was as deep as that room and was being filled in; there was no smell from it and it was practically miles away from any inhabited house. The only people who could complain were those passing in the train ...

Mr. Hayles said he visited that apology for a market at Newport on the previous day and found it in a very congested state, with 700 pigs, 400 sheep, cattle of untold number, and a dense throng of buyers and sellers, so that one's feet were about as useless to enable one to move as Chinese lanterns in a tornado (laughter). There was no room to stand, walk, or move, and a pair of stilts would have been necessary to get about. He supposed the difficulty in the way of removing the Market was that the inhabitants living round it loved the smell of sweet lavender and that to them there was no music like that of the lowing of the cattle, the bleating of the sheep, and squealing of the pigs, to say nothing of the 'language' of buyers and sellers (laughter) ... Mr. Hobbs said the Corporation, who were giving their best attention to the matter, could not be expected to move rapidly in considering so important a question.

───────────◆───────────

The Titanic's maiden voyage had been delayed while the Harland and Wolff shipyard in Belfast carried out repairs to the Olympic following her collision with the Hawke. As a result the Titanic left Southampton on its ill-fated maiden voyage three weeks later than intended. The outcome is well known.

In its coverage of the sinking, which is already well documented elsewhere, the County Press reported on the fate of Islanders who had sailed on the Titanic ...

April 20th, 1912
APPALLING SHIPPING DISASTER
LARGEST LINER SUNK. LOSS OF OVER 1,500 LIVES
ISLANDERS IN THE DEATH ROLL
A shipping disaster of appalling magnitude has horrified the world this week, the new White Star liner Titanic, the largest ship afloat, having crashed into an iceberg in the dead of night on Sunday last on her maiden voyage from Southampton to New York, 300 miles off Cape Race, Newfoundland, with the result that this gigantic vessel sank in a few hours, with the loss, it is feared, of over 1,500 passengers and crew ... As far as can be ascertained, eight or nine of

Newport Market, St James Square. 1907. (See page 143).

the crew belonged to the Island, and according to latest reports only two Ryde men are among the 775 who have been saved ... Southampton has suffered very heavily by the disaster, there being hardly a street in which there are not a number of bereaved homes. Many of the lost are married men with families, and relief funds for the sufferers have been opened ... Up until yesterday morning a total of nearly £40,000 had been subscribed ...

THE ISLAND AND THE DISASTER

Unfortunately quite a number of Islanders and relatives of Islanders were among the crew of the Titanic. These included:- Quartermaster W. Perkis, 36, of Ryde (reported saved). Second steward G. P. Wheat of Ryde (saved). J. White, Prince-street, third class steward. Steward William Cheverton, 27, of Mill-street, Newport. Steward J. Longmuir, Ventnor, Steward S. Blake, 25, of Cowes, and Stewardess Mrs. Snape, Sandown. Coastguard Wardner, of Yarmouth, has lost a brother and a cousin, both belonging to Southampton. Amongst the first-class passengers on board the Titanic was Mr. A. F. Nicholson, of Claremont, Steephill-road, Shanklin, who has a large business concern in America, which he periodically visits. He is, unfortunately, amongst the missing. Very great sympathy is extended to Mrs. Nicholson in her bereavement ... A story was circulated yesterday to the effect that Capt. Smith committed suicide when the fate of his great liner was in doubt. This is declared to be a slander upon the memory of a brave man. He refused to leave the ship. When last seen he was on the bridge and he died as an English captain knows how to die, going down with his ship.

April 27th, 1912

THE TITANIC DISASTER

Criticisms are made in America of the ignorance displayed by the Investigating Committee, whose chairman, Mr. Smith, has attracted attention by inquiring 'why the passengers did not take refuge in the watertight compartments', and 'whether the Titanic sank by the bows or the head'.

―――――――◆―――――――

Back in July the previous year (see page 132), the County Press had detailed the fishing activities on the Island and in passing, the report had mentioned the possibility that rainwater run-off from tar-sprayed roads was killing fish. These were no empty words apparently. Mr. Percy Wadham, the local taxidermist (see vol. 1), had submitted evidence of the effect to the Fishing Gazette in an article which the Daily Mail had now reprinted ...

May 11th, 1912

ROAD TARRING AND FISHERIES

Writing in the *Daily Mail* Mr. R. B. Marston, editor of the *Fishing Gazette* calls attention to the 'new danger to anglers and to proprietors of fisheries' in consequence of the tarring of roads. He admits the necessity for dust prevention and points out that the use of asphalt, though dearer, is preferable to that of tar. He says that at present experts themselves seem to differ as to whether ordinary coal tar can be so purified as to be made harmless to fish and insect life - for if you kill the billions of small insects on which the fish exist you may as well kill the fish also. Mr. Marston proceeds: 'Few men have had such sad experience of fish poisoned by washings from tarred roads as Mr. Percy Wadham, who for many years has stocked and preserved the trout waters at Carisbrooke and Newport, in the Isle of Wight. In 1909 the Carisbrooke-hill road, which winds under the famous Castle, was tar sprayed, and as soon as the first rain washed the surface of it, the surface water ran into the trout stream from which the Castle takes its name, and every trout was killed, and the fish could be seen lying about dead below the tar water inlet, both in the stream and the mill dam. There was no doubt about it, because two mill dams adjoining, but above the one into which the tar water flowed, were quite unaffected. Mr. Wadham says: 'The contaminated surface water from tar-sprayed roads seems to be continually poured into the stream after every rain for months after the roads are dressed with tar, for on testing the water four months after the tar was laid it was surprising to find that the water contained such a high percentage of tar gases, which are soluble in water. Recently anglers have formed the nucleus of a defence association, and I hope that it may be the means of protecting our very valuable trout and other fisheries from destruction by this new system of road tarring. It is already too late in the day for the authorities to give us an excuse that they killed the fish in their ignorance, and they must be held responsible for destroying private property as other people are'.

It is only fair to the Rural District Council to say that it is claimed that the 'Tarvia' used by the contractor is innocuous to fish.

By any standards, even in 1912 fourpence an hour was a pitiful amount to pay a man even if he happened to be just a lowly street sweeper. The guilty party this time was Newport Council and a whiff of predjudice was in the air as a potential increase in the sweepers' wages was discussed ...

August 3rd, 1912
NEWPORT TOWN AND WORKMEN AND THEIR WAGES

Mr. Steel moved the adoption of a recommendation of the General Practices Committee to increase the street sweepers' wages from 4d. to 4½d. per hour in view of the greater cost of living, and that the men lose time when not at work. - Mr. Godwin seconded, and said no married man employed by the Corporation should receive less than £1.1s. per week. Ald. Cheverton said it should not go forth that they underpaid their men. Some of the men he would not pay 2½d. an hour, whilst others were worth the 4½d. If they granted that increase all the men should understand that they were expected to be smarter in their work. Some appeared to be news vendors of the town, and the hardest work they did seemed to be carrying their brooms to the Town-hall from a quarter to half an hour before 5.30 so as, he supposed, to get a wash and brush up before they went home (laughter). He should not be honest if he said that all were a splendid lot of industrious workmen. Mr. Munden said ... he had seen men going home to breakfast ten minutes before time ... Mr.Wadham thought they should pay 4½d. till the age of 65, then reduce it to 3½d. and not employ a man after 70 … Mr.Salter said he strongly resented the idea that a man was too old to work at 70, and said old people should not be spoken of in such a disrespectful way. Mr. Ediss was strongly against such a proposal as Mr. Wadham had suggested, and said that a man who had done his duty should rather be presented with a smaller broom when he reached 65 (hear, hear, and laughter). - The proposition was carried.

———————◆———————

Different times have different values. While it was literally possible to abuse children or animals with little or no threat of a jail sentence, the theft of property was a different matter altogether. As Mr. Mundell who had stolen two pence worth of coal was to find out, offences against property were always rigourously prosecuted …

August 17th, 1912

THEFT AND ATTEMPTED SUICIDE

George Mundell, an elderly man, was charged on remand with having stolen coal at the Newport Railway-station and also with attempted suicide. He wept during the hearing of the cases.

Henry John Cooper, manager for Messrs. Wood and Co., coal merchants, of Newport Station, said that the coal produced was similar to what they had in their yard. He valued it at about 2d. The prisoner had no right whatever to take coal from the yard. – P.S. Foyle said that on August 2nd, at about 3 am., he concealed himself at the Railway-station and at about 5.30 am. he saw the prisoner enter the Station-yard and go to Messrs. Wood and Co'.s coal heap. Witness went to him and said 'You have taken some coal from that heap'. Prisoner then took the coal (produced) from his pockets. P.C. Stevens also told prisoner that he saw him take the coal and he replied 'That's right'. Told that he would be taken into custody, prisoner said 'Don't do that. I have got three little children at home'. Witness said he must do it, as he was there as the result of complaints as to coal being stolen. Prisoner said it was the first time he had been there. - In reply to the Mayor, witness said the coal heap was not fenced in. - Prisoner pleaded guilty. - He was further charged with having attempted suicide. - P.S. Foyle said that when crossing over the bridge at the railway approach prisoner broke away from them and mounted the rails of the bridge. Witness and the constable both caught hold of him, but his clothing gave way and he fell into the water, which was 17ft. below and was about 4ft. deep. On reaching the water he ducked his head two or three times, but P.C. Stevens entered the water and got hold of him. The prisoner said 'Let me alone; let me die; let me drown out of it'. Witness assisted the constable to get him out and to take him to the Police-station, where prisoner repeatedly said 'I wish I was dead out of it'. He was medically attended by Dr. Raymond who ordered his removal to the Workhouse Infirmary…. In reply to the Mayor, prisoner's son-in-law, from Portsmouth, said he was willing to take prisoner back to Portsmouth with him if the Bench decided to discharge him. - Prisoner also pleaded guilty to this charge and appealed for leniency, as it was the first crime he had ever committed. 'It was poverty and want that drove me to it' he added. It was the saddest disaster of his life.

The Mayor said they had taken into consideration the fact that that was practically the prisoner's first offence. The charge of theft would be dismissed. As to the second, they had received a medical certificate from the doctor at Portsmouth Prison stating that prisoner wanted looking after, and as his relative had agreed to take charge of him he would be discharged (applause, which was immediately suppressed).

———————◆———————

The previous week, inmates at Camp Hill Prison had staged a mutiny which ended in them being forced back to their cells at sword-point; a few days later the protest had flared up again.

If the County Press ever did have any thoughts on some of the items they reported they kept them to themselves which makes the next item all the more unusual when for once the writer makes his own thoughts quite clear.

The prisoners' mutiny was even discussed in the House of Commons. The ways of the honourable members in 1912 seem uncannily familiar …

Dec 14th, 1912

PAMPERED PRISONERS' REVOLT
RIOTOUS CONDUCT AT CAMP HILL

A serious sequel to the mutinous conduct of the privileged prisoners at the new Camp Hill Prison and the consequent punishment of the offenders occurred on Saturday and continued on Sunday and subsequently. Incensed by deprivation of privileges and close confinement to their cells, some of the offenders became violent and destructive on Saturday and the corridors and Prison yard resounded at frequent intervals with the noise produced by the prisoners in smashing cell windows, wrecking furniture, and volleys of filthy and threatening language from prisoners towards officers moving about in the Prison yard. Having knocked out all the glass in their windows, which can be opened at will by the prisoners, the infuriated occupants of the cells proceeded to demolish the iron window frames which they threw into the yard, together with flowerpots, food utensils, and fragments of furniture and food, which they refused to eat. More than one officer had soup, which was being handed into the prisoners for dinner, dashed back into his face … Some of the men endeavoured to wreak vengeance on those responsible for their safe custody, and there were exciting escapes from serious personal violence directed against the officers by these pampered pests of humanity. Having demolished everything within reach, some of the prisoners made futile attacks on the stout steel grids, which guarded the windows on the outside, and they clung to the bars like monkeys and shouted defiance and insults at the officers, their shouts being heard for a long distance outside the prison walls. This disorderly conduct was continued throughout Saturday and Sunday … The more disorderly inmates renewed their riotous conduct on Monday morning, but the day passed more quietly … During Monday the 'triangles' were removed from the lower Prison to Camp Hill in readiness for the birching which, it was stated, would take place on the following day in pursuance of the sentences passed by the Board of Visitors last week, but this sentence was not carried out we understand, exile from the privileged prison being ultimately decided upon as likely to have a better effect. It is understood that four were to receive a birching, and not flogging with the 'cat' as the ring leaders were thought to richly deserve, and that the remainder of the offenders, comprising about two-thirds of the prisoners, have to undergo dietary punishment and confinement in cells. The cells are now none too comfortable, for the broken windows remain unrepaired so that in some cases wind and rain driving into the cells have added to the punishment inflicted by the authorities.

THE WEEK IN PARLIAMENT
THE MUTINY AT CAMP HILL PRISON

… The well-known Gallery Correspondent of the *Pall Mall Gazette* writes:- Mr. Douglas Hall, member for the Isle of Wight, had a field day in the Commons on Thursday. The House was altogether in a frivolous mood. Hilarious cheers from both sides greeted Mr. Douglas Hall when he rose to ask a question about the treatment of the convicts in Camp Hill Prison, Isle of Wight … the place where the enlightened ideas of Mr. Churchill have been put into operation.

Mr. Douglas Hall wanted to know whether the pampered criminals in this home of rest and luxury were allowed to smoke and chat after meals eaten off tables with floral decorations; whether they could have hot shaving water by ringing electric bells; whether their cells were decorated with photographs; and whether these little luxuries were intended to deter other criminals, or to induce those already there to take up permanent residence.

The question was replied to by the Under-Secretary for the Home Department, and it was significant that he did not answer one of the inquiries specifically put by Mr. Douglas Hall. He took refuge in generalities … Mr. Douglas Hall beseeched the Under-Secretary, with an exquisite touch of comedy, to say something that might set his mind rest about the floral decorations - a delicate thrust that brought appreciative cheers and laughter from a rather rollicking house … The Under-Secretary had to make the ignominious confession that he had no precise information about the flowers. The humour of Mr. Douglas Hall was not yet exhausted. 'Are there not serious complaints from the convicts', he inquired with mock gravity, 'that the bells are not answered?' The Under-Secretary, quite unequal to a duel of this kind, was glad to run away.

1913

Barely 18 months had passed since the union victories of 1911 and as a direct result the union movement had since become more confident and assertive. Another dispute brought J.S.White's yard to a halt …

January 11th, 1913
SETTLEMENT OF THE COWES SHIPWRIGHTS' STRIKE

Yesterday (Friday) it was officially announced that the strike of shipwrights at Cowes had been settled. It commenced 11 weeks ago today (Saturday) and was ended by a compromise which it is hoped will give satisfaction to both parties in the dispute although the final voting showed that there was by no

means unanimity on either side ... An offer by the employers of an increase in the pay of ⅜d. per hour was rejected by the shipwrights. On Thursday the employers increased their offer to ½d. per hour, representing an increase of 2s. 3d. per week of 54 hours ... Much gratification is felt in Cowes at the settlement of the dispute which has resulted in a serious delay in the work at the shipbuilding and yacht yards. The conduct of the strikers has been exemplary, and there has been no picketing or outward demonstration of any kind.

———————◆———————

The outbreak of swine fever showed no signs of ending*. A letter to the County Press back in August 1911 (see page 133) had crticised the feeding of animal remains to pigs but 18 months later nothing had changed ...

February 8th, 1913

PIG FEEDING AND HEALTH

To the Editor of the Isle of Wight County Press.

Sir, - I noticed some weeks back, Mrs. Hollis writing re-Swine Fever at Appleford, says: The pigs on the farm were strictly dairy fed, no offal or other food likely to produce fever being allowed'. I take this to mean, and I think farmers generally will bear me out, the feeding of pigs on flesh is provocative of swine fever. Surely if this fever is to be effectually stamped out such a reprehensible practice should be put a stop to. Why is it that nowadays it is next to impossible to get a piece of decent mild cured breakfast bacon? The answer seems to be because nine tenths of our bacon pigs are fattened on flesh. The bacon offered for sale is hard and lean and with as much taste to it as a salted shaving. Pigs' proper fattening food is dairy produce, not the offal of a butcher's shop, or the refuse of an Albanian town. Isn't it time the Board of Agriculture took it up, if they really mean business? It's no good lime-washing and cleansing sties when their occupants are fed on fever producing food. - Yours truly, INQUIRER.

———————◆———————

Over the years, Captain Scott's expedition to the South Pole has been the subject of books, documentaries and films. In 1913, however, the news of his death took the form of just a few short paragraphs in the County Press which were not even given a headline. The brief report appeared in a column of general news items, sandwiched between an article headed 'Prolific Ducks' and an advert for Doan's Backache Kidney Pills ...

February 15, 1913

The British Antarctic Expedition search party on November 12th sighted the tent within which were the bodies of Capt. Scott, Dr. Wilson, and Lieut. Bowers. Seaman Evans died from concussion of the brain and Capt. Oates from exposure. Capt. Scott left a message stating that he and his comrades had been willing to give their lives to the enterprise for the honour of their country and he appeals to his countrymen to see that those dependent on them are properly cared for.

* Britain was finally declared free of swine fever in 1966, only for a case to emerge in 2000.

The erection of a suitable memorial to the Antarctic victims is under discussion … The British Antarctic Expedition Committee has issued an appeal for funds for the relief of the dependents of the South Polar victims, and newspapers are already responding.

————————◆————————

THE WEEK'S NEWS

ST HELENS. AN EXTRAORDINARY EGG. - A black Minorca hen belonging to Mrs. F. Morris has laid an interesting specimen of an egg. To all appearance it was normal, but on being opened it was found to contain another egg inside with a hard shell.

19,200 GUINEAS FOR A PICTURE - At Christie's sale yesterday, Gainsborough's picture, The Market Court, realised 19,200 guineas.

SAUCY DEFENDANT - James Bartlett, St. Helens, pleaded guilty to a charge of having cycled without a light at 11.45 p.m., on April 5th at Station-road, St Helens. – P.C. Summers said that when he called to defendant asking him where his lights were, he replied 'Next to my liver'. He afterwards dismounted and said he did not know it was a constable who had spoken to him. Defendant who said he was sorry that he was saucy to the constable, was fined 1s. with 1s. costs.

THE TORPEDO - found on the shore at Brook last week was conveyed to Portsmouth by a Government despatch boat.

BIG GUN REMOVED - After covering three miles in exactly three weeks the new 9.2 in. gun was hauled into the Needles Battery on Tuesday. The utmost care was taken by the men of the R.G.A to prevent damage to the roads, the gun, which weighs 32 tons, being hauled from Fort Victoria to the Needles on a trolley over thick planks placed on the roadway. It could therefore only be moved a few yards at a time and this accounts for the long time in transit. As far as we have seen, the roads were not damaged at all.

————————◆————————

For the first time, the boat service attracted criticism …

April 12, 1913

STEAM-BOAT TRAFFIC

To the Editor of the Isle of Wight County Press.

Sir, - May I ask for space in your paper in order to ventilate what may be properly called a public grievance. I allude to the state of things existing in the steam-boat service between Portsmouth (Southsea) and Ryde. On Saturday evening I had to wait on Clarence Pier for the 7.30 steamer. We were all expecting one of the newer and larger boats, it being Easter (and, of course, there was a crowd). But no! we saw to our disgust that the boat was one of the oldest and smallest. It was raining in torrents and blowing half a gale; it was almost impossible to remain on deck! The crowd was so great in the alley-ways that moving about was out of the question, and to make matters worse it was almost dark, the solitary oil-lamp, and a bad one at that, being quite inadequate for its purpose. As for the saloon, well! no words can describe it properly; the atmosphere was too awful to remain in, there being absolutely no ventilation. The paraffin lamps gave such a bad light that one could not read thereby; the smell of the oil permeated the cabin, and to make matters worse, oil was dripping on the seats, and a paper which I inadvertently placed under one lamp was soaked with paraffin when I wanted to read it, and I was obliged to throw it away. I wonder how many people had their clothes spoiled without discovering it until they arrived home? Well, to proceed: The floor was covered with luggage, and some ladies were also on the floor, being too ill to move. Many ladies were ill and tried to get aft to the ladies' cabin. Some collapsed on the way, either on the floor or on the laps of other passengers. Those who succeeded were heard to say afterwards that the state of things in the ladies' cabin was beyond description, greatly owing to out-of-date and inefficient appliances therein.

In fact what a fellow passenger remarked to me very aptly described the general state of things on board. He said 'This is more like a cattle-boat 20 years ago than a passenger steamer in 1913 plying between two important South Coast seaside resorts, one being the main entrance to the Isle of Wight'. And I thoroughly endorsed his opinion … If they must run the old 'crocks', let them do so in the day-time; but on dark, cold, and stormy nights the use of these 'year-one' affairs must always cause the most intense inconvenience and often suffering to the public … How much longer are the inhabitants of the Isle of Wight going to remain inactive while they are cut off from the mainland after 7.30 on most days of the winter months? … Yours truly, RYDE RESIDENT.

———————◆———————

What constituted entertainment nearly 100 years ago would not necessarily find a place on the stage today. In the Empire Hall at Cowes* audiences were eager to gaze on the 23 inch high Lady Little …

May 24th, 1913
VISIT OF THE SMALLEST WOMAN IN THE WORLD
The enterprising management of the Empire Theatre, Cowes, of which Mr. A. Orton has charge, arranged an exceptionally attractive programme for this week. At great expense, a visit was arranged of Lady Little, a charming little dwarf, who, it is claimed, is the tiniest woman in the world. There were crowded attendances at all the performances to see this marvellous little woman, who, although over 20 years old, is only 23 inches in height and weighs 10½lb. She was attired in a handsome black velvet gown and displayed magnificent jewellery, the gifts of Royalty and other distinguished people. The dainty little woman showed amazing intelligence in answer to the questions of her chaperone, Mr. H. L. Hilliard, who caused much amusement by the announcement that Lady Little almost daily received offers of marriage. Since she had been at Cowes a gentleman had sent her a postcard offering her his

---

* Located in St Marys Road, Cowes, the Empire changed from a variety theatre to a cinema in the 1920s and today houses the workshops of Spencer Rigging.

hand and heart, and stating that he was prepared to sacrifice everything he had for her sake. He was earning 9s. a week! The Lilliputian lady sounded like a child and was afterwards carried round and introduced to the audience, shaking hands with hundreds of people. She will appear at the matinee this (Saturday) afternoon.

◆

The Freshwater, Yarmouth and Newport Railway Company had never operated their own rolling stock but instead had paid the I.W. Central to operate the line. By 1913 they were firmly of the opinion that the Central was overcharging them and also using underhand methods to escape carrying out necessary maintenance. They took back their line and opened their own station five minutes walk from the existing one*, and for the next 10 years Newport had not one, but two railway stations. It was not an ideal state of affairs for through-passengers who now had to manhandle their luggage out of the Central station, across a road, and along a public footpath to the new station ...

July 5th, 1913

FRESHWATER RAILWAY

The working agreement of the Isle of Wight Central Railway Company on the Freshwater railway-line terminated at midnight on Monday, and on Tuesday morning the Freshwater Railway Company commenced working their own line, the only difference in the service at present being that the trains run to and from the new railway platform at Newport. Fog-signals were exploded on the passing of the last 'Central' train from Freshwater, arriving at Newport at about 10.30 p.m., and the Freshwater Company's trains started on Tuesday morning under conditions which ensured fairly smooth working, having regard to the hurried way in which the arrangement had to be made for the change, the contractor's staff carrying out the work at the Newport Station having to work day and night on Sunday last, so that everything should as far as possible be ready for the alteration. In addition to the two fresh engines and a number of commodious and quite luxurious coaches which the Freshwater Company had imported for their service, a pleasing novelty in the way of a petrol rail-motor, to carry 12 passengers, has been introduced, and the trial trips run with it have proved pleasingly successful. Some inconvenience to through passengers has naturally been inseparable from such a hasty change, but this has been minimised as far as possible by the Freshwater management. This inconvenience can be largely removed by the substitution of an ordinary for the swing-gate at the entrance to the foot-path, which forms the principal means of communication for passengers between the Newport Stations, and in the interests of the travelling public the public authorities, who have control over this foot-path, should take steps to make this very necessary alteration, so that bicycles, perambulators, and passengers' luggage might be got through without having to be lifted over the gate. An indication of the attitude adopted by the Central Railway Company to the change is afforded by a public notice of that Company that passengers must find their own way from the old to the new stations at Newport! ...

---

* The main railway station was located roughly at the turnoff from Medina Way down into Holyrood Street, and the FY&N station was sited on Hunnycross Way opposite the filling station.

Perhaps to mark the centenary of the event, the Hampshire Telegraph printed an account of a duel which had taken place on the Island in 1813. In turn, the County Press had reprinted the account and some weeks later, the grandson of one those involved wrote to the editor providing even more details ...

July 26, 1913
AN ISLAND DUEL
Last week's *Hampshire Telegraph* contained the following interesting account of a fatal Island duel, taken from its issue of July 19th, 1813: The duel which took place yesterday se'ennight, near Newport, between Lieut. Blundell, of the 101st. Regiment, and Lieut. McGuire, of the 6th West Indian regiment, has terminated fatally. Lieut. Blundell died on Sunday noon last. The ball entered the right shoulder in an oblique direction, crossed the back, taking away part of the vertebrae and lodged near the armpit. Mortification, delirium, and death were the consequences. The deceased was the son of J. Blundell, Esq., a merchant in London. The dispute which led to the unfortunate meeting arose, we understand, in the following manner: About a fortnight since, the deceased took a young officer of his regiment to the cottage of his father-in-law (H.White, Esq., of this town) at Niton, to dine with him. In a few days afterwards, Lieut. McGuire, who, as we have stated, was present at the late marriage of Lieut. Blundell said to him, 'I see you can take friends to the Cottage', and for some days afterwards he took many opportunities to insult him, which Lieut. Blundell disregarded. At length McGuire wrote to the officers of Blundell's regiment, describing him as a ruffian and a coward. Upon which, five officers belonging to the regiment (all young Irish gentleman) proceeded to Niton, and sent to Lieut. Blundell, telling him that he had been so highly insulted that he must fight McGuire. This Lieut. Blundell evaded for some hours, but, between 11 and 12 at night, all parties having drank freely, he gave them a challenge to McGuire, with which at between one and two in the morning, they returned to Newport. Lieut. Blundell followed a few hours after to a spot near Carisbrooke Castle, and the duel took place. - On Monday and Tuesday an inquest was taken in the case by Thomas Sewell Esq., the Coroner for the Island, and a most respectable jury; after a full and minute investigation of the circumstances the Jury returned a verdict of Wilful Murder against Ensign McGuire, as principal in the first degree; Ensign Gilchrist, and Lieut. Hemmings, as principals in the second degree; and against Lieut. Kinsley and Ensign Slater, as accessories before the fact. The principals and seconds absconded immediately after the duel and none of them have yet been taken.

To the Editor of the County Press,
THE LAST DUEL FOUGHT IN THE ISLAND
Sir, - Lieut. Blundell and Ensign McGuire were stationed at Niton during the Napoleonic war. Lieut. Blundell had been recently married to a daughter of a Mr. Henry White, then residing at or near Niton. A trumpery quarrel arose between these two young officers about the borrowing of some clothes which one had lent the other, possibly for the purpose of attending the marriage ceremony ... It was alleged that McGuire had insulted Blundell and the officers of the regiment

insisted that he must challenge McGuire ... Neither of the parties concerned was anxious to fight, but their fellow officers insisted that they should do so. They met on the morning of Friday July 9, under the eastern wall of Carisbrooke Castle, adjacent to the bowling-green, in the dry ditch which runs parallel to the wall, an ideal spot for a duel, as neither combatant would have any advantage from the right ... Shots were exchanged without effect, Blundell's pistol having burst. The seconds then went up and conferred with their principals, but there is no record of the conversation. Blundell asked for one of McGuire's pistols. It was given him, and they fired again. Blundell missed McGuire, but McGuire's bullet struck Blundell on the right shoulder blade, and he fell. Gilchrist's servant went for a surgeon, and when he returned with one McGuire and the seconds were gone, but the other officers were still there. Blundell had shaken hands with McGuire and forgiven him before he went. He was then conveyed to Newport, where he died on Sunday following at the Wheatsheaf Inn. On his deathbed he said it was a bad business, that he did not want to fight, but his fellow officers made him do it. The inquest was held by Thomas Sewell (my grandfather) ... At the next Assizes held at Winchester, McGuire, Dillon, Gilchrist, and O'Brien were found guilty of wilful murder and sentenced to death. They were, however, eventually pardoned by the Prince Regent ...   For many years after the event the initials J.B. were annually cut in the turf on the spot where Blundell fell by a person, unknown, but supposed to be the widow. The place where the duel was fought was on the east face of an outwork between two bastions, in the dry ditch running parallel to the wall. I am indebted for particulars of the duel to the Rev. W. J. Stobart, vicar of Carisbrooke, and to Dr. G. B. Longstaff, of Putney, a great-nephew of Lieut. Blundell. - I am, Sir, yours truly, HENRY SEWELL. Bonchurch.

———————◆———————

THE WEEK'S NEWS

EXTRAORDINARY OCCURRENCE - Mr. G. Russell, of Gatehouse Farm, experienced an unusual incident this week. On Sunday one of his cows gave birth to a calf, under normal conditions, and on Wednesday the same cow presented him with another calf.

A NEWSPAPER GOSSIP says few people have a more gruesome hobby than King Alfonso of Spain; none other than gathering together the objects associated with the various attempts against his life. Among other items, he possesses the teat of a feeding-bottle, with which an attempt was made to poison him at the age of eight months, the walking-stick with which a discontented servant tried to brain him, pieces of the bomb thrown at him in Barcelona, the skeleton of one of the horses killed by the bomb attempt in the Rue de Rivoli, Paris, and fragments collected in the street after the explosion of the infernal machine hurled at the Royal carriage on his wedding day.

NED FAULKNER, an old-age pensioner, aged 82, who has to walk three miles every Friday into Aymestrey (Herefordshire) to draw his pension, is always accompanied by a pig, which follows him like a dog and lies down outside the Post-office while he transacts his business.

OLD ISLAND RACE CARDS - Mr. Henry Way, of Pyle, possesses an Island race card of July 31st, 1811. At this meeting there were only two races and the sports did not start until 4 o'clock. There seems to have been a fear of a plague of dogs as the card conveys the intimation that 'all dogs seen on the course will be shot'. Another notice strange to present-day ideas is that 'Any person seen cutting the ropes will be prosecuted' ...

A mushroom grown at Wareham, Dorset, measuring 47½ inches round and weighing 8½ pounds, was brought to Covent Garden on Monday.

———————◆———————

Newport Councillors, backed by local traders, were in favour of relocating the St. James's Square cattle market to a new site. A public enquiry was held* to hear evidence from all interested parties ...

December 13th, 1913

NEWPORT MARKET REMOVAL
IMPORTANT PUBLIC INQUIRY

Practically the whole of Tuesday was occupied by Mr. R. C. Maxwell, barrister-at-law and Local Board Inspector in hearing arguments to enable the Corporation to remove the cattle market now held in St. James's-square, Newport, to another site ... The Town Clerk opened his case and said that as far back as July 1904 the Local Government Board had held an inquiry as to a loan for asphalting the market, and had stated that they were strongly of the opinion that the market should be removed to a place which was not a public highway ... Mr. Frank E. Whitcher, mayor the previous year, said the market was held in one of the main through roads of the Island and with the development of motor and other traffic it was an increasingly serious thing to bar the use of the highway to traffic for ten hours every Tuesday. That meant the diversion of traffic round by St. Thomas's-square, an extra distance of some 300 yards ... Mr. Leonard Jordan, a member of the firm of Jordan and Stanley, wholesale and retail grocers and provision merchants, with one of their shops in St. James's-square, said that for over 20 years he had taken a prominent part in the agitation for the removal of the market ... The medical officer was instrumental in circularising the town with handbills asking the inhabitants to do their best to prevent the plague of flies. It was obvious that a large number of flies came into the town with the pigs and other animals and remained there after the departure of the animals from the market (laughter) ... not only was the thoroughfare closed to vehicular traffic, but the footways in the Market-square were blocked by children with sticks worrying the animals, and loafers and others, as well as dealers and traders whose business took them there, and customers of business premises were prevented from having free access to those premises.

Mr. Hiscock: You are a specialist on flies? (laughter).

---

* Before the Council decided on schemes which would have long lasting effects on the community they sometimes involved the public in the decision making process by way of public enquiries or polls. In 1907, for example, the Ward estate had offered Cowes Council first refusal on the purchase of West Hill House (since demolished). Cowes residents were consulted by a poll and voted overwhelmingly for their money not to be used in such a way. The Council obeyed.

Mr. Jordan: No ... With the exception of Thursday, which was the early closing day, Tuesday was the worst day for trade in his experience ... Mr. Sydney Wadham, managing director of Messrs. Wadham & Sons, of St. James's-square said he had been in the house furnishing business in premises facing the market-place for 28 years ... The market not only prevented their own vehicles from loading and discharging outside the shop, but also prevented customers in motor-cars and carriages from approaching. He was of the opinion that his firm lost a considerable amount of business that way ... James Linington, who said he had been the collector of tolls in the market for the past eight years, said the market was crowded seven or eight times a year perhaps, but at other times there was heaps of room (laughter).

The Town Clerk: What is the state of things when vehicles are being unloaded?

Witness: Rotten, sir (laughter). They wait until it is nearly 11 o'clock and then all come together, so it is their fault (laughter).

The Town Clerk: Is there are plenty of space for poultry now?

Witness: No, because we get the RSPCA people on to us. We used to put a dozen in a pen, but now we're not allowed to put more than six in, so the pens take up more room.

The Town Clerk: With regard to the pigs being brought in, is there any difference lately?

Witness: Yes. At one time you could get hold of a pig's tail and whip him out of the trap into the pen in no time (loud laughter). Now the 'cruelty man' says we have to lift it carefully out, and it takes three times as long to unload the pigs. They used to take hold of the pig's tail and out he would come, but that was cruelty now (renewed laughter)....If people came a little earlier it would get over a lot of the trouble but unfortunately in the Isle of Wight they are too slow (laughter).

Mr. Hiscock: I did not know they were painted quite so black as that.

Witness: They are, sir; I am an Isle of Wighter myself (loud laughter).

Mr. J. H. Linington, ironmonger, of St James's-square, said the removal of the market would be disastrous to trade and depreciate the value of property in the market and be detrimental to the prosperity of the town, and especially to his business. Edwin Carwardine, Lamb Inn, gave similar evidence. He might have to move his house if the market were moved ...

The Inspector said he had made a full note of everything, including the jokes, and he would give careful consideration to the matter.

1914

THE WEEK'S NEWS

How a cat frustrated the efforts of a well-known Island veterinary surgeon to complete the post-mortem examinations on a pig was related in an RSPCA case at the Newport Court Petty Sessions on Saturday by the veterinary surgeon concerned. He explained amid laughter that unfortunately his cat had eaten the portions which he had taken from the pig for further examination. Puss, happily, has survived the stolen meal.

According to a German scientist quoted by the Medical Press, a 150lb. human being is worth £1 11s. 3d. That is, in terms of his constituent elements. His fat is worth 10s. 5d.; of iron there is hardly enough to make a nail an inch long. There is sufficient lime to whitewash a pretty good-sized chicken-house. The phosphorus would be sufficient to put heads on 2,280 matches, and there is enough magnesium to make a pretty firework. The average human body contains enough albumin for one hundred eggs. There is possibly a teaspoonful of sugar and a pinch of salt.

Skunk will be very largely worn during the coming season, and will be found by reason of the increased demand to be somewhat more expensive than in previous years. There is also a notable tendency, one of the leading furriers says, to wear the un-dyed furs, such as red fox. Stoles will be larger than ever, and muffs show no tendency to return to the normal proportions of a few seasons ago. The most popular kind of muff will be that of velvet edged with fur to match the stole.

To the Editor of the Isle Of Wight County Press. WHY SHOOT IT? - Sir, - In a daily paper I read that a Nutcracker, a bird seldom seen in England, was shot at Hamstead, Isle of Wight. But why shoot it? It seems to be the fate, more or less, of every rare bird that visits our Island, at once to be shot. I am, Sir, yours truly, 'LOVER OF BIRDS'.

———————————◆———————————

Although electricity was transforming everyday life, it was more usual for it to be found in the workplace rather than at home, the cost still being far beyond the means of most people. Still a comparative novelty, a demonstration of its benefits could always command a large audience …

March 14th, 1914
ELECTRICAL EXHIBITION
The Isle of Wight Electric-light and Power Co. Ltd, held an exhibition at 24, Union-street last week with a view of showing the inhabitants of the Island the uses to which electricity can be put in the home for lighting, heating, and cooking. Amongst the domestic uses of electricity illustrated were vacuum cleaners, suitable for private houses as well as large establishments. Electrical radiators, convectors, and fires for heating rooms were also shown. The use of this power in the laundry was ably demonstrated by one of the employees of the Vectis Laundry, whose services were obtained by the courtesy of the manager. She showed how ironing can be cleanly and rapidly done by this means. In Ryde alone there are over 100 electric irons in successful use. Under the new system of charging for electricity the cost is under ½d. an hour if the current is kept running through the iron the whole time. The irons can be connected to the existing lamp-holders, and thus obviate the expense of extra wiring. The rooms were lighted throughout with metal filament lamps fitted with Holophane reflectors. The centre window contained a vacuum cleaner, from which the casing had been removed to show the simple little electric motor

which does the work. The feature of the window which attracted most attention was the food of various kinds which had been cooked in the electric oven. One of the latest designs of the high-efficiency metal filament lamps of 2,000 candle-power was suspended over the pavement. It is doubtful whether such a light had before been seen in Ryde. Mrs. Mole, of London, gold medallist and holder of many diplomas. demonstrated electric cooking to a large audience. The cooking was so excellent and apparently so simple that the general question put to Mrs. Mole was 'How much does it cost to cook by electricity?' She explained that as the Company supplied electricity for cooking at a low rate of 1½d. per unit under contract the cost was no more than by any other existing method. The quality of the cooking can be judged by the fact that there was keen competition to purchase all the food cooked ... The Electric-light Company are to be congratulated not only on their excellent demonstration in Union-street, but also for throwing open their works in Bennett-street to enable those interested to see how electricity is manufactured, and for the courteous manner in which the engineer and his assistants looked after the visitors.

———————◆———————

TOWN AND COUNTY NOTES

Steps will shortly be taken by the Royal Society for the Protection of Birds, with the active co-operation of the Trinity House authorities, to erect perches and racks on certain selected lighthouses on our coast to help preserve the lives of migratory birds. Such protective appliances already exist at St. Catherine's in the Isle of Wight. They were put up last year after the early spring migration had taken place. The apparatus is the invention of Professor Thijsse. It is his contention that a large proportion of the vast number of birds which perish at lighthouses do so, not through flying directly at the lantern, but by circling about it till they become exhausted and fall into the gallery of the lighthouse, or the sea.

Striking evidence of the remarkable increase in motor traffic was given at the monthly meeting of the Yarmouth Town Trust on Monday, March 23rd. The clerk (Mr. J. A. Cole) stated that nearly 700 motor-cars were landed or shipped at the quay during last year. Yarmouthians find that they have been treating the motorist too lightly in the matter of tolls when compared with other places in the island, and have consequently increased their charges. Probably the great majority of cars come into the Island via Yarmouth, as landing there is more convenient.

TEN YEARS DELAYED IN THE POST - On Tuesday morning, 30th June, a picture postcard, bearing the post-mark 'Ventnor, 8.p.m., 14th July, '04' was delivered at the Grapes Hotel, Sun-hill, Cowes. The distance from Ventnor to Cowes is about 15 miles, and the card has been nearly ten years in the post. The card, which is in splendid preservation, is addressed to Master Cyril Rohr, the son of a former landlord, and it was sent by J. Clements. There is no Cowes post-mark on the card. Mr. James Hopkins is the present landlord of the Grapes Hotel.

———————◆———————

Exactly a year earlier the steam-boat service from Portsmouth to Ryde had come in for criticism for its lack of passenger amenities (see page 152). A year on, a driver praises its performance as a car ferry ...

April 11th, 1914

MOTORISTS AND THE ISLAND

To the Editor of the Isle Of Wight County Press.

Sir, - I noticed a statement in a recent issue of your paper to the effect that the Southampton to Cowes route was better than Portsmouth to Ryde for the conveyance of motor cars. I have been a sailor for 15 years and a motorist for ten, and my views are exactly contrary to those expressed in your paper. I think that one can safely say that the great majority of cars going to the Island come from London or near there. The Ryde route is therefore shorter. I have crossed fairly frequently during the last four years, and have found that the average time of crossing, including loading and unloading is about 45 minutes, though I have known it to take an hour. The question of cost cannot be controversial, as the Ryde route is so much cheaper. As for ease of transport, I have never had the slightest difficulty on the Ryde route. The car is run straight onto the barge at Ryde, and straight off at Portsmouth. I have never used a horse, or heard of one being used, and I do not believe for an instant that one is kept. On the Cowes route my car was put on board a passenger steamer by a crane, and the ship had to be placed in position by using the engines - a very slow job. The car was placed so that bogies had to be used at Cowes to turn it round in order to disembark, which is very bad for the steering gear. It is also very slow. The only tarpaulin supplied was so hard that it was impossible to put it over paintwork. Excellent tarpaulins are provided on the Ryde route. I may add that I have no interest whatsoever in the Ryde service, pecuniary or otherwise. I enclose my card and remain, - Yours faithfully, J.P.G.

———————◆———————

Strange But True. - This joke appeared in the issue of April 11th, 1914 and so is approaching its 100th birthday ... Unless it is even older ...

MacBull: I shall be a gay grass-widower for the next two months; the wife's gone for a holiday to the West Indies.

O'Bear: Jamaica? -

MacBull: No, it was her own idea.

———————◆———————

Strange But True again ...

June 27th, 1914

EXTRAORDINARY INJURY BY A FISH

Mr. James Wheeler, of Providence House, Norton-green, Freshwater, is lying at his home suffering from a poisoned and lacerated leg, as the result of an extraordinary attack upon him by a fish. He and a friend named Birt Cotton were fishing with a draw net from the shore at Bouldnor on Saturday when they landed three large flat fish of the skate species, each weighing about half a hundredweight. The first two were secured, and Wheeler was pushing the other in to the shore with his boot when it struck at him with its tail, on which is a long horny spike, very sharp, and with serrated edges. This was thrust through trousers and underclothing into the calf of Wheeler's left leg with great force, penetrating about 3in., the serrated edges causing a very nasty wound as it was withdrawn. The wound bled profusely, and as it is known that such fish are highly poisonous, Wheeler's companion and Messrs. R. May and S. Flint, who were near, quickly rowed Wheeler, who was in agonies, to Yarmouth, where Dr. Thomarson cleansed and dressed the wound. Later he was removed home, and, attended by Dr. Hopkins, is progressing favourably, although probably he will be unable to use his leg for some three weeks. The prompt medical attendance, and possibly the fact that the spike had first to pass through the man's trousers, lessened the effect of the poison. It was evidently a sting-ray, sometimes called a fire-flare, described by one authority as one of the Trygonidæ family, the tail of which is armed in its middle portion with a sharp, flattened, bony spine, serrated on both sides, and capable of inflicting a very severe and dangerous wound. Amateur fishermen should beware of such fish, and as they were netted quite close to the shore they might possibly be a source of danger to bathers.

------------◆------------

The next morning was a Sunday and as Mr.Wheeler was beginning his recuperation, Archduke Franz Ferdinand of Austria was riding in a motorcade to City Hall in Sarajevo. A grenade was thrown at him by a would-be assassin and landed on his car but by good fortune it simply rolled off to explode under the following one, leaving him unharmed.

Whether he would be so lucky a second time may have crossed the Archduke's mind for a brief instant when just 35 minutes later he was shot dead by a second assassin who had a much better aim. As a direct result, Austria declared war on Serbia, which in turn led to the start of World War One a few weeks later.

Back at the County Press stories of dogs in distress could, for now, still find a place amongst the ever gloomier international news …

July 11th, 1914
A TOUCHING DOG STORY
Miss Violet Kirby, of Hazelbrae, who was for some time local secretary of the RSPCA, has a Scotch terrier which has survived a wonderful experience. In company with another dog it has been in the habit of hunting for rabbits on the cliffs near St. Lawrence. Last Sunday Miss Kirby left the dogs to their sport and returned home. On Monday the younger of the animals came back to the house in a very dilapidated condition and showing evidence of distress. A search was thereupon instituted for the other dog, but all efforts were unavailing up to Thursday morning when a postman named Hatcher heard moaning near the cliff. The spot is one of the most dangerous along the Undercliff, and is known as 'High Hat'. Two working men named Charles Sweetingham and William Downer obtained a hundred-foot rope, and Sweetingham was let down over the cliff to search for the animal. He was on the point of being pulled up when he heard a very faint moan and discovered the animal practically dead in a

rabbit burrow with just its face and the top of its head peeping out. He had literally to cut the dog out of the hole. It was nearly dead; its fore-legs were stripped of flesh and flies had eaten its head and face nearly raw. The poor thing has been given food judiciously, and is now well on the way to complete recovery, after being four days without food or water. Sweetingham and Downer have been generously recompensed by Miss Kirby.

———————◆———————

Although no one knew it at the time, Miss Kirby's dog had made history in its own little way for it was to be the last time for four years that space would be found for gentle stories of domestic pets in peril; more serious issues were soon to fill the pages of the County Press. In the days following, Germany declared war on France and Russia. Pre-existing alliances between different countries came into play and as a result Britain declared war on Germany.

For the next four years the County Press was almost exclusively given over to reporting the war, only the Towns and Villages columns being sacrosanct. All other local news was subject to either appearing in a shortened form or not appearing at all. When the August 1st edition of the paper appeared, Britain was just three days away from that declaration of war.

The County Press prepared its readers for what was to come with prophetic and eerie accuracy ...

August 1st, 1914
THE INTERNATIONAL CRISIS
Recognising the grave possibilities of the situation, we announced on Sunday morning at the head office of the *County Press* and at several of our branch offices that the Serbian reply to the demands of the Austrian Government was considered unsatisfactory. Events during the week have developed with alarming rapidity, until yesterday the reports came to hand that Russia, Germany, and Holland were mobilising, and the most pessimistic telegrams stated that well-nigh the last hope of averting the most disastrous war in history had gone.

———————◆———————

Events moved quickly and had an immediate effect on the Island, Cowes in particular ...

August 8th, 1914
THE ISLAND AND THE INTERNATIONAL CRISIS
THE WAR AND COWES WEEK
YACHTING FESTIVAL ABANDONED
The extremely critical European situation caused an abandonment of the Cowes-week, which would otherwise have commenced on Monday. The falling through of the great yachting Festival, which, in all the circumstances was inevitable, of course caused the keenest disappointment in yachting circles and to the inhabitants of Cowes in particular. The decision to abandon the regatta, which was announced on Sunday afternoon, following the receipt at the Royal Yacht Squadron of the message from the King, caused little surprise. With the

The Cowes-week from Town Quay pontoon, 1906. (*See page 163.*) Photograph by Alfred Arnold.

prospect of war increasing hourly, the absence of several racing yachts, the recalling of naval and military officers to their ships and regiments, and the calling up of many Naval Reserve men serving on the yachts, there were grave doubts on Saturday as to the advisability of holding the regatta ... The grim topic of war was on everyone's lips, and it was impossible to devote attention to yachting and other pleasures usually associated with the Cowes Festival ... As can readily be imagined the abandonment of the regatta week, which is quite unprecedented, was a very serious blow to the town and the loss to the tradespeople is incalculable.

EXODUS OF GERMAN VISITORS

The outbreak of hostilities on the Continent will mean a serious loss of visitors to Island resorts. On Monday evening, at very short notice, the Kaiser's youngest son, Prince Joachim, who was spending a holiday in Shanklin, as he usually does during the summer, received an urgent summons to rejoin his regiment of Prussian Guards. The Prince left the Royal Spa Hotel, where he had been staying, in a motor-car, and hastened to Ryde Pier where he was able to catch the late boat to Portsmouth. On Wednesday several German families hurriedly left Ventnor. There has been a wholesale clearance of Austrian waiters from local hotels.

A new column, 'The Island and the War' made its first appearance. Like the items headed 'Town and County Notes', these are compilations drawn from more than one issue ...

THE ISLAND AND THE WAR

GERMAN WITHOUT A PERMIT - At the Newport Police-station on Wednesday Victor Ubinger, German hotel employee, formerly of Ventnor, was remanded till today (Saturday) on a charge under the Aliens' Registration Order of failing to obtain the necessary permit to remain in the Island. P.S. Evans stated that he arrested the accused at Newport on Tuesday after he had been told by the police at Ventnor the previous day that he must obtain a permit. The Sergeant said that prisoner was in rather difficult circumstances, and it was in his own interests to be remanded for a few days.

BIG CAPTURE OF GERMANS OFF YARMOUTH - On Saturday afternoon the Red Star liner Lapland, flying the Belgian flag, came down the Solent and anchored off Yarmouth. On Monday at about midday, a government tug was seen to approach her, and later it was learned that 120 Germans among the crew had been transferred to the tug under an armed escort. These prisoners of war were conveyed to Gosport, where they were incarcerated in a fort.

A young lady who was sketching the river scene at the Newport Quay on Monday afternoon was taken to the Railway-station by soldiers on duty at the railway-bridge over the Quay, but later she was allowed to return to her sketching.

The prisoners from the Camp Hill Prison who have been assisting in the fortification works on the east coast of the Island were cheered by passengers as they left the train at Dodnor to return to Camp Hill on Saturday.

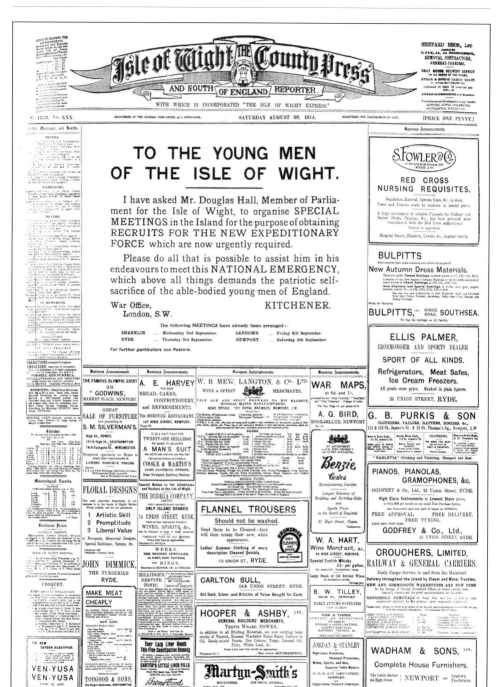

Isle of Wight County Press
AND SOUTH OF ENGLAND REPORTER.

WITH WHICH IS INCORPORATED "THE ISLE OF WIGHT EXPRESS."

No 1559. Vol. XXX.   REGISTERED AT THE GENERAL POST-OFFICE AS A NEWSPAPER.   SATURDAY AUGUST 29, 1914.   REGISTERED FOR TRANSMISSION BY POST.   [PRICE ONE PENNY.]

TO THE YOUNG MEN OF THE ISLE OF WIGHT.

I have asked Mr. Douglas Hall, Member of Parliament for the Isle of Wight, to organise SPECIAL MEETINGS in the Island for the purpose of obtaining RECRUITS FOR THE NEW EXPEDITIONARY FORCE which are now urgently required.

Please do all that is possible to assist him in his endeavours to meet this NATIONAL EMERGENCY, which above all things demands the patriotic self-sacrifice of the able-bodied young men of England.

War Office,
London, S.W.

KITCHENER.

The following MEETINGS have already been arranged:—

SHANKLIN — Wednesday 2nd September.   SANDOWN — Friday 4th September.
RYDE — Thursday 3rd September.   NEWPORT — Saturday 5th September.

For further particulars see Posters.

WARNING TO THE PUBLIC - The Press Bureau warn the public against placing the slightest reliance in the many rumours current daily regarding alleged victories or defeats and the arrival of wounded men or disabled ships in this country. They are, without exception, baseless. The public may be confident that any news of successes or reverses to British arms will be communicated officially without delay.

Much anxiety is felt by Mrs. Leftwich, of High-street, Cowes, for the safety of her daughter Miss Edith Leftwich, who is a governess in a German family at Munich.

RYDE - ANOTHER PUBLIC-HOUSE CLOSED - Acting under the orders of the general officer commanding the Portsmouth and I.W. Defences another public house has been closed from November 24th, for 14 days, for having sold a bottle of intoxicants to a soldier contrary to orders.

SEAVIEW - A TORPEDO ASHORE - On Saturday morning a live torpedo, some 20ft. in length, washed in opposite the Yacht Club and caused considerable excitement. Mr. Richard Newell waded into the sea waist-deep and steered it clear of the rocks, and eventually it was brought ashore and lodged in Mr. Newell's boat store.

On the North sea in the early hours of September 20th, three cruisers, HMS Aboukir, Cressy and Hogue were sunk by German submarines with heavy loss of life. A subsequent Naval Board of Inquiry found that a contributory cause was neglect on the part of all the senior British officers involved, particularly by their failure to follow instructions to zigzag on their course. A survivor's account appeared in the County Press ...

September 26th, 1914

LOSS OF THREE BRITISH CRUISERS
TORPEDOED BY GERMAN SUBMARINES
HOW ENGLISH SAILORS CAN DIE

... A stoker of the Cressy says: 'We knew the old ship was done for, and she was settling slowly down on her side. The gunfire slackened owing to the utter impossibility of firing in that position, and rifles were served out to some of us in order that we might aim at the Germans if they came to the conning towers of their boats. All of us took off our clothes, for we could see it would have to be a swim or nothing. The commander and officers walked about among the men, calm and cool as you like, talking to us as if nothing had happened. The boat seemed to take a long time to sink, but suddenly turned right over on her side and some of us scrambled up on that. The last I saw of the commander was when he was walking about on the side of his ship, laughing, with nothing on but his cap. I believe he was saved. A little way off there was an English trawler rescuing some of our fellows. A positive hero the skipper of the boat was. It was a Lowestoft boat. As soon as he got some of our men out of the sea the Germans tried to torpedo him. But he never stopped his work ... nothing was too dangerous for him. The Cressy went down about three-quarters of an hour after she was first hit. There was a raft floating alongside as she went down, and I got on that; there were a dozen of us on it in all, but we found it was still fastened to the Cressy, and we had to get off it quite quick. Only two of us are alive now. I swam about for a long time, holding on to bits of wreckage, but every now and then a wave would come up behind and whack a bit of timber in your neck. Nasty, that was. And then there were the dead bodies, hundreds of them, floating around'. He paused here, then brightened up suddenly and dragging something out of his pocket, said 'See what I have saved - my stump of clay pipe. I had it in my mouth all the time. I'm never going to part with that now. But the Germans, know what they did? Why, when we were in the water swimming for our lives, they came up to the conning towers of their boats and laughed at us. Yes, jeered. I wish I'd had a rifle then. I'd have fired at them somehow. But the best thing I saw was the coolness of a little cadet. Not more than 14 he looked. He drifted near me, he and a seaman clinging with their hands and elbows on the same bit of wood. I never seen anything so calm as that lad. He was talking to the seaman with him. 'Well' he says 'we've got to carry on like this, and if we die we shall die game'. and with that he begins to talk about everyday things on the sunken ship. 'What's the new chief engineer like'? he says, and chats about little incidents in the mess. Only 14, a little light-haired boy. I hope he was saved ...

Within a day of declaring war on France, Germany invaded Belgium and then several days later, France itself, and in just a few short weeks British and German soldiers, sometimes less than a hundred yards apart, were shelling each other from cold, muddy trenches. Events had moved so fast that at one point the French Government were forced to hire taxis to take soldiers from Paris to the battlefields of Marne.

Within weeks of the war starting, the first letters home began to arrive from the front line. Initially at least, the letters appear to have been uncensored and the County Press were to print page after page of remarkable first-hand accounts of Islanders' experiences in the trenches. The quality of the letters is such that it was difficult to decide which ones to leave out; they all make compelling reading. To see grainy images of the war on a television screen is one thing, but reading the actual words of young men from the Isle of Wight writing first-hand of their grim, fragile lives is quite another ...

October 24th, 1914
INTERESTING LETTERS FROM A YOUNG ISLAND SOLDIER
THE 'COUNTY PRESS' AT THE FRONT

Lance Corpl. Jack Ryall, son of ex-Police Sergt Ryall, of the Island Constabulary, who has been through several of the hottest engagements at the Front with the 1st King's Royal Rifles, writes to his mother at Cowes: 'I am still pegging away and living in hope. We have been having some rather unpleasant experiences lately. I expect you read all about our latest battle, which I think was bigger than the one at Mons. The German artillery fire has been the only success. Their rifle fire has been badly directed. In our last battle I had a nice firing position, and in case of a retirement I was practically safe. The Germans came up a little way and ran back in a wood again in dozens. As soon as they showed doubt we gave them such a reception, which they could not get over and then their machineguns made it bad for us and played a nice little game. I counted five myself within 200 yards, but their shots appeared to fall very short, which was all the better for us ... I received your letters safe and two County Press. Smoking gives you a lot of comfort when you are in the trenches with only shots and shells flying about. I am very well up to the present. The Germans have not moved from here yet, but before we finish our tour in France we are either going to make sausage meat of them or wait until November 5th and burn them. Whilst I have been out here I have seen the finest, and also the saddest, sights of my life' ... Under date October 9th, he writes 'As we have been rather quiet during the daytime with the Germans, I thought about going over to the trenches and offering them a few of my chocolates and getting a light for one of my smokes, as I never had a match. You see some amusing incidents during service out here. The Germans were shelling a field opposite us for an unknown reason, for there were only a few dead cows there' ... Writing again on October 13 he says: 'I had a letter from Aunt Charlotte, and she said 'Poor little Jack. I don't expect you can smile now like you used to'. She ought to have seen me pick a bold German over for her reply. Ryall had a smile like a Cheshire cat. I will just tell you how it happened ... We were bobbing down enjoying a nice piece of bread and jam. Presently we looked up and actually saw a German standing right up out of his trench. It was very brave of him, but I had a 'peck' at him together with a sergeant. I could not swear we brought him down, but in any case he shifted from his place remarkably quick ... Sometimes I think that if I come through safely I must have 14 lives, but I have been very lucky in all these big scraps up till now, and if I stop one in a bit of a squabble it will be very hard lines, I think. Remember me to little Will and tell him not to worry about Kaiser Bill. When we go into Berlin we will smoke him out. If we should get on the move again I shall be able to write only occasionally, but do drop me a line, also the County Press.

In the same issue an editorial reflected on the Kaiser's sincerity ...

It is now quite evident that when, only a few years ago, the Kaiser visited England, he was plotting war against us while professing friendship for us. Sweet words were on his lips, but in his heart was bitter hate ... It is doubtful whether the world can show at the present time a more treacherous creature, and I would venture to suggest that his effigy at Madame Tussaud's should be labelled 'The German Judas' and put into the Chamber of Horrors.

It seems the first death of an Islander in uniform took place not on the battlefields of France but in a freak accident in St. James Square, Newport when an electrical spark ignited gas in underground cable ducts. Ironically, he had just been declared medically unfit for service ...

October 24th, 1914

STARTLING STREET EXPLOSION AT NEWPORT
TERRIBLE DEATH OF A TERRITORIAL BANDSMAN

On Saturday night the residents of Newport and crowds of shoppers were startled by a terrific explosion in the vicinity of the Market-place, and not unnaturally, some in the streets, including several soldiers, at first imagined that the capital of the Island was being made the object of an airship raid. They were even cries of 'Zeppelin' and shopkeepers in the localities complied with a suggestion made by soldiers that they should put out their lights. One or two gazing skyward even went so far as to declare that they had seen an aircraft. But all this proved to be imagination, as it was soon discovered that the explosion was not due to an enemy's bomb, but arose in the inspection chamber* under the electric-light standard outside the front door of the old County Press office, facing the Market at the junction of Pyle-street and St. James's-street, and, unfortunately, it had fatal consequences. The explosion occurred soon after 9 and was plainly heard within a radius of about a mile. The streets were very busy at the time, many people were in the Market and passing up and down St. James's-street near the scene, and several had narrow escapes. Those in the vicinity were greatly alarmed and rushed away from the danger, some falling in the scramble, whilst another crowd surged up through the Market to see what had happened. The electric light in a portion of the district was defective, and it was when a fresh fuse was put in at the pillar-feeder in St James's-square to remedy this that the explosion occurred. According to eyewitnesses, Bandsman Edward Belcher, of the 'Princess Beatrice's' Isle of Wight Rifles, son of Mrs Belcher, a widow of Lower High-street, was walking up Pyle-street at the time and arrived close by the electric-light inspection chamber at the time of the explosion, which blew high into the air the heavy concrete iron-framed cover of the chamber. This cover went well above the roof of the old County Press office, and whilst deceased was staggering under the shock of the explosion and probably looking round to see what had happened, the descending cover struck him on the head and shoulder and crushed him into the gutter. Several soldiers close by went to his assistance but unfortunately life was extinct ... The deceased was on the point of leaving the Territorials, having been certified medically unfit for further service, and he proposed to return home from Sandown on the following day ...

---

* Explosive sewer gases find their way into cable ducts. To this day contractors about to work in manholes or underground ducts must carry out a test for the presence of gas before starting work.

The war began to affect everyday Island life just 12 weeks after it started. An un-named correspondent recorded in some detail what it meant for the inhabitants of Ryde ...

November 21st, 1914

RYDE IN WAR TIME

A pen-picture of Ryde in war time would have to be very comprehensive indeed to embrace all that is going on around us. In common with the rest of the Island we have been mixed up, so to speak, with the material effects of the war from its very commencement. These might have assumed the form of minor inconveniences at first, such as the stopping of late boats, a very interrupted communication with the mainland, the cessation of the band performances in the Esplanade-gardens, and so forth; but as time went on our association was hardly enviable. Visitors left the town in hordes, and others were persuaded not to come; in fact our season was crippled, and today, after 15 weeks or so, circumstances are heaped upon us in such volume that it is utterly impossible to divert our thoughts from the war ... Our blinds have to be drawn at certain times, and there are other things we have to do in this direction if we wish to keep the borough constable on the right side of the front door ... One may suppose that the enforced lowering of lights in business establishments is hardly appreciated, but it has to be tolerated. And generally speaking the tradespeople vie with one another in inventing various devices to confine the light to their wares, and so comply with the order. A red shade over the light is now the most favoured and is a great improvement on the green, which took upon itself a particularly nasty habit of giving bilious appearance to all those folk on inspection bent. If our half-lighted streets fail to bring things sufficiently home to us we have the search-lights operated from the mainland, playing havoc with the pattern of the wall-paper in our bed-rooms throughout the night ... Those who shop in the morning have their attention temporarily diverted by the appearance of the latest news outside the County Press office ... The casual frequenter of the Pier has the war on the sea brought home to him whenever he fancies a stroll in that direction as torpedo-boats frequently put in for provisions and water. The hospital-ships proceeding to and from Netley serve to remind one of the horrors of the whole thing, and closer association in this respect is provided by the landing of wounded for treatment at the several hospitals in our midst ... In the early part of the summer a ratepayer in the borough wrote to the Council complaining that the trees in St. Thomas's Churchyard had grown so high that the public in certain streets of the town were unable to see the clock on the Town-hall. It is surely pardonable to wonder whether this same person has taken it upon himself to complain to the military authorities now that the town clock is in total darkness at night ... In the ordinary times the faddist, the crank, and the grumbler will wage a battle royal over things of this category, yet in these days he deems it wise and consistent to hold his peace. It's an ill wind. Of course there are other far more forcible reminders that war is being waged without; the casualty list, unfortunately, is all that is needed to bring that home to us ...

G. R.

RECRUITING FOR THE ARMY VETERINARY CORPS.

2000 MEN are now **REQUIRED** for the **ARMY VETERINARY CORPS.**

Candidates for enlistment should be men of steady character, who have been accustomed to horses, and who are able to ride.

Pay will be at ordinary Army Veterinary Corps rates.

Age limits will be from 40 to 47 years.

Suitable men under 40 years of age may also be accepted who are ineligible for combatant units.

All standards of height and chest measurement will be waived provided men are organically sound and fit to perform the work required.

Separation Allowance will be issuable under the usual Army conditions.

Apply **Central Recruiting Office,**
Woodleigh, Castle Road, Newport, I.W.

1915

The County Press accounts of life at the Front are a gift to military historians and probably deserve a book of their own. Far from the details of war being kept back from the public, the fact is that soldiers' letters home gave full and frank accounts of life on the battlefield; probably more so than the authorities would have liked sometimes. Here, the sad and surreal Christmas truce of 1914 is recounted by a Newport soldier …

January 2nd, 1915
NEWPORT MAN AND CHRISTMAS TRUCE IN THE TRENCHES
BRITISH AND GERMAN SOLDIERS FRATERNISE AND EXCHANGE GIFTS

Rifleman Mallard, of the machine-gun section of the Rifle Brigade, in a letter dated December 26th, from the trenches to his parents at Newport, says: 'About half-past 4 on Christmas-eve we heard music, and gathered that the Germans had abandoned their trenches; but our artillery spoilt the effect by dropping a couple of shells right in the centre of them, so you can guess what became of the band, for we did not hear it again. We were wondering if the Germans would agree to a couple of days peace, and as soon as it was dark we were surprised to see Christmas trees stuck on the top of their trench, lit up with candles, and all the men sitting on the trench. So, of course, we got out of ours and exchanged a few remarks with the Germans and invited them to come over and have a drink and a smoke but we did not like to trust each other at first. After a bit, however, three of our officers started to go over to meet three German officers who were approaching them, their way being directed by searchlight from the German lines. It made a fine picture to see those six officers meet between the two lines, shake hands, and smoke each others' cigarettes in the glow of the searchlight. All the boys gave a tremendous cheer and became quite excited over it. After a bit the officers came back, bringing with them souvenirs from the Germans. Then it was the turn of the troops, and they swarmed over to meet each other, shaking hands and exchanging nick-nacks. I noticed that some of the Germans were using British-made matches. We took them out some tea and cocoa which they eagerly accepted, but not till we had drunk some of it. They are very 'cute' boys; most of them very young. We agreed not to do any shooting until midnight on Christmas night. Our going over to them quite altered their opinion of the English soldier, and now they think a lot more of us. On Christmas Day we agreed to play a football match and we got a football, but their colonel would not let them play, so we had a bit of a game on our own … In the evening we gave each other sing-songs till about 10 p.m. That ended our Christmas of 1914, which was very enjoyable, considering the circumstances. Just after midnight we could hear the sound of bullets as they hit the ground, so we knew the game had started again, and our artillery set the ball rolling this morning … I have a couple of cigars given to me by a German yesterday which I am keeping for father'.

---

* British commanders vowed that such a truce would never take place again. To ensure there would be no repeat performance, in subsequent years artillery bombardments were ordered every Christmas Eve to keep the men occupied.

The letters the soldiers were writing home continued to provide graphic details of day-to-day life in the trenches …

January 9th, 1915
SANDOWN MAN'S TRIALS IN THE TRENCHES
Mr. Fred Thomas, son of Mr. and Mrs. Thomas of St. Leonards, Leed-street, Sandown, is serving with the 8th Royal Irish Hussars, 3rd Cavalry Brigade of the Indian Expeditionary Force. In a letter to his parents he says: 'We have just come out of the trenches again. It was something cruel. I was very nearly perished when we came out. I had a sleep and when I woke up the next morning my feet were like a pair of boxing gloves. They were swollen up to about six times their ordinary size … It is something awful out here to see the slaughter and destitution wherever you go - homes completely wrecked all over the place and all the dead lying about as well … I didn't have much of a Christmas. We didn't come out of the trenches until a couple of days before Christmas. On Christmas-eve I slept in an old barn on some straw, and I was jolly thankful to get it. PS. I have just been in the trenches again. One poor fellow in the next trench said he would have one last shot at the Germans before he was relieved. A bullet split his head open. Another one was taken out of the trench with both legs and arms blown off by a shell'.

———————◆———————

A whole world away, nestling in the peace and quiet of the back of the Wight, the bird-rests fitted at St. Catherine's lighthouse two years ago* were proving a success …

January 23rd, 1915
BIRD-RESTS AT ST. CATHERINE'S LIGHTHOUSE
The chief officer at St. Catherine's Lighthouse makes the following report as to the use of the bird-rests and perches erected by the Royal Society for the Protection of Birds … 'These birds, attracted by the bright light of the lantern, flutter around it until, dropping down from exhaustion, they perish in the gallery or lost in the sea … The use of the perches had been great enough to intimate that there is never likely to be such another night's destruction as that in April 1913, when the representatives of the Society were shown the remains of 500 small travellers from overseas who had fluttered out their small lives in the night and had been picked up dead in the Lighthouse gallery … They were undoubtedly of value in the saving of bird life, as the number killed was small compared with the quantity killed during migrations before the perches were erected … They are still in position and have been made use of considerably by the birds previous to their migration flight southwards'.

———————◆———————

* The perches are no more. Up until the 1980s at least, floodlights playing on the base of the tower encouraged the birds to land safely on the grass there.

To the irritation of the War Department, accounts of the Christmas truce continued to appear in provincial newspapers right across Britain, the County Press included. ...

January 30th, 1915

RYDE MAN SHAKES HANDS WITH GERMANS ON CHRISTMAS DAY

Pte. Alan P. Conacher, 2nd Battalion, Seaforth Highlanders has written to his parents. Under the date of December 26th he says: 'After lunch we were very much surprised to see the Germans leave their trenches with no arms or equipment and come halfway to meet us. They gave us cigars and we in return gave them cigarettes, &c. They shook hands with us, wished us a merry Christmas and asked us not to fire for three days. We told them we would not if they did not; up to the time of writing they have kept their word. I had a chat with some of them, who spoke English very well. They said they were fed up with the war and wished it was over. Some of them were very fine men; they would pat you on the back and say 'Good comrades, very good British soldier'. Some of their officers were there and exchanged greetings with our officers. But fancy, in the greatest war in creation, going out to have a chat with the enemy and the next day we may be killing each other ...'

———————◆———————

One of the worst fates that could befall a single girl during these years was to become pregnant. An illegitimate child could bring shame and ruin, not to mention poverty, and led to many scared and unhappy young girls going to desperate lengths either to prevent a birth or to conceal it once it had taken place. The discovery of tiny bodies concealed in all manner of places was a common occurrence; over the years they had been discovered in attics, copses, shoeboxes and paperbags. This time the hiding place was the railway tunnel at Ryde ...

February 13th, 1915

BABY'S BODY FOUND IN RYDE RAILWAY TUNNEL
BELIEVED TO HAVE BEEN THROWN OUT OF RAILWAY CARRIAGE WINDOW

A gruesome discovery was made by a Joint Companies' foreman-platelayer whilst walking through the tunnel at Ryde on Sunday morning. About 300 yards from the entrance he noticed a bundle lying in the permanent way. Closer investigation proved it to be the dead body of a baby, that of a male child about 14 days old. It was well-developed, and quite decently clothed. It is conjectured that the body was thrown alive from the window of a railway carriage between 12.30 and 9 p.m. on Saturday ... The inquest jury returned a verdict of 'Wilful murder against some person or persons unknown'.

(Four weeks later, Annie Jolliffe of Yafford, 'a domestic servant', was charged with wilful murder and bailed to appear at Winchester in June, see page 176).

———————◆———————

Charles Seely, later to become Sir Charles, had grown wealthy as the owner of coal mines in Nottinghamshire. He moved to the Island in 1859 and purchased Brook House in the village, along with most of Brook and Mottistone. Public spirited, and the founder of the Seely Library service, he left just over a million pounds when he died, and a large estate ...

May 1st, 1915
PROPOSED SALE OF THE SEELY ESTATE IN THE ISLAND
We are authorised to announce that one important sequel to the lamented
death of Sir Charles Seely, Bart., will be the sale of the extensive family estate in
the Island, with the exception of that portion in the Brook area, which will be
retained together with Brooke House and the new mansion on Brook Hill. As is
well known, this is the largest landed estate in the Island, consisting of large and
valuable farms in the south, west, and centre of the Wight, and comprising an
area of nearly 13,000 acres ... Whilst the sale will doubtless afford fortunate
tenants of the estate an opportunity of becoming their own landlords, there will
be a feeling of general regret at the severance of the happy relations between a
generous landlord and tenants which for so long have obtained on this model
Island estate. None will regret the coming change more than the many
labourers on the estate, who owe so much of their improved conditions to the
ever kind and generous solicitude of both the late Sir Charles and his esteemed
father.

———————————◆———————————

The trial of Annie Jolliffe took place at Winchester ...

June 19th, 1915
MANSLAUGHTER AT RYDE
Annie Jolliffe, 23, domestic servant, was indicted for having feloniously killed
Charles Rowland Jolliffe at Ryde on February 6th.
In presenting the facts of the case to the jury, Mr. Harris, prosecuting, said
prisoner gave birth to a son at a Salvation Army institution in London on
January 26th ... and left to return to her home at Yafford on February 6th ... On
arrival at Ryde Pier she was stopped by P.C. Hodges, acting as alien officer, and
questioned as to her nationality. The officer noticed that she was carrying a
baby. On arrival at Newport she met Mr. Sprake, the Chale carrier, who knew
her well and she was not then carrying any baby. On the following (Sunday)
morning ... the body was found in the tunnel. Counsel proceeded to say that the
child was only slightly injured, and in the opinion of the doctor, death was due
to shock and exposure ... Mr. Emanuel then called the accused, who said that
her parents had lived at Yafford for a long time. When they heard of her trouble
they were very cross. She went to London in December, and before returning in
February she wrote home asking her people to meet her at Portsmouth
Harbour. As they were neither at Portsmouth or Ryde she became very much
upset, and scarcely knew what she was doing. She fed the baby at Portsmouth,
and when going through the tunnel at Ryde dropped it out of the train, hoping
that someone would find it and bring it up. She did not take it home because
her parents did not like the idea ... Mr. Emanuel made a very impassioned
speech to the jury ... There were very sad circumstances about the case - first
the unhappiness at home when the girl knew she had fallen, being sent to
London among complete strangers, and also the non-arrival of her parents to
meet her when the trouble was over. The last was a terrible disappointment to
her, and having reason to believe that her parents were still angry with her she

could not contemplate the serious results of dropping the child out of the train. The fact that she had fed it just previously showed very strongly that she did not wish to kill it. Then she did what hundreds of others in similar circumstances did - told untruths. Counsel pointed out that when all the sad circumstances were considered it must be obvious that her mind was not normal at the time, and therefore she should not be convicted on the capital charge.

The jury found her guilty of manslaughter, and His Lordship passed sentence of 12 months in the second division.

———————————◆———————————

Mr. Floyd was an East Cowes Town Councillor.* He was an outspoken man who spoke freely about what he felt was the truth, and the reports of the Council meetings over the years contain many of his frequent outbursts. Always keen to have his opinion heard, he was no shrinking violet and did not suffer fools gladly. Unfortunately, neither did his fellow Councillor, Captain Derham ...

June 29th, 1915

MR. FLOYD AND CAPT. DERHAM

A DISORDERLY SCENE. - The General Purposes Committee reported that Capt. Derham had not yet been able to obtain a suitable boat for the bathing place. Capt. Derham said he did not know of a suitable boat anywhere...he knew of a 13ft. boat, but they wanted £10 for it. He did not think there was any chance of getting a suitable boat. Mr. Floyd said that to the best of his belief that matter had been put in the wrong hands.

Capt. Derham: I believe it has.

Mr. Floyd was confident a boat could be bought. There were plenty advertised for sale at Freshwater from 10ft. to 16ft. in length.

Capt. Derham: Do you think I am going to Freshwater to look for a boat?

Mr. Floyd: If a member is asked to find a suitable boat he will to try to do so.

Capt. Derham: I have done so. If you think I am going to be such a —— fool as to wander all over the country looking for a boat, you never made a bigger mistake in your life.

Mr. Floyd: If I was such a pig as you ——.

Capt. Derham: What! You call me a pig, you——.

Leaving his seat, Capt. Derham picked up a chair and, holding it over his head, threatened to strike Mr. Floyd, saying, ' If you don't withdraw and apologise, I will hit you over the head with this'. Taking the cushion from the chair he threw it at Mr. Floyd. The latter also picked up a chair, with the evident intention of retaliation, and an ugly scene threatened. Members rose from their seats and for a few moments there was a scene of intense excitement. Capt. Derham, holding the chair over his head in a threatening manner, persisted in his demand for a withdrawal of the expression 'pig' and an apology from Mr. Floyd ...

The Chairman (to Mr. Floyd): Will you withdraw the word 'pig?'

Mr. Floyd: I will willingly withdraw. I was not alleging that Capt. Derham was a pig.

---

* Mr. Floyd, after 40 years service as a councillor, was convicted in 1917 of dealing in stolen scrap metal and was jailed for six months. On release he attended the next available meeting but was immediately forced to resign by the other members, Captain Derham included.

At the end of the meeting Mr. Floyd and Capt. Derham crossed swords again while discussing another item on the agenda. Eventually the meeting closed.

Mr. Floyd: We have come here to do business.
The Chairman: Not for a lot of twaddle (laughter).

August, 1915
THE WEEK'S NEWS
ILLEGITIMACY - The Chairman of the Local Government Board said a lot had been written and said about war babies, but he was very pleased to say that they were not suffering from that epidemic in the Island. There had only been 16 illegitimate children born in the Island during the last quarter. The average for a number of years would be considerably over 12. - Mr. Minter said that the report was very satisfactory, having regard to the remarks which had been made. - The Chairman: When you consider the thousands of military men stationed here during last year, it is very satisfactory (hear, hear).

VILLAGE NOTES - We have received a complaint that in one Island village an 'apparently strong and healthy man, with no ties or dependents', has been engaged as an enumerator when 'his fit and proper vocation should be fighting for his country'.

BRIGHT SUNSHINE - Of the 180 sun stations in the British Isles only about half a dozen have had as much sunshine as Totland Bay this year, with its 1,150 hours.

COWES - During August there have been between 70 and 80 patients at the King Edward's Convalescent Home for Officers at Osborne House.

The tourist trade on the Island had always depended in part on German visitors and their absence was having a pronounced effect on visitor numbers, particularly in Ventnor. An article in the Daily Mail reflecting on this fact and also the Kaiser's apparent intentions for the Island was reprinted in the County Press. It was written by Charles Hands,* a famous London journalist who knew Ventnor well ...

August 21st, 1915
'AS OTHERS SEE US'
THE ISLAND WANTED BY THE KAISER
In an article by Mr. Chas E. Hands, published in yesterday's Daily Mail, the well-known journalist writes:-
The Germans have not come this year, and the yachtsmen are sailing in other craft, so the garden Island is suffering severely. But it would not be surprising

---

* Hands knew Ventnor well having first visited in 1908 while researching a newspaper article. He fell in love with the Island, returning many times and eventually retired to Ventnor where he died in 1937. An obituary in the *New York Times* declared 'Charles Hands died today in Ventnor, Isle of Wight where he had lived for many years. He was one of the most famous reporters Fleet Street ever produced'.

if after a time the loss of the two main sources of income did not bring, both to Ventnor and Cowes, a new and greater prosperity. Ventnor, no longer polluted by Germans, may proclaim its beauties with stronger appeal than ever to English holiday-makers as Ryde and Cowes, which have ceased for the present to be the autumn monopoly of the opulent yachting class, may revert to the use and enjoyment of the nation at large. But so far, the English people have not discovered the Island.

The proportion of its visitors who are making their first acquaintance with the Island is said to be greater than ever before, so that even though its visitors are fewer its clientele is being extended by the war. The time will come when this little strip of Paradise Coast will be as thronged as other Channel watering-places, but at present it has the supreme recommendation that it is entirely cleared of Germans and possesses the further advantage of not being overcrowded by the English. According to the Town Clerk, whose information is exact, the proportion of Germans among the summer visitors in the years before the war was about two-thirds, and among the remaining one-third a considerable number were French and American. According to the old fly-driver, who also ought to know, the proportion was 12 Germans and five Americans to one English visitor. Ventnor in the summer was practically a German watering-place.

But there is a good reason to know that the German middle-class fashion for Ventnor and Shanklin as summer holiday resorts were organised and stimulated by Germany as a cover for the spy system. Among the hordes of tourists from industrial Germany came, it is now known, men and women who were not there for their health. They knew every nook and corner of the Island, every twist and footpath of the cliffs and downs, everything that to the experienced eye could be disclosed of the defences of Portsmouth and the ways of the Navy ... There is no doubt whatever in Ventnor and Shanklin that one of the aims of German naval policy is the possession of the Isle of Wight and its conversion into a Heligoland fortress ... a commanding breakwater from which the traffic of the Channel could be blocked and controlled - a Gibraltar of the Channel. The Kaiser, they believe in Ventnor, desires the Island for his own. It is a possession worth aspiring to.

The Germans want it and have infested it, but their devastation has come to an end. There will never more be a German season on the Undercliff. The English have it now all to themselves.

———————◆———————

Unregulated drinking hours were seen as a serious threat to the war effort. Eventually the concerns led to a wholesale revision of Britain's licensing laws ...

September 11th, 1915
OFFICIAL WARNING TO PUBLICANS AT COWES AND EAST COWES

Licence holders at Cowes and East Cowes have this week been served with the following notice signed by the Chief Constable. 'The General Officer Commanding Portsmouth Garrison desires me to inform you that many complaints have been received as to the excessive drinking among the crews of the transports and munitions workers at Cowes and East Cowes. Unless prompt measures are at once taken by the licensed victuallers and others to prevent this drunkenness, the General Officer Commanding informs me that he proposes to make an Order under Paragraph 10, Defence of the Realm Regulations, curtailing the hours of opening to the same as are in force at Southampton'.

The hours during which licensed premises are open at Southampton are from 12 (midday) to 2.30 and from 6 to 9 p.m., and 'treating' by anyone is absolutely forbidden. The brewers have had notices printed and exhibited as a warning to all concerned.

Sergeant Arthur Odell wrote to his parents giving a grim and moving account of day-to-day life in the trenches. Written fluently and powerfully, with the occasional flash of wry humour, his words make compelling reading. It is an affecting letter, written almost matter-of-factly by someone resigned to his grim existence …

September 25th, 1915

NEWPORT SERGEANT'S RACY LETTER
THRILLING TALE OF TRENCH TERRORS

Sergt. Arthur Odell, 6th. Berkshire Regiment, formerly employed in the machine department of the 'County Press', writing from Flanders to his parents at 12 Crocker-street, Newport, says: You ask how things are looking up here. Well, business is about as usual. By that I mean that there is a few minutes 'hate' on either side every morning at sunrise and every evening at sunset, varied by a mine now and then, but as for anything serious, that come at any moment … I received your last letter the day we went into the trenches last time, and we were there for 14 days in a veritable hell all the while. We had hardly been in there half an hour before they started shelling us, and kept it up for over 12 hours. After that it was quiet for a while, and then we had showers of bombs and rifle grenades day and night for two days. On the third day they exploded three mines under us, and kept us up all night. On the fourth night we had our first taste of trench mortars, or 'sausages', as they are called, and one sergeant, one corporal, and three men were killed … Now a word about mines. It generally happens like this. You are standing in a trench when suddenly you find the ground moving, and before you can move yourself the earth seems as if it has shifted back a foot and then fallen forward with a bump. Then it does the same thing the other way, and then, either under you or in front, it opens and belches out a tremendous burst of flame and smoke and tons of muck. After the smoke clears away you see a huge crater, big enough to put two or three horses and carts in, and then, if you don't pull yourself together and get on what is left of the parapet and open fire you find a mile of Germans coming at you with fixed bayonets. Oh, we do see life! The funny part about it is that I have yet to find a man the least bit funky when there is anything doing. One seems to lose all fear then and only thinks of bagging as many of the enemy as possible in the shortest time. But I must admit that it is a bit 'nervy' to walk along the trenches at sunrise or sunset, knowing that it is only a matter of being in the right place to avoid going for a joyride on the top of a sheet of fire and smoke. Still, it's all in the game. As for bombs and rifle grenades, I don't mind the former, as you can generally see them coming, but the other beastly things are far different. You are in your trench when you suddenly hear what seems to be a dove cooing. If it's your first experience of them you probably look round for the dove, only to find that the coo ends in a devil of a bang and lumps of metal flying in all directions. After the first experience it is rather amusing to see everybody dive into the nearest hole when one is heard coming. 'Sausages' are about as much like sausages as a cat is like a horse. They are nothing more or less than an old oil-drum filled with high explosives, and get their name from their appearance as they twist over and over in the air. You can see them coming day or night, as they have the fuse outside and you can see it burning. But God help anyone who is near when they burst, as they blow everything handy into fragments. Last, but not least, are the 'whiz-bangs' (shrapnel shells). Personally, I don't worry much about them now, as I have had one or two narrow escapes from them, and find that unless they catch you fair and square their bark is worse than their bite. The Germans had the range of our trenches to a bee's whisker, and it was none too pleasant. The night we came out of the trenches I had a narrow escape. I was doing my turn of patrol … when suddenly I found myself lying face downwards in the mud and slush. I jumped up in a great 'tear' as I thought the men had tripped me up, and then saw a head come peeping out of a funk-hole and a voice said 'Did it hit you, sergeant?' I then found that a shell had burst just behind me, and a lump of the base was stuck in the tail of my overcoat. I've got the nosecap of it now, and it is a splendid specimen … I was more than pleased to receive the County Press, as we get very little London news out here, let alone news from the old Island'.

Happily, records show that Sergeant Odell survived the war, eventually returning to the Island to live here for the rest of his life.

Within days of the war starting the Government passed the Defence of the Realm Act. It was a powerful piece of legislation that enabled them to seize any land or property judged necessary for the war effort and even allowed them to take over the railway network. Amongst other things, it led to the introduction of British Summer Time, censorship, and early closing for pubs. Strictly prohibited were the flying of kites (they could attract Zeppelins), the feeding of bread to wild animals (a waste of food), buying binoculars and lighting bonfires.

Also prohibited was 'Causing the disaffection of the civil population', and this was to be the undoing of Arthur Morris of Ryde who, in a rash moment, had announced to his workmates 'God bless the Fatherland' and then for good measure had added '—— King George' …

November 6th, 1915

ELECTRICAL ENGINEER CALLS FOR CHEERS FOR THE KAISER

Arthur Morris, electrical engineer, employed at the I.W. Railway Company's Locomotive Works and living at 9 Abingdon-road, Ryde, was charged with attempting to cause disaffection among the civil population of the Works, contrary to the Defence of the Realm Regulations, on October 8th.

Ernest Bartlett, a driller employed at the works, said he heard the defendant say the Kaiser was the best man in the world. Witness turned to him and said 'What about our King?' Defendant replied '—— our King - three cheers for the Fatherland'. He also said '—— King George'.

East Cowes blacksmith George Arnold (behind donkey) and customer, 1907. Photograph by Alfred Arnold. The Blacksmith's Arms, Newport derives its name from Arnold's forge, located there from 1870 to the late 1880s.

The Magistrates' Clerk (Mr. John Fardell): What gave rise to those statements? - Witness: I don't know. - Q. Were there are many of you present? - There were several. - Q. In what part of the works did this take place? - In the blacksmiths' shop ... Mr. Thirkell (defending): Q. Is there are generally a lot of talking going on there? - Not that I am aware of. - Q. Sometimes a bit of joking goes on, surely? - Yes, but not on a subject of that sort; there might be a few words passed in a joking way ... Q. Didn't defendant go to Walter Herbert's bench about this time and Herbert said to him 'Hello, you —— Chinaman, have you come to 'pinch' something? - I did not hear it. I was there when he said the words about our King. If there was any talking at all he ought not to have said that ... Q. Did you meet the manager sometime after this? - Yes; we went to see the governor in the works and he said he was treating it as a joke. I should not think there was much joking in it. - Q. You are only a witness, but you can make the case as bad as you like. Did you not hear the defendant say to Herbert 'You have not got anything worth 'pinching'? - I did not ...

Police Sergt. Ryall said he saw the defendant in the same evening at Abingdon-road. He told him that it had been reported to the police that a short time ago he made statements derogatory to the King and in favour of Germany, and that he would be prosecuted. Defendant replied 'I took a note of what I said and I have apologised to the works foreman and also to the works.... I am sorry I said it; it was more in a joke than anything else. Defendant, on oath, in reply to Mr. Thirkell, said he was a loyal British subject and that the words were used in joking. He was born in England and had never been out of the country. His father and mother were English. Mr. Thirkell: What did Herbert say to you when you went to his desk? - He said 'You Chinaman, what have you come to 'pinch?' - Q. And what was your answer? - 'You have not got anything worth 'pinching'. He said 'You are like the Germans; they 'pinch' anything ... Q. What remark did you make then? - I said 'God bless the Fatherland'. Q. Was that meant to be a joke? - Certainly ...

The Bench retired, and on returning into Court the Mayor said the magistrates had found defendant guilty of a very serious offence. It was a very grave thing to admit he said what he did say before those men. The Bench were going to fine him £5, or in default one month's imprisonment. He hoped it would be a lesson to him to be more loyal to the King. Defendant was allowed a fortnight to pay.

1916

January, 1916
THE WEEK'S NEWS
WEASEL OUT OF BOUNDS - At Newport on Monday was witnessed the unusual sight of a weasel running along the High-street and vainly trying to enter shops, whose doors were fortunately closed. Mr. W. H. Fry, who was passing with his coal van at the time, knocked the animal over with his whip and it was killed before it had done any mischief.

A VICAR'S SURPLICE ON FIRE - While the Rev. C. Bostock, formerly curate of Newport, was preaching his sermon at Lymington Parish-church on Sunday evening, electric wires in the pulpit fused and set on fire the Vicar's surplice.

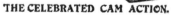

The current was switched off and the flames were quickly extinguished before any serious damage was done.

A bottle of whisky which before the war started could be purchased for 3s.6d. per bottle now costs 4s.6d.

A London chemist, asked for cold cream on Wednesday, said the price had doubled during the past 24 hours.

Mr. Nicholas Mursell, the proprietor of the Castle Inn, has in his possession a licence granted in the 4th year of the reign of Queen Anne by Her Majesty's groom porter, Thomas Archer, authorising the then landlord of the inn, Joseph Haskell, 'to keep and retain and have in and about his house, for the recreation of such as may play thereat, a cock-pit from the 29th September, 1705'.

———————◆———————

Voluntary enlistment had initially been enough to supply the Government's demand for soldiers but by the end of 1915 almost half a million British soldiers had already been killed and the number of recruits began to dry up. As a result, conscription was introduced for single men between the ages of 16 and 41 (the call up of married men started three months later), and an appeals procedure was put in place for those requesting exemption from service. Weekly tribunals were held in public, for all to see and hear, and in addition, full details of the hearings, sometimes occupying nearly a whole page, appeared in the County Press every week ...

February 26, 1916
ISLAND TRIBUNALS

Mr. Andrew Thomson of Cowes, the well-known yacht handicapper and broker, applied for the postponement to a later group of his gardener, A.E. Sweetenham, of Church-road, Gurnard, on the grounds that his services were indispensable. He had made every effort to find a temporary substitute, and the only man he could get was not fit for the work. He wanted him for domestic needs, providing vegetables for house use. He attended to the flowers himself ... The recruiting officer's report was: 'I dissent. Nothing to warrant postponement'. - The Chairman: Sorry to inconvenience you, Mr.Thomson, but the Tribunal is against you. Your man had better join up as soon as he can.

John Griffiths, coal exporter, Union-street, Ryde, applied for exemption for his son, Thomas Archibald Griffiths, who assisted in the business. It was explained that this was a reserved occupation, and a provisional exemption was granted.

Marcus Leal, a gardener, living at 45 West-street, Ryde, applied for exemption, but was refused.

Col. Howard Brooke made an application on behalf of A.J. Newbury, his chauffeur, who is in group 10, and a provisional exemption for one month was granted.

Harry Caws, butcher, High-street, Cowes, who stated that he had two boys in the Army and another in the Post-office in South Africa, was granted an exemption for his son, who manages the business. - The Chairman said he was entitled to an exemption conditional on his son remaining in his employment. - Mr. Caws: Thank you; much obliged.

Mrs. Crozier, of Westhill, Yarmouth, appeared in support of the application for exemption of A. J. Maloney, described as an electric-light plant manager, aged 29. She said he was the sole support of his father, who was paralysed. She took him on after her chauffeur went to join up. She was not using her car now. Dr. Carlyon: Could you not get a man over military age to look after the electric-light plant? - Mrs Crozier: I suppose I could, but I shall have a great bother. - The application was not granted.

———————◆———————

Some were not impressed by those seeking exemption from service ...

April 8, 1916

A SOLDIER'S VIEWS ON EXEMPTION CLAIMS
To the Editor of the Isle Of Wight County Press.
Dear Mr. Editor, - On reading the reports of the proceedings of the Island Military Tribunals I was surprised to see that so many young men have been encouraged by their employers to get exempted from serving their country. Although so many men have given up home and everything to fight for the country and maintain the reputation and good name of the Island, such people as these are letting it down. Men of the Wight, don't let us down now that we are getting the upper hand! Help your comrades and don't hold back. - Yours, AN ISLANDER DOING HIS BIT.

———————◆———————

Despite those stirring sentiments, not everyone wanted to go to war. Conscription meant that objections on religious or moral grounds now became an issue and 16,000 men in Britain registered as conscientious objectors. Military Tribunals were held in towns and cities up and down Britain to inquire into each man's circumstances. Of the nearly 9,000 men who appealed, 4,500 were sent to do work of national importance such as farming, 17 were sentenced to death (afterwards commuted), 140 were imprisoned for life and 50 were jailed for 25 years. Prison life was not easy for the conscientious objectors and 70 of them died in jail. To go before the Island tribunals knowing it would be in the full glare of the community was clearly not a decision to have been taken lightly ...

April 8, 1916

ISLAND TRIBUNALS
H.J. Woods, 21, jeweller and outfitter, of Sandown, was another appellant against non-combatant service on conscientious grounds, and he complained that some members of the Local Tribunal prejudged his case, one member remarking 'We can't waste any time. Let us get on with the next case'. Whatever the punishment he would take no military service. His objection was inherited from parents, grand-parents, and great grand-parents. - By the Chairman: His objection was not based on religious but on moral grounds; he belonged to no religious body. He had talked freely about his views, and had received many insulting letters. Even when they sang patriotic songs at school, he felt it was more like singing to gods - heathenism (laughter) - than anything else. If an officer came to their shop and wanted an outfit they would not supply him. Their trade had been practically boycotted since the last appeal. He was afraid he could not do agricultural or any other work which the authorities suggested to him as being of national importance. - The Chairman: You

must go on with your jewellery and outfitting? - Yes (laughter). - Q. You don't think that at a crisis like this you should conform to what the authorities think is best for you to do? - I could not go by what the majority say ... He could not do farming or other work, as he might be releasing others for service ... He was a teetotaller, and conscientiously objected to taking any intoxicants (laughter). - The Chairman: If you took intoxicants you might be assisting the revenue (laughter) ... Appellant's father said that appellant in his youth was a Boy Scout until he took him out of it owing to the military tendency. His father and grandfather suffered for conscience sake, and as early Bible Christians. It was in them and they could not get it out ... appellant was brought up to believe that fighting and quarrelling were vices and killing your fellow man was a crime. - The Chairman said the appeal must be dismissed. – Appellant: May I further appeal? - The Chairman: You had better apply to the Military authorities. – Appellant: Before I go to prison? - Lieut. Ward: You will get a fortnight's reprieve (laughter).

E. W. Edwards, 22, grocer's assistant, of Cowes, appealed on the ground of conscientious objection to military service. The Local Tribunal exempted him from combatant service only. He held those objections on moral and religious grounds. Since he went before the Local Tribunal several people had threatened to close their accounts with his employer and at his request his employer reluctantly released him. Whilst he objected to military service he felt that everyone was bound, in a peaceful country, to assist that country in some way or another, though he could not undertake Medical Corps work, as he could not allow his conscience to be directed by any military authority. - The Chairman said he would be exempted from military service on condition that he engaged in work of national importance. A list of occupations would be produced later, and he could select one, and for that purpose the case would stand adjourned.

Mrs. Baker, a widow, supported the appeal of her single son, *T.J. Baker*, a grocer's porter, who was her sole support and had a conscientious objection to fighting, though he would be willing to do munitions work ... The Chairman said the appeal would be dismissed. – Applicant: Can I appeal again? - The Chairman: I am afraid not. – Applicant: This is not justice. In Russia they don't take a widow's son, and our own Government said they would not take him. What about that? - The Chairman: Our decision has been given, and I am afraid we must abide by it. - The mother concluded by stating that she had written to Lord Kitchener once and she should write to him again.

———————◆———————

Not everyone who was opposed to going to war necessarily felt that way for moral or religious reasons. Some just simply didn't want to go ...

August 19th, 1916
RYDE MAN WHO WANTS NOTHING TO DO WITH THE ARMY
Edward Frank Pocock, Bath-chair man, 3 Temperance-place, High-street, was charged with failing to report himself for military duty. P.S. Ryall said that when asked why he had not joined up the defendant said he did not intend having anything to do with it. Lieut. Jacobs, from the Recruiting Office, Newport, proved the defendant should have reported on July 24.

The Mayor: What have you to say about it? – Defendant: Really and truly I don't want anything to do with it. - The Mayor: I don't suppose you do; there are lots of people like you. – Defendant: I don't see why I should be forced to have anything to do with it, do you? - The Mayor: It is the law of the country. You will be fined 40s., and handed over to a military escort. – Defendant: How can I pay 40s. if I have not got it? You cannot get blood out of a stone, you know. - The Mayor: It will be deducted from your pay.

In 1913 the Cowes shipbuilders J.S.White & Co. decided to move into aircraft production. It was a brief experiment that lasted only five years but during that time they manufactured over 200 small aircraft, mostly small seaplanes for the Royal Navy. Aviation was still in its infancy and those brave enough to act as test pilots did so in the knowledge that theirs was a high-risk occupation ...

September 9th, 1916
SHOCKING AVIATION FATALITY AT NORTHWOOD
TWO COWES BROTHERS KILLED

Cowes and district suffered a painful shock on Thursday afternoon when it became known that two brothers of a highly esteemed local family had been killed in a sensational aeroplane accident, which tragically cut short careers which had given promise of winning fame in the aviation world. The victims were Mr. Ralph Oliver Lashmar, aged 29, pilot, and Mr. Allan Frank Lashmar, aged 24, observer, sons of Mr. and Mrs. W. J. Lashmar, of 1 Upper Moor-green road, Cowes, who were making a trial flight in a new aeroplane. The tragedy occurred just before 1 o'clock on Thursday, when the brothers were making the second flight with a large new machine in the Northwood district. The machine ascended soon after midday, and, as on Wednesday, when the first flight was made, everything went well at the start and the machine rose to a great height, the trial promising to be a great success. Suddenly, however, as the machine was descending in a wide sweep something apparently went wrong with one of the wings when the aeroplane was still at the height of 700 or 800 feet, the result being that it got out of control and dived rapidly to the ground, capsizing as it crashed to earth in a mangle field off Cockleton-lane, Northwood. The machine was badly smashed and its occupants were so terribly injured that death was practically instantaneous, though the younger victim appeared to be breathing slightly on the prompt arrival of those who were nearest to the scene of the fatality. In its descent the machine passed over Cockleton-lane greatly alarming Mr. Wyatt, of Gurnard, who was driving past in his market van. He was one of the first to hurry to the scene of the wreck, which was about 150 yards from the highway and near the plantation. A telephone message for help was sent to the Military Hospital at Parkhurst, and Dr. Denton was quickly summoned from Cowes and attended, but, alas! the men had gone beyond medical aid, and the military motor ambulance arrived and conveyed the bodies to Mr.W. G. Thomas's mortuary at Cowes, in charge of P.C. Gamble, to await the inquest.

A large number visited the spot during the afternoon and evening to get a view of the wrecked machine ...

THE INQUEST

The inquest was held by the Deputy Coroner (F. A. Joyce, Esq.) last (Friday) evening at the Congregational Schoolroom, Cowes. Mr. C. F. Hiscock represented the deceased's employer's firm, several directors of which were present....William Lashmar, father of the deceased, said his son Ralph had been engaged as an aviator for two years, and Allan had been flying for the firm for about a year. Both had had considerable experience largely with seaplanes, and were thoroughly competent.

The expert in charge of the aviation department said the deceased men, with a new machine, which was carrying half its full load, left the ground about 12.45 on Thursday on their second trial flight with it ... the machine rose to a height of 6,000 feet in a wide circle, and then with the engine shut off it glided down to within about 600 feet of the ground. The deceased then opened up the engine again and commenced to make another circle in his descent, when something appeared to go wrong and the machine made a spiral nose-dive, ending in a side-slip as it came to the ground.

By the Coroner: He was not able to say in what respect the machine went wrong.

Q. Was it the breaking of the wings? - It appeared that the tips of the wings turned upwards, but I have since proved that that could not have happened. Two Government inspectors had examined the wreckage and found that the wings' wires and struts were intact, which showed that the wings did not fold upwards. The official inspectors were perfectly satisfied that the accident was not due to faulty material or to the construction of the machine ...

The Coroner said no doubt the deplorable occurrence was the result of an accident but they had not been able, from the facts available, to arrive at the cause of the accident. The machine was carefully tested and examined before the flight, and the pilot was most experienced and competent ... The jury returned a verdict of 'Accidental death'.

The Foreman said the jury wished to express their deepest sympathy with the bereaved parents of those two young men, who met their death in defence of their country just as much as if they had died facing the foe (hear, hear). The jury might add as some consolation for those responsible for designing and building the machine that in their opinion no blame could possibly attach to them, and they hoped that the accident would not deter the carrying on of the firm's enterprise (hear, hear).

1917

In 1914 when the war started, women were still unable to vote, something they had in common with lunatics and convicts. Their demand for the vote was eventually helped in no small measure by the fact that they had made an immense contribution to the war effort, and shortly after the war ended women over 30 were granted the vote.

For women it was to be the beginning of the beginning but for some men it was more like the beginning of the end ...

ISLE OF WIGHT COUNTY COUNCIL.

VENEREAL DISEASES.

ALTHOUGH these Diseases occur as the result of immoral conduct, they may be spread in other ways. The effects upon the individual and upon the race are grave and far-reaching. It has been demonstrated that prompt recognition and systematic treatment will enable the patient to avoid these grave after-consequences. Arrangements have been made for FREE TREAT- MENT FOR ALL. Persons suffering from these diseases can have treatment UNDER CONDITIONS OF SECRECY. Treatment Centres have been provided at General Hos- pitals, at which many other diseases are also treated. A Treatment Centre is now avail- able for this District at the Royal I.W. County Hospital, Ryde. Poor persons may be provided with their railway fares when requisite. Every patient's identity will be kept secret, and patients will be known by number, not by name. No hospital letters or recommends will be required. Further information as to these facilities, as to hours and days of attendance, and copies of a special leaflet on the dangers of Venereal Diseases can be obtained from the County Medical Officer of Health, Dr. J. P. Walker, Public Health Offices, Richmond House, 3 The Strand Ryde. Applications may be made to him by telephone (Ryde 322) from any Call-box or by letter. If desired, replies will be addressed to persons at any Post- office, " To be called for."

February 24th, 1917
FIRST THINGS FIRST
To the Editor of the I.W. County Press.

Sir, - 'A Member of a Woman Suffrage Society' in your issue of February 10 considers that it 'would be against the best interests of the Empire' if women are not enfranchised before the next General Election. Does she mean that it would be in the best interests of the nation that 14,000,000 women should be endowed with political power, when there are barely 12,500,000 men in the Kingdom? May I remind her that all those matters she mentions - drink, education, child welfare, housing, &c., are being dealt with already by numbers of public spirited men and women all over the country, through the local governing bodies. Is it possible to enfranchise 'numbers of the best women' - as your correspondent desires - without eventually including all the women of the country, whose instincts, aptitudes, ambitions, and desires are domestic and maternal, and not in the least public or political? In the best interests of the nation and Empire the division of labour between the sexes, which gives the care and responsibilities of the home and the children to women, and the duties and dangers of upholding the laws and protecting the State to men, will prove the natural and proper condition. I am, Sir, yours truly, CITIZEN.

TOWN AND COUNTY NOTES
FISH DESTROYED BY THE FROST - Since the thaw a large number of grey mullett, many weighing 3lb. or 4lb. each, have been found floating on the salt creek between St. Helens and Bembridge Railway-station, killed by the pond being frozen. It is pitiable to see such a quantity of good food spoiled in these times.

WILD FOWL - A large flight of wild grey geese paid a visit to Forelands and settled in the field there on Monday. On being disturbed they proceeded out to sea. None have been seen since 1895 when a flight of five birds settled on the Harbour land, and many a sportsman then realised what 'a wild goose chase' meant, not one being bagged. Several of the smaller Brent geese have been shot in the Harbour this winter.

Large quantities of sprats are being offered for sale in the Island. They are said to have a high nutritional value and, being rich in oil, are particularly suitable for a winter food.

Some of the conditions under which Island men have been serving in Mesopotamia are disclosed in a remark made by a man in that country to Lieut.-Colonel Godfrey Collins, who said that for nine months he had not seen a woman, tree, or stone.

As a result of a money prize offered at Barcombe to the person who could kill the largest number of cabbage butterflies within ten days, over 4,000 were destroyed, the winner of the prize accounting for no less than 1,395.

On Tuesday morning, a balloon, with an anchor attached, flew over Bembridge during the heavy gale and went in the direction of Seaview, where the anchor did damage to the roof of Kenilworth in two places, ripping off the tiles and hurling them amongst the small crowd of onlookers. The huge gas-bag, with its appended ropes and grappling irons then flew over Upton and Ryde. At Froglands Farm, Carisbrooke, the trailing grapnel caught the iron framework of the wind water-wheel, pulled it over, and damaged it badly. It eventually made its way across the Solent to the mainland.

THE ISLAND AND THE WAR
The Germans reported 4,037,692 casualties in their official lists for January.

It is possible that the Government may use Dartmoor Convict Prison as a work centre for conscientious objectors.

Colonel Sunderland, J.P., of Ravensden Grange, was fined £100 at Bedford on Saturday for feeding pigeons and fowls with corn fit for human food.

I.W. WAR AGRICULTURAL COMMITTEE. - NOTICE TO FARMERS. Farmers requiring the Loan of Horses and Men to cultivate additional acreage for the 1918 harvest are hereby given notice to apply to the Executive Officer, 8 Southsea-terrace, Portsmouth. Forms and further particulars will be sent on application. A.E. THURGOOD. Executive Officer.

Instead of applying for exemption, or registering as a conscientious objector, some used the ploy of being economic with the truth in their efforts to avoid going to war. Mr. Wells, described in court as one of the largest potato growers in the South of England, had given the wrong age on a government form the previous year and when the truth was eventually found out he was summoned to appear in court the very next day to explain himself. Ironically, it was revealed in court that had he told the truth in the first instance he would almost certainly have been granted exemption as a matter of course ...

March 10th, 1917
ISLAND POTATO GROWER AS MILITARY ABSENTEE
ALLEGED AGE FALSIFYING IN GOVERNMENT RETURNS
Reginald Frederick Wells, farmer and potato grower and merchant, of Cridmore and Newport, defended by Mr. C. F. Hiscock, who surrendered to his bail on the charge of being an absentee under the Military Service Act, on entering the dock was called upon to answer a second charge, namely that on November 16, 1916, he unlawfully and knowingly, in making out an Agricultural Census return, gave false information concerning his age.

Supt. J. H. Galloway said that on the previous afternoon defendant came to his office respecting another matter, when he drew defendant's attention to the Agricultural Census form in question, on which defendant's age was filled in as

47, whereas he (the superintendent) had reason to believe his age was very much less. He charged defendant, who replied 'I did not think it was of any importance, and I did not know my correct age' ... Mr. Hiscock said Mr. Wells was probably the largest potato grower south of Cambridge. For reasons which need not be explained at that moment, he did not submit himself for military service. The unfortunate part was that had he known at the time that he was liable for military service he could have gone to the local Tribunal and he would no doubt have obtained some form of exemption because it was in the national interest that one occupying so important a position as a food producer, should be allowed to go on with his business ... Mr. Hiscock said all he could urge was that defendant had very large business obligations which were of paramount importance, not only to him, but to the country, and, whatever their decision, he appealed to the Bench that the defendant should be allowed some short time to close up the retail business and make necessary arrangements, as far as possible, before joining up ... He was an uneducated sort of man, who had built up a very large business, but was not aware that even his birth certificate might be obtained. That would show what was in his mind and that no useful purpose could be served by saying that he was 47 ... They were some 22 men at work for defendant, and if he was marched off to Winchester it would mean chaos, and defendant would be a very heavy loser in regard to the obligations he had entered into.

The Chairman (to defendant): The sentence of the Court is that you be fined £10, and handed over to the military authorities. – Defendant: May I ask a question?

The Chairman: It is too late now. That is the sentence. Stand down.

Defendant: My men have not been paid.

------------◆------------

Officers at the front were well used to writing to the mothers of soldiers under their command. Usually they wrote to convey bad news, but not always ...

May 19th, 1917

THE ISLAND AND THE WAR

Mrs. Parsons, of 9, Victoria-road, Newport, has received the following gratifying letter from Lieut. Butler in praise of the gallant behaviour of her son, Rifleman Ernest Parsons, Hampshire Regiment: 'I am taking the first opportunity to write and tell you of the truly heroic conduct of your son, who has been my servant for nearly 18 months. Two days ago our battalion attacked some enemy trenches over a mile and a quarter of grassland, without any sort of cover whatever for the whole distance, and particularly during the last half we were under a tremendous fire of every sort, rifle, machine-gun, shrapnel, and high explosive shells. Your son stuck with me and was as cheerful as he always has been. When within 200 yards of an enemy redoubt I was hit in the side, your son at once dressed my wound, and whilst he was doing so I was again hit in the shoulder, and my clothes and equipment were hit in four places, and the peak of your son's helmet was carried away by a piece of shell. No words can do justice to the extraordinary coolness of your son under the most intense fire. He looked after me as a nurse does a sick and frightened child, telling me not to bother about my wounds or getting back. 'I'll get you back all right, sir; don't you bother'. After fixing me up he helped me back to cover, under fire for a mile, carrying my equipment, &c., as well as his own things, including his rifle. Once under cover he dressed my second wound and took me right back to the casualty clearing station. How he escaped being wounded himself I shall never be able to understand. You know the opinion that I have always had of the qualities of cheerful willingness to undertake any duty that your son possesses; he has now been tried under the severest possible conditions, and has proved himself to be a son of whom any mother should be far more than proud. My sincere wish is that the day is not far off when you will have him back with you at home. I am sending this letter through my mother for her to know that I practically owe my life to your boy'.

———————◆———————

During the war years, checkpoints were put in place at every port of entry to the Island. They were manned by police or military personnel whose task was to enquire into passengers' nationalities. The task was approached very seriously and a sense of humour when replying was not recommended ...

June 16th, 1917
SOLDIERS AND THE ALIENS ORDER
Private Stanley Lawson, A.S.C. (M.T.), of Southampton, was charged with giving false information under the Aliens Order. – P.S. Snow said that at 3.15 , the 28th ult., defendant, when landing from the steamer at Cowes, was challenged as to his nationality and said he was a German. - The Clerk (Mr. John Fardell): Do you challenge all soldiers? – Witness: We do sometimes, but sometimes the provost-sergeant sees them off from another gangway. - Q. What is the object of questioning a man in His Majesty's uniform? - It is quite possible for an alien to come in uniform. We frequently have Belgians coming over and send them back. - The Clerk: I only wanted to know. - Defendant wrote that, being in uniform, he did not realise that the question was seriously addressed to him. His officer wrote that defendant's action was no doubt due to his facetiousness. - Defendant was fined 5s.

PAYING FOR HER JOKE
Elisabeth Wyard, of Southampton, a well-dressed woman, was similarly charged, and replied 'What I said was a joke. It was the first time I have been to Cowes'. – P.C. Denham said he was at the Pontoon, Cowes, when defendant arrived by the 3. 15 p.m. boat. He challenged her as to her nationality and she said 'German'. She afterwards said she only did it for a joke. - Defendant said when the constable asked 'British?' She said 'German' as if it were a joke, and she did not realise the importance of it till afterwards. - The Chairman: Do you mean you said it in a joke? - Yes. – The Chairman: I am afraid you will have to pay for your joke. - Fined 10s. or seven days.

———————◆———————

In 1890, Mr. Leddicott, who ran a curiosity shop in Holyrood Street, Newport, had come under fire when it became known that he had on display in his window what were said to be some of the remains of Princess Elizabeth, the daughter of Charles I, who had died at Carisbrooke Castle (See vol. 1, page 61). The question of who had removed the remains, how Mr. Leddicott had come into possession of them and what eventually happened to them was never explained at the time. However, nearly 30 years later, the curious story was briefly mentioned in the 'Occasional Jottings' column, which appeared each week under the byline 'Stylus'. Readers responded straight away and their replies and research finally provided the answers ...

September 1st, 1917
THE REMAINS OF PRINCESS ELIZABETH
'Stylus' writes: In a recent note it was mentioned that a report by the late Dr. Wilkins of his examination of the remains of the Princess Elizabeth was published by the late Mr. Leddicott ... I have not hitherto had the good fortune to meet with a copy of Mr. Leddicott's report of the post-mortem examination of the poor Princess's remains. I regret this, inasmuch as it might furnish us with another reason which induced Queen Victoria to grant permission for such being allowed ... I read in the brochure published by Dr. Wilkins, in 1859 - a year or two later than the examination - 'that the remains of Elizabeth, the daughter of Charles the first, were interned in St Thomas's church. During the building of this church great care was taken to preserve the remains of the unhappy Princess inviolate!' It is further stated by Dr. Wilkins 'that the Princess died from the disease called rickets'. Canon Venables writes in his *'Isle of Wight Guide'*, in a footnote, p.80, 'I am informed by those who were present when the coffin of the Princess Elizabeth was opened during the recent re-building of Newport Church that there was scarcely a bone in her body of its proper shape' ... Some years since, under the heading 'A Romance of the Grave', the *Pall Mall Gazette* published, with much detail, the story of the removal of Princess Elizabeth's remains from St Thomas's Church, Newport, and of what occurred subsequently ... Here is how the removal is described:- 'Owing to some alterations in the church, the coffin was removed from the vault and deposited in a shed, the door of which was locked. In this shed it lay for some time, that is, until the alterations to the church were completed. And during its sojourn here a remarkable thing happened. One dark night some four or five persons, one of whom was a doctor, a member of the Royal College of Surgeons, marched clandestinely to the shed, forced the lock, and carried the coffin with its poor remains on a wheelbarrow to the doctor's house. Here it rested two days, during which time the doctor accomplished his object, which was a medical examination of the body of the Princess. The body was then replaced, but the story leaked out, and the doctor was pressed by the authorities. He, however, gave the solemn assurance that he had replaced the body intact, and the matter was hushed up. Some time afterwards the doctor published locally the result of his investigations, but the publication was suppressed through the influence of the Town Council of Newport, who were thrown into a state of alarm'.

After the doctor's death, 'Stylus' writes, it was found that a rib bone and a lock of hair had been taken from the remains, and these were discovered in a jar at the doctor's house with a written statement to the effect that they were taken from the body of Princess Elizabeth. As already stated in the *County Press*, these relics came into the possession of the late Mr. Leddicott, of Newport, 'who', to resume the story as told in the Pall Mall, 'declared that he had been worried to death about them. The real persecution began when a gentleman from Clapham called at the shop and offered, first £5, then £10, and finally an even higher bid for the jar. Mr. Leddicott refused saying the relics were not for sale. Whether it was owing to information given by this disappointed curio-hunter or from some other source, the Home Office next intervened, and Mr. Leddicott received a visit from a detective, who made an attempt to frighten him into parting with the relics. This was unsuccessful, and subsequently he received a letter from the Home Office, dated April 3rd. 1890, which said: 'The attention of the Secretary of State having been drawn to the fact that you are exposing in the window of your shop a bone purporting to be a bone of the Princess Elizabeth, who died at Carisbrooke Castle, I am directed to point out to you the indecency of exposing fragments of human remains, unlawfully abstracted from the coffin of a known individual of high rank in past times; and I am glad to say that the Secretary of Estate would be glad to hear that the fragments had been replaced either in or alongside the coffin where it is now deposited'. In his reply Mr. Leddicott denied that he had exposed the relics in his shop window. 'I am willing to admit', he proceeded, 'that it is unseemly to expose human remains under ordinary circumstances, but I would remind you that such remains are to be found exposed in Government and other museums, and are kept as precious relics by religious persons. I am a dealer in curiosities, and this bone of an historical personage is in my hands as such. I have no power to return it to the coffin, or to place it alongside; and if I had, I do not understand why I should be called upon to do so. I may add that it has been in my possession over nine years. During that period I have on several occasions been offered large sums of money, but would not part with it'. Attempts to gain possession of the relics were made subsequently by many other people, and the Vicar of the parish went so far as to make a bold claim for them. He was routed, however, and the curiosity dealer remained master of the field'.

But while defying Government and other authorities, Mr. Leddicott at length submitted to the gracious influence of Queen Victoria and Princess Beatrice, and he surrendered the relics, the hair being deposited in the Isle of Wight Museum, while the rib bone, enclosed in a silver casket, was reverently restored to the tomb in St. Thomas's Church in the presence of the Royal Governor of the Island.

———————◆———————

It was announced that a large part of the grounds of Norris Castle at East Cowes was to be cleared of timber to make way for a housing development. A thousand trees on the wooded slopes below the Castle were sold and felled to make way for the 200 proposed houses. In the event, like so many other schemes of those times, the plans came to nothing and not a single house was built …

September 29th, 1917
NORRIS CASTLE ESTATE DEVELOPMENT
Considerable interest centred in the offer by public auction of the first portion of the Norris Castle Estate for building purposes, and the sale of a portion of the timber on this historic estate. The sale was held at the Fountain Hotel, Cowes under instructions from Mr. Edwin Parker, solicitor, of Newport, who recently purchased the fine old Castle from the executors of the late Sir Richard Burbridge with the object of developing it for building purposes to meet the needs of the district … The sale of upwards of 1,000 trees, principally finely grown ash, as well as beech, elm, oak, &c., attracted a representative attendance of timber merchants, ship, yacht, and aeroplane builders, and the trade generally, war conditions having compelled a greater reliance than ever before in living memory on home-grown timber … Messrs. Morey and Son were the largest purchasers securing about half the quantity offered, and other considerable purchasers were Messrs. Alexander Sharp and Co. Ltd and Messrs. J.S. White and Co. Ltd. The 20 lots which found purchasers realised well over £1,000. The purchasers have to cut and remove the timber. The land offered for building comprised about 20 acres in 209 building plots running through the estate to the Solent at Old Castle-point, and it was stated that the vendor proposed to construct a new road, to be called Norris-road, through the centre of this land, leading to a promenade on the seafront, and also a cross-road, to be known as Vincent-road, near the sea … It would not interfere in any way with the amenities of the Castle, which was entirely shut off by a belt of trees; it remained to be seen how that should be dealt with. The proposed new road would be a boon to the residents of East Cowes and the immediate neighbourhood, as it would enable them to reach a magnificent promenade on the seafront.

Since the beginning of the war the nature of cases heard in the Island courts had changed dramatically. Serious crime had almost completely disappeared and the Island's police were kept busy bringing charges that seem quite trivial compared to pre-war times. They included 'Riding a bicycle on the pavement', 'Pilfering a piece of cake valued at 5½d.', 'Committing a nuisance by playing football in the street', 'Stealing two lettuce', 'Obtaining two cakes by false pretences' and 'Embezzling 3s.3d'. Despite the rather trivial nature of these and similar offences, juvenile crime was seen as a major problem and councillors requested that the Home Office allow the birching of older children …

September 29th, 1917
POLICE MATTERS
BIRCHING JUVENILE OFFENDERS
… The Standing Joint Committee had addressed communications to the Home Secretary stating it was desirable that the age limit for birching juvenile offenders should be extended having regard to the increase of juvenile crime during the war … Mr. Hayden asked whether it was seriously considered that birching would be a remedy. He hoped they would not assent to a general system of birching as a cure for that sort of thing. They wanted to find the cause of wrongdoing, and then they might find the remedy … Mr. Mears said no one who noted the great increase in juvenile crime could deny that the need for some such step was imperative. Mr.

THE ISLAND AND THE WAR.

◆

THE WEEK'S CASUALTIES.

KILLED.

J. W. Raeburn, Canadian Force Newport)
Pte. A. Ricks, R. West Kent Regt. (Newport)
Pte. A, Rogers, Hants Regt. (Sandown)
Dvr. G. H. Tyler, R.E. (Gurnard)

PREVIOUSLY REPORTED MISSING, NOW REPORTED KILLED.

Lieut. E. Clayton. R.A.F. (Ventnor)
Pte, L. Kinshott, Hants Regt. (Ryde)
Lce -Cpl. G. H. Woodford, D.C.L.l. (Newport)

DIED OF WOUNDS.

Gr. H. T. Carter, R.G.A. (Cowes)
Cpl. A. J. Froud, R. Sussex Regt. (Cowes)
Gr. E. J. Harwood, R.G.A. (Yarmouth)
Pte. F. G. Henstridge, R. Warwickshire R. (Shanklin)
Pte. W. G. Peck, London Regt. (Newport)

DIED OF WOUNDS AS PRISONER OF WAR, PREVIOUSLY REPORTED KILLED.

Pte. W. Gladdis, R. Berkshire Regt. Cowes)

DIED AS PRISONER OF WAR, PREVIOUSLY REPORTED MISSING.

Spr. F. Draper (Ventnor)

DIED AS PRISONERS OF WAR.

Pte. A. Brett, Worcestershire Regt. (Shanklin)
Gr. F. E. Diffey, R.F.A, (Newport)
Gr. A. Warren, 1/5th Hants R.F.A. (Havenstreet)

DIED.

Pte. L. A. Williams City of London Regt. (Ryde)

MISSING.

2nd-Lieut. O. J. Tolman, R.A.F, (Whippingham)

INFORMATION DESIRED.

REPORTED missing on Sept. 27th, in France, 2nd-Lieut. O. J. Tolman, 22 Squadron R.A.F.—Any information gratefully received by his mother, Mrs. W. H. Grace, Alverstone, Whippingham, I.W.

COWES.

Mrs. Gladdis, 4 Castle-road, has received official news that her son, Pte. Gladdis, was not killed in action on March 23rd, as reported, but died from gunshot wounds in the lung on April 6th as a prisoner of war in hospital at Le Cateau.

We regret to announce that Gunner Herbert Thomas Carter, R.G.A. (Siege Battery), son of the late Capt. Ivo Stodhard Carter and of Mrs. Beere, of Pandora, Arctic-road, was admitted to hospital, seriously wounded in the chest, on September 25, and died shortly afterwards, aged 24. Although so young, he had had eight years' service, six and a half of that time in India, but had only been 11 weeks in France.

Another promising young townsman has made the supreme sacrifice on the Western front, namely, Corpl. Archie John Froud, third and youngest son of Councillor J. Froud, of St. Giles, Park-road, who, on the 26th ult, died in hospital at Rouen from wounds received in the chest and right leg during the heavy fighting on the 21st ult. He was going on well when, unfortunately, the effects of gas poisoning developed, and he suddenly succumbed.

GURNARD.

Driver George Henry Tyler, R.E., of Portland House, has been killed by a bomb on the Western front.

NEWPORT.

Lance-Corpl. George H. Woodford, D.C.L.I., aged 26, the eldest of four fine soldier sons of Mr. H. Woodford, 31 Royal Exchange, who had

been missing in France since October 4th, 1917, is officially presumed to have been killed.

Pte. O. H. Hutchings, Wiltshire Regiment, the 19-year-old son of Mrs. E. B. Hutchings, of 98 Hunnyhill, has been severely wounded in legs, side, and right arm by shell fire on the Western front, where he was temporarily buried in a dug-out by shell explosion. Both legs have been amputated above the knee.

Mrs. Ricks, St. Aubyns, Staplers, has received the sad news that her husband, Pte. Alfred Ricks, Royal West Kents, aged 41, was killed in France on August 27th. He was formerly proprietor of the well-known restaurant in Lower High-street.

Mr. Alfred Peck, T.C., of the Britannia, Hunnyhill, has received the sad news that his third son, Pte. William George Peck, London Regiment, aged 22, died on the 24th September as the result of wounds received in Palestine. He joined up 3½ years ago, and, after serving on the Western front, went to Salonica, where he saw considerable service, and was afterwards transferred to Palestine. It was in the dash on Nazareth that he was fatally wounded. His officer spoke highly of this promising young soldier.

Official and other Notices.

Hayles thought the trouble arose through lack of parental control owing to the absence of fathers on service, and that it would pass away with the war. Ald. Fellows said birching had been enforced by law for many years, but what they were dealing with now was the fact that there was no punishment for the young hooligan too old to be birched under the present law, except fining the parents. The recommendation simply aimed at punishing indecent conduct on the part of young blackguards, who richly deserved a thrashing which they would never forget; it was a scandal that the law did not effectively deal with them (hear, hear).

1918

Meat, pork in particular, was in short supply during the war years. The shortage led to new feeding practices on the farm ...

January 5th, 1918

WAR-TIME PIG FEEDING

The present scarcity and high cost of feeding stuffs render inevitable a revision of methods of pig-feeding. In the past the pig has received large quantities of food substances, such as potatoes, barley, maize, and peas, which might have been used directly or in the form of flour or meals for human consumption. So long as the supplies of these foods left a surplus above the requirements for direct human consumption no objection could be taken to this course, but now that such a surplus no longer exists the use of such materials for pig-feeding must be regarded as wasteful and contrary to the national interest. It could only be justified if it could be shown that an actual increase of food supplies could be obtained by feeding these materials to the pig. Experience shows, however, that it takes about 7lb. of concentrated food to produce 1lb. of pork or bacon. Yet 7lb. of cereals would yield about 5lb. of flour or 7½lb. of bread, and this is sacrificed to produce 1lb. of pork which has actually less nutritive power than 1lb. of grain ... Today the pig must be restricted as far as possible to materials which cannot be used for human beings such as grass, roots, acorns, silage, bran, pollards, sharps, damaged grain, fishmeal, dried yeast, dried grains, malt culms, oil cakes, and meals, together with waste products such as whey, food refuse of all kinds, and surplus vegetable matters from the garden or allotment ...

━━━━━━━━━━◆━━━━━━━━━━

January 1918

NOTES AND QUERIES

NOTICE. - I will give Five Pounds to any charitable institution for substantial proof of the person or persons who were the instigators of the libellous report that I have been guilty of Hoarding Provisions contrary to regulations issued by the Food Controller. - (Signed) E. SIMMONDS, Freemasons' Tavern, Newport, I.W.

DEATH OF A FORMER TOWN CRIER - An old inhabitant has passed away in the person of Mr. Henry Toms, who died on Tuesday at his residence in West-street, aged 74. He was a native of Brading, and for many years acted as town crier. The funeral took place on Friday.

AN ALLEGED NUISANCE - A correspondent, signing himself 'Contemptible' writes: A stroll down Newport Mall after the regular 'early morning dog-parade' is enough to disgust a pig. Can any of your readers suggest and insist on a suitable remedy?

HOMING PIGEONS SHOT - Complaints have reached us that valuable homing pigeons have been lost or injured in the Island through being shot. Many of these birds are either on war service or are being trained for it. When it is pointed out that a message carried by a pigeon which recently alighted in the Island resulted in the rescue of airmen in trouble at sea it will be realised how wicked is the shooting of such birds. It is not generally known that anyone shooting these birds is committing a grave offence under the Defence of the Realm Act, and is liable to a heavy penalty.

ISLAND LABOUR PARTY FORMED. - At a meeting in the Guildhall, Newport, Mr. W. Berryman announced that it had been decided to form the Isle of Wight Labour Party. For a considerable time the Island had been backward, as regards trades unionism and Trade Union representation ... They had the will and the power to make the Isle of Wight Labour Party one to be feared and to be thankful for ... Until they realised their strength they could not hope to obtain the emancipation of the working classes from a state of serfdom ...

Miss Fortyodd had been aroused from her slumbers by a rather awkward burglar. Thinking to quiet her, the burglar said, gently: 'I don't want you, lady; only your money'. Whereupon Miss Fortyodd sniffed contemptuously and replied: 'Get out; you're just like all the rest of them'.

————————————◆————————————

An anonymous officer wrote home with a poignant account of how British and German soldiers at the Front had met for once as fellow men rather than as soldiers ...

February 9th, 1918
AN ISLANDER'S EXPERIENCES AT THE FRONT
An Island artillery officer, writing to friends at Newport, says: 'Well, we have at last been relieved, so shall be out of action for a few weeks. We have had a very bad time this last spell. Many who went into action with us have not come out. I never want to see Passchendaele again. I generally strike upon some ghastly spot like that. (It is possible that we leave this front altogether; I only hope it comes off.) I had quite an experience a few days ago. It is rather a long tale, but may interest you. Nowadays they occasionally attach artillery officers to the infantry for a couple of days, and vice versa, just to get an idea of how the various branches of the Service carry on. Well, I struck a lively day. The battalion I was with was going into the line that night. It took us 7 hours to get up 3½ miles, the ground being so bad that we were all linked together on a long rope, so that when one got stuck in the mud there was some hope of getting out again. The last mile was waist deep. We arrived at 11p.m. and completed the relief. I might say here that it had been raining for the last 24 hours. Of course

there are no trenches in this part of the line, only posts - shell holes connected up. We got three men stuck in the mud up to their chests, and couldn't get them out till 9 a.m. the next day (10 hours). They were only kept alive by having rum taken to them every two hours. The curious part was this. When dawn broke both our own posts and those of the Bosche were so bad that the men couldn't stick in them, so they came out and stood on top; the Bosche did the same; and there we were, standing in the open within 40 yards of each other, grinning. There wasn't a shot fired. Of course, while these three men were being pulled out we were working under a Red Cross flag. We didn't have sufficient stretchers, so old Bosche brought one across halfway, dumped it down, and walked back. I thought it was awfully good of him …'

———————◆———————

The County Press was suffering badly from wartime shortages. Not only was paper very expensive, it was in very short supply meaning smaller issues and correspondingly less space to run the advertising which generated so much valuable revenue. The price of the paper which had been one penny for nearly 30 years had only recently been increased to 1½d. but times were so desperate that the public were now being asked to pay an even higher price, and this time for a smaller paper …

March 9th, 1918
THE 'COUNTY PRESS' AND PAPER RESTRICTIONS
On Saturday last the Royal Commission on Paper issued a revised list of regulations as to the importation, distribution, and priority of supply of paper and paper-making materials. Under these regulations the weight of paper suitable for newspaper and other printing available during the coming year will be further reduced to only a sixth of pre-war supplies. And not only is the supply available drastically limited, but the cost is at least four times greater than before the war.

Under these circumstances, having to face what the *Daily Mail* describes as the greatest crisis in the history of newspapers, the proprietors of the *County Press* appear to have no alternative but to increase the price to 2d. per copy from the end of the current quarter and to reduce somewhat the size of the paper. They hope to retain the interest of all their old friends, and that they will assist them to bear the heavily increased cost of production … They can greatly help by circulating their own copies amongst friends at home or by sending them to friends away from the Island instead of purchasing copies especially for the purpose …

———————◆———————

In December 1917, the steamship La Peru ran aground off Niton and to the delight of the locals jettisoned large quantities of her cargo in what proved to be a successful attempt to refloat her. The cargo, pork destined for British troops, came ashore and was swiftly gathered up by the waiting crowds, nine of whom were later prosecuted at Newport for 'not delivering salved goods to the Receiver of Wreck'. The prosecutions, seen as harsh by many, caused a great deal of bad feeling.

Twelve weeks later it was the turn of West Wight residents to fill their larders when an American ship, the War Knight, carrying large quantities of pork and lard invoiced to the British government, was involved in a collision in the Channel and was subsequently towed to Freshwater. On arrival she was sunk by gunfire to extinguish a fire which had broken out and this caused the hull to split open. Her precious cargo floated ashore and the beach became a hive of activity as large crowds removed the goods before the Customs men did. House to house searches were carried out over the next few days and two months later 30 prosecutions took place on the same day. The train to Newport, carrying the accused, was referred to as the 'Bacon and Lard special' ...

May 18th, 1918

WRECK PORK AND LARD

Joseph Grist, 50, gardener, Freshwater, was charged with failing to report the finding of wreck.

Mr. J.C.W. Damant said he prosecuted in this and 29 similar cases under the Merchant Shipping Act which provides that anyone finding or taking possession of wreck should, as soon as possible, deliver it to the Receiver of Wreck, the maximum fine being £100. A large ship from America,* with a cargo of pork, lard, &c., consigned to the British Government, collided at the back of the Island about March 24th, and subsequently stranded at Watcombe Bay, Freshwater. The cargo rapidly began to wash ashore ... It was nearly all cases of lard and shoulder and pieces of pork ... The lard was packed in cases of 56lb. each.

Also prosecuted in similar circumstances that day were Charles Harding, Frances Chiverton, Fanny Crooks, Jessie Cox, Eleanor Keeping, John Kellaway, William Baker, George Pitman, Joseph Salter, Queenie Taylor, Minnie Pragnell, Frederick Coley, Mary Jane Rayner, Charles Calloway, Helen Inglis, Florence Sayer, Mabel Whatley Emily Turley, Arthur Cotton, Charles Houlder, James Gillan, Frederick White, Mary Kennet, Helen Coles, Jane Drudge, Walter Gillan, Gertrude Stanley and Mary Jane Effemy.

———————◆———————

Those who removed cases of pork and lard in commercial quantities, and there were several, were never traced and unlike those above, who by and large simply removed only what they could carry with their hands, the commercial operators escaped prosecution. Many in court protested that the authorities had 'found out the sprats while the whales go free' but despite their pleas virtually all were found guilty and fined sums ranging from £1 to £5.

A sympathetic correspondent wrote to protest ...

SALVING PORK AND LARD

To the Editor of the I. W. County Press.

Sir, - Had the magistrates who were on the Bench on Saturday known the true facts concerning the cases which they had brought before them by the Customs regarding the few people, out of the many, who secured pieces of pork that washed in on the shore from the wreck at Freshwater, they would have been more lenient and taken quite a different view of the matter. The wreck was towed into Freshwater Bay on fire on Sunday the 24th March, and she was burning for several days. On the following Wednesday, Thursday, and Friday some of the cargo began washing ashore all along the coast. The pieces of pork in question

* Wartime restrictions in the form of a news blackout meant that not a word of the original stranding had appeared in the *County Press* at the time it occurred. For most people, the first they knew of the events on the beaches was when this report of the court cases appeared many weeks later. The same was true of the *La Peru* incident, the initial stranding going unreported.

were smothered with black grease from the burning ship, and, with sand and seaweed added to the grease, some of it looked quite unfit for human food. The people who took it to their homes and cleaned it deserved credit instead of punishment in trying to clean them to save food, which otherwise would have perished on the shore where scores of pieces are now rotting and are being devoured by seagulls. There were no notices whatever in Compton Bay, Brook, or Chilton warning people not to take anything from the shore, neither were there any officials on the coast, as the Coastguards were all away on active service, and the local coast-watchers had no instructions either to take reports or prevent anyone from taking anything from the shore. - I am, yours truly, W.W.H.

The County Press also felt that justice had not been seen to be done ...

In one or two of the cases before the County Bench on Saturday, against persons for failing to report or deliver up the pork and lard salved from the recent wreck, there appeared to be some doubt whether the defendants did or did not actually report what they had done. While there is no legal excuse for ignorance of the law, and, in cases of wholesale wreckage like this, the reward for legitimate salving is fairly generous, every reasonable step should be taken to let the public know the regulations, and to make compliance with them as easy as possible. In these days of food shortage the public should be encouraged in salving every possible ounce of food. The adoption of any dog-in-the-manger policy by the authorities by failing to salve themselves and discouraging the public from doing it, is against the interests of the community.

———————◆———————

August, 1918
TOWN AND COUNTY NOTES
DOGS WOOL FOR SOLDIERS. – Miss K. Blechynden, of Ryde, appeals to Island dog-owners to send dogs' combings to be sterilised and spun into yarn for making cardigans, socks, and stockings for sick and wounded soldiers. The wool should be perfectly clean, as long as possible, combed free of mats, with soiled pieces cut out, different varieties and colours separated, and packed loosely. They should be sent to 77, Swanmore-road, Ryde.

A Queen Elizabeth shilling, dated 1582, in a very good state of preservation, has been dug up by Mr. Young in his garden at Round House, Fairlee.

A Sutton's main crop cabbage, cut in the County Asylum on Thursday by Mr. H.C. Cross, who is in charge, weighed just over a quarter of a hundredweight (28¼lb.) and measured 47in. round its solid heart. How is this for a record? It will be on view at the Asylum today.

Major Robert Loraine, the actor-airman who has just been wounded at the Front, will be remembered as the first aviator to land in the Island in an aeroplane. (See page 125) ... During the eight years that have elapsed since that visit, aviation has developed so rapidly that it is no longer necessary to make long journeys to see aeroplanes in flight; in fact, we have become so accustomed to them that we hardly trouble to look up now when we hear the droning of their engines.

COWES. A VERY PLUCKY DEED. - On Thursday, a lad named Harold Day, aged 16, of Beckford-road rescued Nora Baker, aged 13, of Victoria-road, from drowning in the sea off the Green, although he had his right arm in a sling, having broken it a fortnight ago. The girl, who had got out of her depth, was sinking for the last time when the lad, who had to swim with his left arm, reached her. Both were exhausted when they reached the shore. During part of the time the girl's legs were round the boy's injured arm. Mr Powell, a gentleman visiting Mornington Hall declared that this was the pluckiest deed he had ever heard of or seen.

--------◆--------

For some months now the war had been moving firmly in the Allies favour. Germany had by now suffered 6 million casualties and during August over 100,000 German troops had been taken prisoner. The German High Command realised the war was lost but instead of the unconditional surrender expected of them by the Allies, Berlin wanted a negotiated peace with honour. In a spirited editorial the County Press, like most of the country, made its disapproval clear ...

August 31st, 1918
A DICTATED PEACE
... Since July 15th ... the Allied troops have gone steadily from success to success. In five days we made a greater advance than was accomplished in eight months of desperate fighting during the first Battle of the Somme. The Allies have had no such month since the war began, and the British have had no such week as the last. Never, until now, have we had the satisfaction of pursuing and harrying on a large scale masses of dispirited and defeated troops ... While it is to be hoped that we have now seen a definite turning point in the war, it is most satisfactory to observe that the determination of the Allies to fight on until the safety and liberty of the world is assured, is manifestly stiffening ... We have to make the German people, the swashbucklers of Europe and the enemies of civilisation, realise, and the whole world realise, that they are beaten: A peace by negotiation for us at least would mean industrial ruin, economic vassallage, and national disaster. A negotiated peace on German terms would mean that we should be compelled again to let Hun trading organisations live upon our vitals and German workmen grow fat while British workmen starved ... If we carry on with even greater determination ... we shall reap the harvest of unimaginable rewards - the final deliverance of the world from the oppression of a pitiless brutality.

--------◆--------

Two months later, with the end of the war finally in sight, the County Press once again gave voice to popular feeling ...

October 12, 1918
THE BEGINNING OF THE END
The weeks pass swiftly by, and each now brings a quick and dazzling series of victories to the Allied armies ... To gain time for reinforcing their battered

troops and strengthening their shattered lines, the Germans have asked, through President Wilson, for an armistice … The President has already declared that there could be no negotiation with those who forced this war upon us, and, in effect, he endorses a mourning parent's recent declaration that we have not sent our sons to die for the sake of a peace acceptable to Germany; their blood calls for complete victory and unconditional surrender …

A month later the war was finally at an end. All through the war years the County Press had been a beacon of calm and measured reporting, never losing its poise or composure and it certainly wasn't going to lose its self-control now by running vulgar headlines. Fittingly, in a masterly piece of restraint it confined itself to marking the end of the war by simply printing the headline 'End Of The War' in a slightly larger than usual typeface.

Aside from that, it was business as usual with dignity intact, and that week's issue looked no different to any other despite the fact that it must have been the most welcome and closely read edition in the paper's history …

November 16th, 1918
END OF THE WAR
An armistice signed at 5 a.m. on Monday, November 11th, brought to an end the greatest war of history. Six hours later hostilities ceased on all fronts, on the 11th hour of the 11th day of the 11th month of the year …
ARMISTICE SIGNED
HOSTILITIES CEASE
After lasting nearly four years and four months the Great European War, carefully organised and provoked by Germany virtually came to an end on Monday by the signature of an armistice.* This event was notified to the British public by the subjoined official communique issued from the Press Bureau at 10.20 on Monday morning. The Prime Minister makes the following announcement: 'The armistice was signed at 5 a.m. this morning, and hostilities are to cease on all fronts at 11 a.m. today' …
KAISER SIGNS HIS ABDICATION WITH A SHIVER
A telegram received via Amsterdam on Saturday states: The Kaiser signed a letter of abdication at headquarters this morning in the presence of the Crown Prince and Hindenburg. He was deeply moved. He had resisted all earlier attempts to make him sign, until he got news of the latest events in the Empire. An urgent message from Scheiddeman was handed to him, which he read with a shiver, and then he signed, saying, 'May it be for the good of Germany.
… The ex-Kaiser, accompanied by a numerous suite, crossed the Dutch frontier at about 2 o'clock on Sunday afternoon. The party travelled in about a dozen luxurious Imperial motor-cars, which bore signs of having travelled far and fast … immediately after crossing the frontier the members of the party left the motor-cars and walked to Eysden Station, the ex-Kaiser leaning heavily on his stick. His hair has become entirely grey, and with his ashen face and drooping figure he

---

* Exact casualty figures are not available but the names on the Island's town and village War Memorials suggest that between 1,500 and 2,000 young men and boys from the Isle of Wight were killed in the war.

presented a pitiful spectacle. He wore the uniform of a Prussian General, but his appearance was very far from that of a Prussian General. Many of his company were armed with rifles and Browning pistols. The Imperial train arrived and the ex-Kaiser boarded the train … After a short sleep in the train Willhelm took off his military uniform and dressed himself in private clothes … It is understood that the Dutch government will raise no objection to the ex-Kaiser and Kaiserin remaining in Holland, they now being regarded as private persons, and therefore entitled to the same treatment as immigrants from other countries.

AMALGAMATED MILITARY TRIBUNAL

The first, and in all probability the last, sitting of the Amalgamated Military Tribunal for the East Wight was held at the Town Hall, Ryde, on Monday … Fifteen cases were heard for exemption from military service and all related to Ryde men …

All the applications were granted.

————————◆————————

Finally the County Press was able to print the headline that everyone had waited so long to see …

November 16th, 1918

ARMISTICE DAY IN THE ISLAND
NEWPORT

Newport's reception of the glorious news of the armistice was marked by a spirit of thanksgiving, and formed a fitting counterpart and sequel to the memorable church services on Remembrance Day in August … The joy was quickened by the reading of a notice from the Mayor (Ald. F.E.Whitcher), stating that in the event of the armistice being signed on Monday he recommended that all business should be suspended from 11.30 till 2 o'clock, so that an assemblage of inhabitants should take place outside the Guildhall at midday, to be followed by thanksgiving services in the churches … The first news that the armistice had been signed came from Parkhurst Barracks, Government messages having precedence in the abnormally congested telegraph service. Whilst the crowd assembled in front of the Guildhall and rejoiced in the good news, the official confirmation was posted in the County Press window. The Union Jack, with the Red Ensign, was quickly run up over the Guildhall by Town-Sergt. Osborn amid the cheers of the onlookers and this was the signal for the appearance of flags in every direction. They fluttered from flag-staffs, waved from strings stretched across the street, and were carried by many of the juveniles, whilst red, white, and blue ribbons were worn in various ways. By midday the crowd had increased, until it filled all the space round the Guildhall and stretched far up the High-street and into St Thomas's-square. Then the Parish-church bells added their contribution to the rising enthusiasm by a joyous peal, and there was much handshaking on all sides as friend met friend and rejoiced in a tremendous sense of relief which the glad tidings brought.

But here and there in the happy throng there were sad faces and moist eyes for dear ones who will never return, and a generous sympathy went out to these bereaved ones …

RYDE

The anxiously looked for news that the armistice had been signed was known soon after 10 o'clock, the first public intimation being posted outside the office of the County Press in Union-street. The good news spread like wildfire, and in a very short time the main streets were bright with flags, and private houses in other parts of the town were not long in following suit. Soon after 11 o'clock the bells of the Parish-church rang out a joyous peal and ... a good sprinkling of the population made their way to the Town-hall about noon in the expectation that the Mayor would make a public pronouncement of the inspiring news that hostilities had ceased ... The highly elated assembly outside sang patriotic airs and cheered vociferously. As the day wore on the streets became crowded with pedestrians; tricolour favours were much in evidence, and the enthusiasm and high spirits of one and all was but a natural outburst of hope long deferred. In the evening coloured fires lit up the semi darkened main thoroughfares, and fireworks were let off promiscuously, the juvenile portion of the community taking a prominent part to their hearts' delight in this direction ...

COWES

The news of the armistice was received here, as elsewhere, with huge delight. Quite early on Monday rumours were rife, and when, as the morning wore on, the rumours developed into certainty, the excitement became intense. Almost as if by magic flags appeared in all quarters, until there was not a street without its gay display either from windows or in lines overhanging the roads. On every flag-staff banners of rejoicing floated in the breeze, and the brightness of the display brought back vivid recollections of the many occasions before the war when Cowes was en fete.

In the yards the workers, as by one consent, 'downed' tools, and the streets were at once crowded with throngs of both sexes and of all ages, shouting and cheering, singing songs, waving flags, and doing everything imaginable to express their gladness. A number of soldiers (wounded and otherwise), together with a party of rural munitions workers, formed quite a little procession of their own, making the streets literally ring with their songs and cheers. The hooters of the works added their quota to the enthusiastic din, while even the schoolchildren joined in, for quite a large number of them, as they came from school, formed up in wide columns and marched along the streets cheering vociferously.

———————◆———————

Finally, an official notice in that week's issue confirmed that at last it really was all over ...

RECRUITING SUSPENDED
CALLING-UP NOTICES CANCELLED

The Ministry of National Service makes the following announcement: The Government has decided that all recruiting under the Military Service Acts is to be suspended. All outstanding calling-up notices, whether for medical examination or service, are cancelled. All cases pending before tribunals should be suspended.

Further Reading

Newport Remembered, Bill Shepard, IW Natural History and Archaeological Society, 1984.

Maritime Heritage: White's of Cowes, David L. Williams, Silver Link Publishing Ltd, 1993.

Cowes & Northwood 1750-1914, Rosetta Brading, R. Brading, 1994.

Niton Calling, Niton Women's Institute, Lightbowns, 1971.

Shipwrecks of The Wight, J.C. Medland, West Island Printers Ltd, 1986.

Back of the Wight, Fred Mew, The County Press, 1934.

Black On Wight, The Story of an Island's Newspaper, Maurice Leppard, The Isle of Wight County Press, 2000.

Memorials & Monuments on the Isle of Wight Web Site, www.isle-of-wight-memorials.org.uk

A complete set of back issues of the *County Press* can be viewed on microfiche at the County Records Office, Hillside, Newport, or at the *County Press* offices in Pyle Street, Newport.

Also available

Yesterday's Papers
Life in Late Victorian England
From the pages of The Isle of Wight County Press
by Alan Stroud

The County Press started reporting the events of the Island and its inhabitants over 120 years ago. With the passing of time the journalists' work, originally meant to have a life of only seven days, has become a valuable source of Island history. It opens a contemporary window onto a way of life that has all but gone.

These first hand accounts of the day-to-day life of Victorians, written with surprisingly few inhibitions and often in the smallest and most revealing detail, provide a history not found in textbooks. This is the Victorians writing about themselves, quite intimately on occasions. They wrote uncluttered by today's attitudes and opinions, with no other agenda than to provide a straightforward account of the week's news.

If there is any lesson to be drawn it is that while times may change, human nature doesn't.

ISBN 978 0 85361 671 9 **£11.95**

... a unique insight into day-to-day life in Victorian England; the paper's location is irrelevant, as just about every paper in the country serving a more rural area must have had similar stories. We tend to think of the late Victorian era as a time of rapid progress, happy citizens and civilised behaviour, especially compared with the present day - wrong! The reports here turn such thoughts on their head, many covering virtually the same incidents as found in today's papers, the degree of highly intrusive reporting being greater, and considerably less sexually inhibited than today. A really fascinating book ... *Camden Miniature Steam Services*

... some cracking stories from the period 1884 ... to 1901, the year of Queen Victoria's death. From tales of crime and loutish behaviour, terrible tragedies and notorious murder cases, to the reporting of Parliamentary debates, the Royal Jubilee and the Cowes Regatta, *Yesterday's Papers* contains a diverse range of fascinating articles. *County Press*